Communicating with children and young people

Making a difference

Michelle Lefevre

BASW
BRITISH ASSOCIATION
OF SOCIAL WORKERS

First published in Great Britain in 2010 by

The Policy Press
University of Bristol
Fourth Floor
Beacon House
Queen's Road
Bristol BS8 1QU
UK

tel +44 (0)117 331 4054
fax +44 (0)117 331 4093
e-mail tpp-info@bristol.ac.uk
www.policypress.co.uk

North American office:
The Policy Press
c/o International Specialized Books Services (ISBS)
920 NE 58th Avenue, Suite 300
Portland, OR 97213-3786, USA
tel +1 503 287 3093 • fax +1 503 280 8832 • e-mail info@isbs.com

British Library Cataloguing in Publication Data
A catalogue record for this book is available from the British Library.

Library of Congress Cataloging-in-Publication Data
A catalog record for this book has been requested.

ISBN 978 1 84742 282 8 paperback
ISBN 978 1 84742 283 5 hardcover

Cover design by The Policy Press.
Front cover: image kindly supplied by www.istock.com
Printed and bound in Great Britain by Hobbs, Southampton.

Contents

List of tables, figures and boxes

Tables

Figures

Boxes

Acknowledgements

A number of people have assisted me in completing this book by helping me to formulate ideas and providing support. I am grateful to them all, but especially want to thank the following people: Barry Luckock, Suzy Braye, Elaine Sharland, Rebecca Watts, Andy Mantell, Viv Cree and various people from The Policy Press read drafts and provided guidance. My professional doctorate colleagues kept me writing with their encouragement and own hard work. Many students and practitioners have shared their dilemmas and challenges in direct work and have inspired this book. Particular respect and gratitude is owed to the children and young people I have worked with throughout the years who patiently allowed me to learn how best to communicate with them. Finally I want to thank my partner, Claire Lucius, who was unfailingly supportive and encouraging and read the whole typescript through.

Setting the scene

Introduction

The importance of effective mutual communication between social workers and children and young people can no longer be ignored. It is now clear that, if they are to make a real difference to their lives, practitioners must be able to relate to children and young people, listen to them, support them and fully involve them in matters that concern them. Indeed this can be a matter of life and death. Inquiries into the abuse, neglect and non-accidental deaths of children and young people reveal time and time again how risks to them may be increased if professionals charged with their care and protection do not spend time getting to know them, finding out what they think and feel, and trying to make sense of their experiences (Ofsted, 2009).

Numerous research studies report that the quality of professionals' engagement with children and young people and the extent to which they are able to facilitate their participation are significant contributors to the quality of assessments, planning and service provision. Young people want to be actively included when decisions are being made about them. They also have a right to this, as set out in Article 12 of the United Nations Convention on the Rights of the Child (UNCRC): a right to express their views in all matters which affect them and for these views to be taken into account. As outlined in Chapter Two, this principle has now been enshrined in law, policy and practice guidance across children and young people's services in the UK. So, finding out what children and young people are thinking, feeling, hoping and fearing, about wider service planning as well as decision making which affects them directly (DH, 2002), is now a statutory requirement as well as a tenet of ethical practice. Involving young people in these ways makes practical good sense, too, as it draws on the insider expertise children have about their own lives (Braye and Preston-Shoot, 2005).

Certain groups of children and young people, such as those who are at risk of harm, those who require services to maintain and promote their welfare (including disabled children), those involved with judicial processes and those who are looked after, have specific entitlements to effective communication with social workers. As discussed in Chapter Three, many of these children and young people have been able to give a clear indication of what they want and expect from their social workers; for example, those in care have outlined their need and preference for information, consultation, support, reliability and a trusted interpersonal relationship (DCSF, 2007).

And yet, despite these policy aspirations and clear practice guidelines, it is clear that even experienced social workers do not always feel confident in their skills and nor do they or their employers necessarily appreciate the importance of their communication and direct work with children (CSCI, 2005). The focus and content of qualifying courses, high caseloads, administrative burdens from the Integrated Children's System (ICS)[1] and inadequacies in workplace supervision have meant that the training, guidance, support and uninterrupted time with children and young people required for high-quality practice are not always there (Gibb, 2009a). However, the profession is now at a turning point; the social work role is being redefined and new commitments are being made to raising the standard of qualifying training, enhancing access to continuing professional development (post-qualifying, or PQ, training), improving workload management systems, reducing bureaucracy and providing high-quality supervision (Burnham and Balls, 2009; Gibb, 2009b). These should provide an opportunity for the policy aspirations and legal requirements for communication with children and young people to be fully realised.

This book aspires to help both less confident practitioners and those in their qualifying training become better informed and more capable in the complex and varied approaches to communication and direct work they will need to meet the ethical aspirations and statutory requirements of their redefined role. In particular, it aims to enthuse readers to develop the most powerful resource they have to offer in their practice with children and young people: themselves.

How communication skills are defined in this book

Chapters Four and Five consider in more depth what might be meant by capability and effectiveness in communication. In order to begin, however, it is helpful to set out here in brief some of this book's key ideas in relation to this. One definition of skilful communication and engagement with children and young people is that outlined in the *Common core of skills and knowledge for the children's workforce*, which the Department for Education and Skills (2005) has set as non-statutory guidance for those working in children and young people's services in England:[2]

> Good communication is central to working with children.... It involves listening, questioning, understanding and responding to what is being communicated.... Communication is not just about the words you use, but also your manner of speaking, body language and, above all, the effectiveness with which you listen. To

communicate effectively it is important to take account of culture and context, for example where English is an additional language. Effective engagement requires the involvement of children … in the design and delivery of services and decisions that affect them. It is important to consult with them and consider their opinions and perspectives from the outset. A key part of effective communication and engagement is trust….To build a rapport with children … it is important to demonstrate understanding, respect and honesty. Continuity in relationships promotes engagement and the improvement of lives. (DfES, 2005, p 6)

The *common core* provides a useful baseline, but, as will become apparent, this book views communication as a more complex set of processes than the rather straightforward procedures outlined above. Activities such as 'informing' or 'listening' rarely involve just simple one-way actions but tend to be interactive and intersubjective[3] by their very nature. In social work, as in everyday life, there are often misunderstandings or misinterpretations of what has been said, shown, heard or witnessed. Children and young people often struggle to convey clearly what is important to them and workers may not fully understand what it is they hear or see. The reverse is also true: practitioners are not always able to find child-friendly ways of explaining difficult or sensitive issues, leaving children unable to make sense of the information presented.

These complex communicative processes mean that it is not enough for workers to have a set of standard techniques to draw on when the situation demands. Instead, an approach customised to the needs of the particular child and situation is required. Workers will need to develop both themselves and their practice in a range of ways if they are to achieve this personalised approach. Communication with children and young people is often more effective if it takes place within a relationship where they have developed sufficient trust in their workers to feel safe discussing their fears, hopes, distress and concerns with them (Winter, 2009). This means practitioners must engage with children and young people at a real, human level and carry out professional tasks such as assessments in a child-centred manner. This relationship-based approach can support the fundamental ethical principles underpinning child welfare practice outlined above.

These principles begin to highlight how effective communication depends not just on *what workers do*, but also on *who they are*, the person inside the professional (Lefevre et al, 2008a). This book aims to inspire practitioners to develop the kind of personal qualities and emotional availability and capability that make children and young people feel safe enough to risk communicating with them about issues that matter to them. It also aspires to create a sound ethical basis to professional practice that ensures that workers respect and promote not only children and young people's needs but also their rights. Practitioners will also be able to use this book to develop their knowledge base, learning more about the different ways in which children and young people communicate, what might get in the way of two-way communication and evidence-informed approaches.

Focus of the book

While theoretical perspectives and research findings underpin the discussions through this book, the deeper understanding and self-development which is aimed for will be best promoted through an interactive engagement with the reflective exercises and vignettes which present practice dilemmas and illustrate points made. Readers will be encouraged throughout to reflect on their current professional context so that their understanding of particular children and how best to work with them can develop through the book. Children and young people will be partners in this endeavour; their expertise on what constitutes effective communication will be drawn on through quotations and findings from studies in which their views and experiences have been heard.

Who is this book for?

Social workers will find this book particularly relevant and helpful as the practice vignettes used draw on some of the statutory roles and tasks that render their interactions and interventions with children and young people particularly challenging. However, it is also likely to be useful for other front-line workers within integrated children's services who work in line with the same *common core* as social workers. As the practice vignettes used within the book are set in England, there are consequently more references to English law and policy rather than that pertaining in other parts of the UK. However, such references have been kept to a minimum as a way of making the book more accessible to social workers elsewhere and to professionals from other disciplines.

What is meant by 'children and young people'?

The terms 'child' and 'children' are often used as shorthand in this book to refer to both children and young people. This is not to minimise the often significant differences between them. Age is likely to be a significant factor in the mode of communication used; interactions with most four-year-olds should employ simple concepts and vocabulary and might need to be play-based, whereas conversations with some 15-year-olds might be more similar to those with an adult. Any attempt to work with both in exactly the same way could confuse younger children and leave teenagers feeling patronised. One 14-year-old, who had been through a child protection investigation, for example, spoke of how annoyed she had felt about workers speaking to her "as if I was a little kid" (quoted in Bell, 2002, p 5).

Age also confers different legal rights and responsibilities in certain aspects of the law. For example, the age of criminal responsibility is eight in Scotland but 10 in the rest of the UK; young people can legally gamble, have sexual intercourse and marry at the age of 16,[4] but cannot drive until 17, or vote, buy fireworks or have a tattoo until aged 18.

However, those commonly referred to as 'children' or 'young people' share three common factors. The first is that all those up to the age of 18 are covered by legislation designed to safeguard them, promote their welfare and facilitate their participation. Second, they share the common legal and social status as minors, that gives them less power and control over what happens to them and limits the extent to which they can participate in society.

The third is that children and young people have a particular need for information, interactions and discussions to be tailored to their individual needs and ways of communicating. Of course, workers should always take into account language and cultural differences between themselves and service users of all ages, and ensure they are working in line with their cognitive capabilities, primary language and modes of expression. However, there is an additional layer for workers to consider with children and young people, as, even into their late teens, they are still moving towards maturation in a developmental pathway unique to their own attributes, potential and environmental experiences. The mode and method of workers' communication will need modifying over time, often quite rapidly, as children and young people learn and change. Practitioners should be wary of imposing pre-formed assumptions about what a child or young person might comprehend based on a conversation six months ago when now they may be able to understand and discuss more complex matters. Particular care also needs to be taken in work with disabled children and young people, neither to have expectations set by developmental norms which are not appropriate for *this* child, nor to expect too little and consequently make too little effort (Stalker and Connors, 2003).

On the occasions when a reference is made only to 'young people' in this book it is generally to distinguish the particular needs, rights, responsibilities, capabilities and experiences of those in their teenage years.

The broad principles of effective communication that are discussed in this book apply to children not only across the full age range (that is, 0–17) but include the full spectrum of children and young people in terms of characteristics, life experiences, capacities and intentions. Disabled children, young carers, unaccompanied young asylum seekers, black and minority ethnic children, lesbian, gay, bisexual and transgender (LGBT) young people, and so on, are all children first. For this reason there are not separate chapters in this book dealing separately with those particular groups. Where specific issues arise for children and young people with particular needs, experiences and characteristics in an assessment, for example, they are discussed alongside generalist principles for assessment with children.

Structure of the book

The next few chapters consider key concepts, definitions, research findings and frameworks for communication that are then applied to different aspects of the social work role with children in the later chapters. Chapter Two considers the place and importance of communication and direct work with children and young people within contemporary social work practice in children's service settings. Chapter Three summarises and analyses findings from a range of research studies in which children and young people have been able to say what they think counts as effective communication by professionals. Chapter Four presents some theoretical perspectives on communication that underpins later discussions. Chapter Five further unpicks and explores the notion of effectiveness in communication and presents a 'core capabilities' model for good practice.

There then follow two chapters that are aimed particularly at preparing practitioners to begin their work with children and young people. Chapter Six offers an opportunity for readers to appraise their existing skills and knowledge and to determine which aspects of the core capabilities set out in Chapter Five they most need to develop. Chapter Seven focuses on workers' preparations for communication and direct work with individual children and young people within particular contexts.

Some key aspects of communication within the social work role are then explored in the final few chapters. Direct methods such as conversations and approaches to interviewing are covered in Chapter Eight, with an emphasis on assessment. Indirect approaches to communication, such as observing and interpreting children and young people's demeanour, play and behaviour, are discussed in Chapter Nine. Use of play, activities and creative techniques to communicate throughout assessment and intervention are explored in Chapter Ten. The final chapter (Chapter Eleven) considers how communicative capability lies at the heart of effective social work practice with children and young people.

At the end of every chapter there are some key questions for readers to consider. Some of these are reflective in nature, designed to develop readers' self-awareness and self-development. Others will relate more to the content of the chapter and will require a careful reading of the text. Further reading and resources are specified at the end of every chapter. These include relevant policy documents, theoretical papers and research reports that have been referred to within the chapter, as well as guides and resource materials that can aid skills development and/or facilitate direct work.

Conclusion

This chapter has set out in brief terms the reasons why this book is so necessary at the present time: to enable practitioners to develop the knowledge, personal qualities, values and skills needed to meet their statutory requirements for effective communication and direct work with children and young people. These will be outlined in more depth in the next chapter, along with an exploration of what can make communication so challenging. The objectives, focus and structure of the book have also been summarised so that readers can select particular chapters to meet specified learning goals, if they so wish. However, there is much to be recommended in reading the book through sequentially, as key principles and theoretical principles are developed through earlier discussion.

Notes

[1] A conceptual framework and approach to supporting practitioners and managers (in England) in undertaking assessment, planning intervention and review (DCSF, 2009). It is particularly used as shorthand for the electronic case record system developed to record, collate, analyse and provide information, a system now being modified in the light of substantial criticism (see Gibb, 2009b; Broadhurst et al, 2010).

[2] The *common core* is shortly due to be introduced across children's services in Wales.

[3] This concept will be explored more fully in Chapter Four, but, broadly speaking, 'intersubjective' here refers to the way in which the subjective perceptions and preconceptions of two individuals are brought together during an episode of communication in order for shared understandings to be sought.

[4] Marriage requires parental consent at the age of 16 in England, Wales and Northern Ireland, although not in Scotland.

Key questions

1. What are your main learning goals in reading this book? What kinds of knowledge, values, personal qualities and skills do you most want to develop in yourself?
2. What do you already know about how professionals' communication with children and young people might need to be different from that with adults?
3. What particular challenges have you already experienced when trying to communicate with both younger children and teenagers? Include examples from either your professional role or personal life. What strategies have you already found to be useful in overcoming these challenges?

Further reading and resources

Archard, D. and Skivenes, M. (2009) 'Hearing the child', *Child & Family Social Work*, vol 14, no 4, pp 391-9.

Laming, Lord (2009) *The protection of children in England: A progress report*, London: The Stationery Office.

Stein, M. (2009) *Quality matters in children's services: Messages from research*, London: Jessica Kingsley Publishers.

2

The importance of effective communication between children and young people and their social workers

"It seems like they have to do all this form filling, their bosses' bosses make them do it, but it makes them forget about us." (boy, 16, consulted by 11 Million, quoted in Laming, 2009, p 23)

Introduction

This chapter considers the nature and place of communication between children and young people and their social workers. Such communication, within the professional and interprofessional context of children's services, is different in many ways from how children might converse with or relate to adults in other family or social contexts. In part this is because the nature of such communication and the professional relationships within which it occurs are dictated by social policy and legislation. These are, themselves, influenced by the prevailing social, cultural and political discourses of the time (Whitfield, 2009). Statutory requirements, policy initiatives, practice guidance and assessment frameworks consequently change over time and cross-nationally, shaping the nature and importance of roles and tasks such as information giving, interviewing, consulting or supporting.

This has led to significant variations in the nature and importance of communication and direct work with children and young people over recent decades. No doubt practice requirements will continue to develop in future months and years with the advent of new policy agendas and social and cultural changes. To clarify the current context and expectations, this chapter uses the vignette of a social work student who is wanting to learn more about the influences which have shaped the contemporary professional role with children in order to help her understand why she should approach her work in a particular way.

Emergence of the social work role with children and young people

Practice vignette: Chloe, the social work student

Chloe, a social work student, has just started her first practice learning opportunity in a local authority children's services department. She has no previous experience in social care and has not studied social policy before so is at the very beginning of forming an understanding of the social work role with children. She asks her practice assessor, Sally, for help with this. Sally suggests it may be helpful for Chloe to begin by learning about some of the key historical influences as this will enhance her appreciation of how the current practice guidelines and cultures came to be developed. Sally starts by outlining to Chloe how the social work role with children developed through the previous century and how findings from serious case reviews and developments in children's rights have been particularly influential.

The way in which children have been seen and positioned within society has changed dramatically in recent times. As recently as the first part of the 19th century children and young people still lacked any legal entitlement to a voice in matters that affected them and their particular needs and vulnerabilities were often ignored or misunderstood. Gradually, through the 19th century, a growing recognition of children's needs, vulnerability and potential led to philanthropic concerns for their welfare and a growing sense of responsibility that they should be rescued from damaging circumstances (Colton et al, 2001). Legislation designed to support children who were experiencing abuse and neglect within their families followed, with the 1889 Prevention of Cruelty to, and Protection of, Children Act leading the way.

As the practice of 'social work' developed in the first half of the 20th century, casework methods and clinical models of practice dominated, influenced by psychodynamic theories and psychotherapeutic principles. The casework approach sought to provide children and their families with a 'helping relationship' as this was seen as central to the success of social work interventions (Mattinson, 1975). Whereas children had previously been thought of as 'miniature adults', their developmentally immature state was now given prominence. This led to an emphasis on their need for care, guidance and protection from abusive adults or dangerous circumstances. Because they were still learning vocabulary and developing formal thinking, a presumption of children's 'incompetence' held sway; they were generally seen as unable to comprehend complex or important matters (Cooper, 1994). The result of these perceptions was that professionals were much less concerned to keep children and young people informed about issues which affected them or seek their opinions about their circumstances or plans for their future (Leeson, 2007). Disabled children and young people were doubly hit by these assumptions of incompetence (Stalker and Connors, 2003).

The establishment of the welfare state in the 1940s, with its aspiration for 'cradle to the grave' welfare services, led to the 1948 Children Act and the establishment of children's departments where the particular needs of children, young people and their families could be attended to (Graham, 2007). Recognition grew that children's negative experiences were not just harmful to them in the moment but had far-reaching effects on their developmental trajectory and adult functioning. Donald Winnicott (1965), who was a paediatrician as well as a psychoanalyst, observed children interacting with their parents and suggested that a child's personality and way of relating to others is formed, for better or worse, through early parenting experiences. Building on James Robertson's observations of children in day care and Mary Ainsworth's research into mother–infant interactions, John Bowlby developed attachment theory to highlight the profound effects on children of separation and loss and how they may be disadvantaged through the lifespan if they lacked a 'secure base' early on (Bowlby, 1969).

The acceptance of these theoretical perspectives and research findings (which, as Chloe is learning on her course, are now supported by neuroscience; see Gerhardt, 2004) meant that the implications of families and societies failing to act in ways which promoted children and young people's welfare could no longer be denied, philosophically at least. Social workers increasingly became concerned with how to understand the impact on children of their experiences and how best to work directly with them and their families. Clare Winnicott, wife of Donald and a social worker as well as a psychoanalyst, was a key influence, promoting the importance of practitioners 'getting alongside' children and young people and building trusting relationships with them. She furthered the understanding of how to get in touch with children and young people's *internal worlds* (inner feelings, perceptions and experiences) while at the same time talking with them about, and intervening in, their real or *external world* environments (Winnicott, 1964). Techniques from non-directive play therapy (Axline, 1969) were also influential; they helped practitioners to engage creatively with children and make sense of their inner worlds through exploring what children might be expressing through their play, stories and drawings.

In the second half of the century, the growth of humanistic and client-centred approaches (see, for example, Rogers, 1951) began to challenge the earlier dominance of psychodynamic theories and the notion of professionals as 'experts'. Casework approaches began to fall out of favour, being criticised for their long-termness of approach, lack of evidence regarding outcomes and downgrading of the expertise of family members (Cooper et al, 2003). As structural analyses of power and oppression moved centre stage in the 1970s and 1980s, the individual and psychological emphasis of psychodynamic casework was felt to potentially pathologise individuals by viewing their problems as solely resulting from personal difficulties rather than considering additionally or alternatively any wider social or political influences such as poverty, racism or homophobia (Trevithick, 2003). The direct work role with children began to be marginalised during this paradigmatic shift. The 1990s emphasis on managerialism, technical-rational approaches and administration further deflected social workers' focus from direct practice (Folgheraiter, 2004), 'diverting [practitioners'] time and attention away from personal contact and towards filling in forms and making telephone calls' (Schofield and Brown, 1999, p 22).

Practice vignette: Understanding the practice context

Chloe has already noticed that this workplace culture is still apparent and she worries that the direct work with children that she is committed to undertaking will not be accorded the respect, time and resources that she would hope for. While acknowledging that systemic problems continue, Sally is able to indicate two significant developments in the latter part of the 20th century which have brought about a re-recognition in policy of the significance of direct work with children and enabled it to take its place again at the heart of social work practice in children's services. The first has been the growing realisation of how the well-being of children and young people may be adversely affected if they are not seen and communicated with directly about their experiences. The second has been the increasing prominence of rights-based approaches that contend that children and young people must be directly involved in assessments, decision making and service planning. She suggests it would be helpful for a student such as Chloe to understand more about each of these developments as they continue to be significant dynamics in contemporary practice, so each is explored in turn.

Significance of safeguarding concerns in re-invigorating social workers' direct work role with children

Some of the most significant legal and policy initiatives in how social workers should be communicating and engaging with children have been provoked by serious case reviews and inquiry reports into the death, serious injury and abuse of children within the family home or substitute care. For example, 'boarding-out' regulations were introduced in 1947 as a direct result of the Monckton Report into the death of 13-year-old Dennis O'Neill at the hands of his foster carers (Home Office, 1945). These were designed to ensure that children in care were visited regularly and that their social workers found out if they had any complaints or worries. The 1975 Children Act followed the inquiry into the death of Maria Colwell, a seven-year-old child who had experienced neglect from her mother and physical abuse by her stepfather (DHSS, 1974). This introduced separate representation for children in care proceedings by guardians ad litem and ensured that their views and concerns were heard directly by the court.

Numerous inquiry reports showed how easily children can be lost from sight when social workers fail to speak directly with them to find out what they are experiencing, feeling and wanting (Reder et al, 1993). The report into the death of Jasmine Beckford in the 1980s exemplifies this. The social worker involved with the family was seen to have 'focused her gaze' on the parents and their concerns and never actually communicated with Jasmine herself (Blom-Cooper, 1985). The result was a failure to comprehend, even see, the harm Jasmine was experiencing.

Children who die at the hands of parents and carers are often the most socially excluded and/or economically disadvantaged, with a significant number, like Jasmine, being from black or minority ethnic groups (Chand, 2000). The more marginalised children are, the more they need professionals to make the effort to engage with their world and to speak with them directly to empower and protect them. And yet it seems that the family lives and experiences of black and minority ethnic children are still poorly engaged with and understood (Williams and Soydan, 2005). As a consequence, there is a danger that white indigenous social workers may fall into one of two traps: either intervening unnecessarily and unhelpfully because they lack understanding of families who have different cultural patterns or norms to them and have pathologised their behaviour; or, by over-relying on cultural explanations of child abuse, they put the most favourable interpretation on parents' behaviour, leaving black and minority ethnic children particularly at risk. Others, too, may fear accusations of racism and hesitate to intervene (Graham, 2007).

Research into the quality of risk assessments of abuse and neglect has also found that social work assessments have not always sufficiently focused on the child or young person in the family (SSI et al, 1997; Cleaver and Walker with Meadows, 2004). Just as with Jasmine Beckford, parents' views and concerns have tended to dominate, perhaps because it is easier for practitioners to hear and engage with what they are expressing. The result is that children and young people's perspectives are often ignored or sidelined, or are never even sought in the first place.

Inspection and inquiry reports have also highlighted how failures to engage and communicate with children living in residential care homes have meant that those experiencing abuse and punitive regimes went unnoticed (NSPCC, 1996; House of Commons, 2000). If key social workers had formed and maintained relationships of trust with these children, they might have felt more able to disclose their plight. In fact, some children did not get to know or even see their social worker at all. In one study from the 1980s only two thirds of social workers had seen the children for whom they were keyworker in the previous year, and far fewer had seen the children alone, so there were few opportunities for important conversations (Rowe et al, 1984). This left children isolated and vulnerable, particularly when their contact with their families and communities of origin was not being promoted and maintained (DH, 1991). Findings such as these later led to statutory requirements that the views and experiences of children in need, at risk and in care should be sought and listened to and that children should be consulted in all matters which affect them.

The inquiry into the way in which children were interviewed about possible sexual abuse in Cleveland (Butler-Sloss, 1988) has influenced social workers' communication with children in a different way. By the late 1980s society was starting to accept that intra-familial sexual abuse occurred and professionals were recognising some of the underlying difficulties which might interfere with children disclosing their abuse, such as fear of the family being split up, worries about not being believed, feelings of guilt or responsibility which were evoked by 'grooming'[1] or a desire to protect other people, such as the non–abusing parent or the abuser (London et al, 2008). However, in their zeal to protect children, social workers sometimes interviewed children in a way that was later classed as abusive and/or elicited unreliable evidence (Ceci and Bruck, 1993). For example, there was legal concern about whether repeated interviewing and leading questions meant children's disclosures might have been exaggerated or even fabricated. The resulting worries about 'false positives' (that is, allegations which were untrue) subsequently reduced the possibility of a prosecution on the basis of a child's testimony. Consequently, even though children were finally being given an opportunity to communicate about abusive experiences, their disclosures were not necessarily believed nor acted on.

To improve and standardise forensic interviewing with child witnesses by social workers and police officers in such situations, legal guidance was issued to ensure that evidential standards commensurate with criminal proceedings were adhered to. Guidance such as the *Memorandum of good practice* issued in 1992 in England and Wales (Home Office, 1992), later revised and updated as *Achieving best evidence* (Home Office, 2002, 2007), was the result. These warn against the dangers of 'leading' children in interviews and provide guidance on encouraging children to provide free narratives about their experiences through using prompts and open questions and only using closed questions to check out information.

Practice vignette: Changing views on childhood

Sally's overview has enabled Chloe to appreciate how failures in communicating with children and young people who are vulnerable and in adverse circumstances have meant their needs, safety and well-being have been compromised. Chloe has learned that this has been one of the most significant dynamics that have led to more recent policy and legal developments. Sally now goes on to outline to Chloe the other key influence leading to statutory requirements for children and young people to be directly involved in assessments, decision making and service planning: the changing way in which children and young people have been seen and positioned within society.

Competing paradigms of childhood

The growing recognition of children's needs and vulnerabilities through the 20th century, outlined above, led to an enhanced awareness of how children may not always have the vocabulary or level of conceptual understanding to name or directly describe their experiences, thoughts and feelings. Consequently one emphasis in professional and in-service training has been on how practitioners should try to help children overcome such barriers to their communication. Workers are advised to acquire expert knowledge about child development and possible psychological obstacles to communication and to take into account the impact of any disability or environmental factors, such as abuse, neglect or insecurity of attachment on children and young people's capacity to express themselves and convey clearly what is important to them (DH et al, 2000; Jones, 2003). Textbooks abound with sensitive, practical and creative strategies for social workers to use (see, for example, Foley and Leverett, 2008; McLeod, 2008). Literature from a psychotherapeutic perspective has additionally emphasised the importance of attending to children's more indirect and unconscious communications, such as what their behaviour, relational style and play might be saying *for* them (see, for example, Wickham and West, 2002; McMahon, 2009).

These approaches have led to important advances in safeguarding and intervening with children in adverse circumstances. However, the focus on children's developmental needs and vulnerability may have in itself created additional barriers, as there is evidence that children's views are downplayed or even ignored in certain situations because of over-protectiveness or a presumption of limited competence (Winter, 2009). Some workers may choose not to engage young children in discussions about sensitive matters in the belief that they are not sufficiently able to make a useful contribution to difficult decisions (Leeson, 2007). Others may want to 'relieve' children of the 'burden' of having to be put in a position where they feel they are having to take sides or betray a loved but abusive or neglectful parent. Adherence to this 'developmentalist' paradigm has come under increasing criticism in recent years for considering children as 'human becomings' rather than 'human beings' (Qvortrup, 1987).

Children as social actors and citizens

Sociologists have in recent years posed an alternative construction of childhood and the capabilities of children and young people. This is one which positions children as 'social actors', individuals who are intentional and purposeful in their own right, who have an important contribution to make to society and to the planning of their own lives (James and Prout, 1997). Rather than seeing children as inherently less capable than the adults who are attempting to communicate with them, this perspective emphasises that children's communicative capability is not a fixed characteristic, but varies according to the attitude and skills of the practitioner working with them (Thomas and O'Kane, 2000). Many research studies support this viewpoint, identifying that, where environmental conditions are provided which facilitate rather than inhibit communication, children demonstrate capability beyond that which practitioners might have expected for their age or ability. For example, children have shown that, when options are posed to them in a more child-centred manner, they are able to consider alternatives and possible outcomes carefully and responsibly (Hague et al, 2002). This is just as true for younger children and those with sensory impairments or learning difficulties; it is the worker's attitude and commitment that counts (Clark and Statham, 2005). Limited expectations can lead to limited results (Stalker and Connors, 2003).

Child-centredness also refers to a practitioner's ability to recognise and respond appropriately to the impact of social factors such as cultural difference, displacement and oppression on children's capacity to engage and express themselves. For example, unaccompanied young asylum seekers' capacity to engage and communicate will depend on: the extent to which practitioners understand how trauma and displacement affects their behaviour, comprehension and relational style; whether a practitioner speaks a young person's language or provides an interpreter; whether the young person's cultural practices and idioms are understood; and the practitioner's capacity to understand and respond appropriately to the young person's fear of oppression, racism and negative responses (Kohli, 2006).

This alternative paradigm of childhood also emphasises children and young people's human rights and their status as citizens, positioning them as 'partners' within social care services who are *entitled* to be consulted and who can make a positive contribution to decision making and service planning. Those who strongly adhere to this rights-based position tend to criticise any attempt to 'relieve' children of the 'burden' of being consulted, arguing that doing so could conceivably reduce practitioners' attempts to communicate with them. Practice which prioritises protection and guidance for children is critiqued as not only infringing children's human rights but as potentially enacting a paradox: ignoring the knowledge and expertise children have about their own lives may actually place children at risk (Holland and Scourfield, 2004; Taylor, 2004).

Competing discourses of childhood

Arguably, an exclusive emphasis on the children's rights/social actor paradigm has its limitations, too, however. While practice from the developmental/vulnerability perspective might veer towards being less alert to children's rights and capabilities, those practitioners may be more likely to consider the *indirect* ways in which children communicate, especially in the face of adversity. If it is accepted that no adult communicates only what is conscious and intended, nor is able to impart clearly everything that they need or prefer (Thompson, 2003), then this must be even more true of children who convey much about their feelings, intentions and experiences through play, metaphor, body language, relationships and other behaviour as well as, or instead of, directly through formal language. This kind of communication tends to receive little or no attention in research and writings that predominantly position children and young people as capable and intentional (Luckock et al, 2006a).

The existence of these competing discourses of childhood has led, unfortunately, at times to polarised approaches being taken, with a 'false dichotomy' being posed between child welfare and child autonomy (Applewhite and Joseph, 1994, p 292; Shemmings, 2000). For example, comments in one national broadsheet newspaper by the then head of Cafcass that children should be allowed to decide which parent they want to live with in cases of divorce or separation because 'children have the insight and maturity to know what they want' (*The Times*, 23 July 2005, p 19) led to an opposing editorial in the same edition which stated that 'It would be unwise to ask children to choose between their parents' as the broader family network were 'better judges' than younger and 'more immature' children and young people were of their own best interests (*The Times*, 23 July 2005, p 23).

Practice vignette: Children as 'beings and becomings'

Sally suggests that Chloe finds a way of integrating *both* perspectives. By considering children and young people as 'both beings and becomings' (Uprichard, 2007), practitioners can concern themselves with both vulnerability *and* capability, both their rights *and* their need for support and protection (Cooper, 1994; Thomas, 2005; Clark and Statham, 2005). This enables the strengths of both positions to be drawn on.

Children as social menace

One further paradigm of childhood is also outlined by Sally; it is one that positions certain children and young people as a form of social menace, as being not only troubled but troublesome, not just 'at risk', but 'risky' (Sharland, 2006, p 247). Statutory roles with such young people, as within youth offending services, are geared particularly to ways of controlling or changing dangerous, criminal or socially 'deviant' behaviours, rather than necessarily addressing other social disadvantages, family strife or emotional difficulties these young people may be facing (Paylor and Simmill–Binning, 2008). Ethical conflicts may emerge for workers where they are not provided with opportunities to uncover and address these young people's underlying individual and environmental difficulties, because they are supposed to focus primarily on their troubling actions rather than their personal troubles. Practitioners may well find themselves struggling to achieve any kind of authentic or productive engagement or communication with young people who are mandated to be in contact with them, have little control over the nature or content of the exchange and consequently feel powerless, disenfranchised or hostile (Corcoran, 1997). And yet it is with these kinds of feelings and experiences workers may well need to begin if they are to identify and help dismantle some of the barriers to communication that stand between them.

More recent developments

Practice vignette: Contemporary developments

In her social work course, Chloe has learned about recent law and social policy which structure guidance and practice in children's services. She asks Sally to help her understand how these relate to the historical influences and conceptual ideas that Sally has already outlined so far. Sally begins by referring to the death of one particular child in England at the beginning of the 21st century, as this has had a far-reaching influence on law, policy and practice with children and young people.

Victoria Climbié, a black child originating from the Ivory Coast, was eight years old when she died at the hands of the great-aunt and her partner with whom she was living. The subsequent inquiry report by Lord Laming into the circumstances which led up to her death found numerous systemic failures across statutory services, but Lord Laming was especially scathing about the way in which professionals, and in particular social workers, had failed to speak directly with Victoria on her own, in her first language, to find out what was occurring to her: 'Seeing, listening to and observing the child must be an essential element of an initial assessment for any social worker', he asserted (Laming, 2003, p 238).

The Climbié inquiry findings were not unique; indeed they echoed the findings of serious case reviews throughout the 20th century. Nor did matters instantly change with Victoria's death. A few years later the serious case review regarding 'Child B' noted similar shortcomings in professional responses and interventions, and reminded practitioners that children 'must be seen alone to allow them to speak freely about their experience and their wishes and feelings' (Westminster Local Safeguarding Children Board, 2006, p 7). It was clear that practitioners' failures to do so adequately were not just caused by individual shortcomings, but also by systemic factors. Developments in policy, law, practice guidance and training were required if practitioners were to be supported in consistently practising ethically and effectively with children and young people.

The growing awareness of such problems led to the Labour government's *Every Child Matters* programme of reform (DfES, 2003) that emphasised, among other things, the importance of 'listening to children, young people and their families' (p 4). This injunction was incorporated into the *Common core of skills and knowledge for the children's workforce* (DfES, 2005), outlined in Chapter One, which was introduced to ensure parity of standards across integrated children's services.

This concern to ensure children are consulted and listened to in assessment, decision making and planning has infused subsequent policy, law and practice guidance. For example, while the *Framework for the assessment of children in need and their families* (DH et al, 2000) had already stated explicitly that children and young people should be active participants in decision making which affects their lives, the interdisciplinary *Common assessment framework* (CWDC, 2008) took this a step further, requiring children's explicit consent to be sought for this assessment and any subsequent referral (unless child protection concerns override any refusal). The *Care matters* White Paper (DCSF, 2007) made proposals for workforce remodelling which would enable social workers to spend more time listening to and building relationships with children and to develop better skills for direct work with them.

Government commitments to promoting children's participation have led to requirements for children to be consulted at wider service planning levels as well as in respect of their own situations (DH, 2002). The *Care matters implementation plan* in England (DCSF, 2008), for example, set out guidance for the introduction of children in care councils, which are now in many areas providing forums for regular, mutual dialogue with children (although this has not yet been consistently implemented; see Lepper, 2010), and mechanisms for involving young people in the recruitment of key staff members. Some of the key principles that facilitate children's participation in consultations are set out in Box 1.

Box 1: Key principles for promoting effective participation by children and young people in consultations for service planning

- Allow enough time for children and young people to develop their understanding of choice and decision making and to become comfortable and relaxed with the person facilitating their involvement.
- Methods must allow children and young people to express their views freely.
- Be aware of sensitivities – some children and young people may find certain issues difficult to talk about and they should not be 'put on the spot' or feel pressurised to contribute.
- Methods of involvement must be accessible to all taking part and in particular must respond to any communication needs. It is often helpful to discuss this with those who know the children and young people well, for example, teachers or speech therapists.
- A wide range of children and young people should have the opportunity to participate.
- Ensure views expressed are those of children and young people themselves and are not influenced or misinterpreted by an adult.

Source: Children in Scotland (2009)

However, legislation, policy and guidance appear not to have removed the significant challenges that remain for practitioners regarding how to communicate, engage and interact with individual children and young people. A workforce inspection a few years ago found that many practitioners seemed to have lost their confidence and belief in their direct practice role with children; the inspectors could, in fact, find few examples of social workers using their skills and relationships to work directly with children (CSCI, 2005). Many children in care are unhappy that they lack the kind of 'continuous personal relationship' with their social worker that would enable them to talk about their worries (Le Grand, 2007, p 5). Some children feel that their social workers are 'difficult to get hold of ... always out, or at least not answering their phone'; they report that telephone messages left for social workers 'often do not result in a call back' or that they 'haven't met their social workers enough to get to know them' (quoted in Morgan, 2006, p 14). Also worrying is some children's impression that they cannot rely on what social workers say or what they promise (DCSF, 2007).

Practitioners have attributed these problems to feeling overwhelmed with administrative tasks and having to report on children's experiences, wishes and feelings according to the timescales of the court, child protection conferences, assessment framework or ICS rather than the pace at which children feel ready to communicate (Leveridge, 2002; Garrett, 2009; Gibb, 2009a; Broadhurst et al, 2010). Being bombarded with the emotional pain and distress of children and their families and required to make complex, finely balanced decisions without time to reflect or adequate supervision may also be evoking defences in practitioners which prevent them from fully engaging with or responding to the experiences of children (Ferguson, 2005; Rustin, 2005). It is now to be hoped that the proposals of the Social Work Task Force regarding the necessity of reducing caseloads and enhancing the quality of supervision (Gibb, 2009b), and the subsequent commitments made by the government to these (Burnham and Balls, 2009), will be taken forward by the Social Work Reform Group to promote the provision of the containing, reflective spaces practitioners need to make sense of children's indirect as well as direct communications and to provide the emotionally engaged interpersonal relationships children want and need.

Conclusion

The practice vignette of Chloe and Sally has been used in this chapter to explore key developments in law, policy, practice guidance and societal views of children and young people which have fed into the contemporary context of children's services. Some of the complexities of effective practice with children and young people and the challenges that practitioners often have in complying with their ethical and statutory obligations have been identified. The chapter has highlighted how both children and young people's rights and their needs may be compromised when effective communication and engagement by professionals is lacking. Legislation, policy and practice guidance now all confirm the importance of skilled communication and direct work with children and young people by their social workers but research, inspections and inquiries continue to highlight professional shortcomings. It is to be hoped that contemporary commitments to providing reflective space, manageable workloads and continuous professional development may now provide the renewed impetus and opportunity for social workers to be able to undertake the kind of sensitive, engaged and effective direct work with children and young people that they want and have a right to expect.

Note

[1] Grooming refers to the ways in which the abuser seeks to ensure the child does not tell what is happening, and might include threats, treats, promises or distorting the child's understanding of what has happened.

Key questions

1. What kinds of things go wrong for children and young people in care when social workers do not get to know them or communicate directly with them?
2. What are some of the barriers that have got in the way of social workers communicating effectively with children and young people?
3. What are the dangers of just focusing on either children and young people's needs or their rights?

Further reading and resources

DfES (Department for Education and Skills) (2005) *Common core of skills and knowledge for the children's workforce*, Nottingham: DfES Publications (www.dcsf.gov.uk/everychildmatters/strategy/deliveringservices1/commoncore/commoncoreofskillsandknowledge/).

Laming, Lord (2003) *The Victoria Climbié Inquiry: Report of an inquiry by Lord Laming*, Cm 5730, London: The Stationery Office.

Uprichard, E. (2007) 'Children as "being and becomings": children, childhood and temporality', *Children & Society*, vol 22, no 4, pp 303-13.

3

Children and young people's views on what counts as effective communication with them

"My perfect social worker would be happy, easy to talk to, and really helpful." (Jamie, aged 10, quoted in Headliners, 2009)

Introduction

Chapter Two considered some of the reasons why it is so important that social workers and other professionals engage and communicate directly with children and young people and what can get in the way of them doing so effectively. In later chapters there will be more detailed exploration of different aspects of communication with children and young people and consideration of how workers may develop the specific knowledge and capabilities they need for their roles and tasks. This requires, however, a baseline understanding to have been set of what might be considered good practice in communication. While Chapter Four looks more broadly at findings from outcome studies and qualitative inquiries with professionals and families, this chapter hears first from children and young people themselves about what they prefer, what has been unhelpful and what they would like professionals to do differently in their communications and interactions with them.

Children and young people's views of professionals' communication

There is now a significant body of research into children and young people's views on the contact they have had with social workers and other professionals in a range of contexts and for a variety of reasons. The 'Further reading and resources' section at the end of this chapter itemises some of these so that readers can consult studies relevant to their particular role. While many of these studies have shed light on what children liked and found helpful, a number also report their dissatisfaction at some professionals' communicative practices. Sources of discontent and frustration include children and young people feeling they have not been given the right kinds of opportunities to talk about their experiences and feelings; have not been provided with enough of the right kinds of information; have not had matters explained in a way which makes sense to them; and/or have not been consulted or involved sufficiently in assessments or decision-making processes.

What children and young people have reported in these studies suggests many practitioners have struggled to effectively engage and involve them in the way that legislation and good practice guidance now requires. Social workers seem to have been more successful in involving and listening to parents than their children (Cleaver et al, 2004). Children and young people's advice is that workers should make sure that they seek, listen to, believe and respect *their* views and experiences (de Winter and Noom, 2003), and do so in ways that are as child-centred as possible.

A child-centred approach

As briefly outlined in Chapter One, a child-centred approach is one that is in tune with the characteristics, abilities and preferences of individual children and young people and enables them to have more control over both the process and content of an assessment or interview. Rather than the tempo of the work being driven by adult- or service-centred timescales, it would be set to the child's pace. Methods would be more akin to children's usual way of communicating rather than solely talking. For younger children this might mean incorporating play or visual methods such as decision charts and stickers. For older young people, talking might need to be undertaken alongside activities such as playing pool or going for a coffee together. Children have described workers who operate in these ways as people who 'know how to talk to children'; teenagers see them as professionals who are able to 'speak to them on their level' (Munro, 2001). By contrast, when workers use difficult words, over-complex concepts, long and complicated descriptions and jargon, rather than short, clear sentences and everyday language, this is off-putting and confusing to children. At the same time, young people do not want professionals to be patronising, speaking down to them, using vocabulary or concepts which assume less capability than they have.

The principle of child-centredness also requires professionals to ensure that children with sensory impairments or complex healthcare needs, who normally communicate via augmentative or assistive systems or technologies, are enabled to do so. This might mean that practitioners should become skilled in these systems themselves, when they will be working with a particular individual for some time, or that they work closely with an interpreter or support worker more familiar with the child to ensure that a mutual understanding is established (Triangle, 2009). If workers do not commit to achieving these aims, then they are effectively disabling children, rendering them less competent in their communication than they have the potential to be (Stalker and Connors, 2003). Disabled children and young people have shared their views on the practices that professionals should avoid (Turner, 2003). These are summarised in Box 2.

Box 2: What disabled children and young people thought would be the worst kind of professional communication

Having someone who...

- thinks they know what is best for you rather than asking you
- doesn't listen
- talks to your parents instead of you perhaps because they think that you would not understand but hasn't bothered to find out if you can
- talks to you but you can't understand them
- isn't very friendly or happy and doesn't smile
- asks you to do things that you know you can't do
- doesn't explain what they are doing to you
- is rude, boring or unapproachable
- has not got any manners
- isn't caring, helpful or interested in you
- doesn't give you the right information
- doesn't follow support through
- doesn't have enough time and is always too busy

Source: Turner (2003)

Organisational cultures may get in the way of child-centred practice. Thomas and O'Kane (2000, p 831) suggest that there has been 'a devaluing or de-prioritising of relatively open-ended direct work with children in favour of structured assessment'. The constrictions of prescribed assessment frameworks can reinforce professionals' lack of confidence or creativity in working with children. This is unfortunate, as these authors found when carrying out their own research with children that:

It is precisely this open-ended work that we found to be most effective in engaging children to express their wishes and feelings. Adults need the freedom simply to spend time with a child, to establish some trust, and to find the best way to communicate with that particular child…. It does need to be relatively unconstrained by other pressures. (Thomas and O'Kane, 2000, p 831)

The challenge, then, may be to consider how more creative methods may be introduced even into time-led assessment structures. Chapters Eight, Nine and Ten give more consideration to this.

The right to be consulted and kept informed

Children of all ages and abilities emphasise the importance to them of professionals communicating directly with them and taking what they say seriously rather than just listening to their parents and carers (Morgan, 2006). Children can be left feeling powerless and frustrated when they are only able to influence what seem to them to be trivial issues, rather than more important matters such as whether they can have more contact with their birth family (Munro, 2001).

Significant decisions are often made in large forums or meetings such as courts, child protection conferences and panels. Many children want to attend such meetings as they want to know what is being said about them and to have their say, but the formal structures and processes do not always facilitate this. Unsurprisingly, children are often intimidated by the size and formality of meetings and are not convinced they can influence the decisions made (Bell, 2002). Some simply do not feel safe to share their wishes and feelings in such forums with professionals they do not know or trust. If information has not been appropriately explained to them in a way they can understand or remember, they may end up feeling that they have been unable to make a valid contribution to the discussion (Munro, 2001). Information and explanation about services and professionals' roles is also crucial (Massinga and Pecora, 2004). Chapter Eleven discusses how to keep children informed and involve them in meetings.

Disabled children have as much right to and interest in assessment, consultation and planning processes as anyone else and are able to fully participate where appropriate methods are used. Young people with learning disabilities, for example, were able to express a range of views in Children in Scotland's (2002) *Citizenship in practice* project. Where creative, flexible methods were used, young people with a range of abilities were enabled to participate. The project team emphasised that a lot of time needs to be spent first, however, developing disabled young people's understanding of choice and what decision making entails as many have not been given prior experience of choices. Box 3 summarises what these young people thought communication with them should be like.

Box 3: What young people with learning disabilities want communication with them to be like

- Respectful
- People using language they understand – "If they're talking about you, you want to know what they're saying"
- Having explained what is going to happen to them
- Having letters addressed to them personally
- Opportunities to participate in meetings about their education
- Information about their health that they understand
- Not being treated like a child
- People talking to them, not their parents
- Being treated the same as everybody else
- Choices being provided and explained

Source: Children in Scotland (2002)

When reports have been written and decisions made, conveying the reasons for such decisions and plans is crucial. Children and young people have a right to information about them and want to be able to understand as much as possible about what has happened and why. Some want to see as much of the reports written about them as possible and to have these clearly explained in their language (Bourton and McCausland, 2001). Writing summaries in clear age-appropriate language for children and young people to keep with them can be particularly helpful as they can keep re-reading these (or have them read to them) when they are trying to make sense of complex issues or situations. Explaining issues and events through drawings or recreating them with small figures may also be very helpful (see Chapters Eight and Ten).

Of course, concerns that younger children and particularly vulnerable young people could be significantly unsettled or distressed by discussion of very sensitive issues may well be appropriate. A careful assessment of what they can manage emotionally and psychologically must be made by those charged with their welfare. Professionals must still, however, remember that children and young people are also distressed and unsettled when there is a lack of any kind of satisfactory explanation, for example, about why there is no contact with their mother when this has suddenly been withdrawn. Even very young children who cannot fully understand what is going on will have feelings about decisions that are made that affect them and will want to have their say (Morgan, 2006). It is essential to consider whether information and discussions are being withheld because of the worker's anxieties rather than the child's. The practice vignette of Adam illustrates how this might happen.[1]

Practice vignette: Making connections for Adam

Adam (age nine) was in long-term foster care and had monthly contact with his mother. He arrived for his weekly play session with me in an unsettled and frustrated mood. I had heard just before the session that the next day's contact was cancelled as his mother was fleeing a violent relationship and had just moved to a refuge some distance away. Adam caused havoc in the playroom, covering himself and most of the room in paint and glue. Open questions about how he was feeling elicited no coherent response, so I asked directly how he felt about contact being cancelled. He became very flat at this and said, "It would have been nice to have seen her before she died".

To understand this comment it was necessary to make connections with Adam's history. Two years prior to this, when he lived with both parents, his father had died suddenly of a drug overdose. Adam had no opportunity to say goodbye and his mother had avoided explaining what had happened. For several weeks all Adam knew was that his father was gone and everyone was avoiding the subject with him.

Adam had made the assumption that his mother's sudden disappearance now was for the same reason: that is, death. His social worker had not told him the real reason why contact had been cancelled as she did not want to re-evoke Adam's memories of the domestic violence he had witnessed between his parents. She had not prepared an alternative explanation so had given vague responses to Adam's questions about why contact was cancelled and when he might see his mother again. Her approach had unwittingly re-evoked Adam's distress at the sudden loss of his father.

Importance of feelings

Fear and uncertainty may affect children's capacity or willingness to communicate. Children and young people are often suspicious (and often with good reason) of hidden agendas when being questioned by social workers (Thomas and O'Kane, 2000). Where there are child protection issues, they may be frightened of the worker's powers (or perceived powers, such as a belief that they will be able to remove them peremptorily from their parents' care).They can become wary or reticent, unsure about the consequences of what they say, watching every word (Bell, 2002). Unaccompanied asylum-seeking young people who are traumatised by previous experiences may also be fearful about any consequences of what they say on whether they can remain in the country.This may distort their usual ways of communication, making them much more silent and watchful than usual (Kohli, 2006).

Older young people can feel particularly uncomfortable, awkward or embarrassed talking about private and sensitive issues, in part, perhaps, because adolescence is a time of heightened self-consciousness.Young people say that they would prefer professionals to come across as comfortable with discussing such matters and un-embarrassable themselves (Freake et al, 2007). To do so, workers will need to feel confident themselves in discussing issues to do with sexuality, sexual health, relationships, substance and alcohol use/misuse and mental health problems (DH, 2004).

A real relationship

Being able to form a real person-to-person relationship with the professionals working with them is a significant factor in whether children and young people feel safe enough to engage and communicate (Munro, 2001; Bell, 2002; de Winter and Noom 2003).They need to know that they have been understood and accepted by their workers. Most will have experienced negative and complicated reactions from others elsewhere in their lives and might expect the same from professionals. So they will only begin to share their muddled thoughts, conflicting or ambivalent views, difficult behaviour and strong feelings when they can feel confident their workers are able to hear, manage and make sense of what they convey. Practitioners can demonstrate their capacity to do this not only through their empathy[2] and appropriate responsiveness, but also through ordinary human qualities such as enthusiasm, warmth, friendliness and humour (Farnfield and Kaszap, 1998; Prior et al, 1999).

Children and young people also want to feel that their workers genuinely care for and are concerned about them, rather than 'just doing a job' and presenting a professional persona. They would prefer practitioners to be someone who can be experienced as 'more like a friend':

> "I would talk to them about everyday things, something I'm really worried about, someone to help support and understand me, someone who would be there if I needed them, someone who would maybe go for a coffee." (unnamed young person, describing their ideal social worker, quoted in Morgan, 2006, p 10)

I have reported elsewhere the views of Jade, an 11-year-old child in care, on this matter (Lefevre, 2008a). She had felt that her foster carer's support worker really seemed to like her as an individual even though he was primarily there for her carers. By contrast, she received the impression that, for one of her key workers, "It was like her job, basically" (p 30). This was far less conducive to her talking about important and sensitive matters.

Practitioners may worry that they will blur the boundaries of the relationship if they are too friendly and compassionate. However, most children and young people do recognise where the professional role begins and ends and are not expecting to be taken to the worker's home to be part of the family or to have a romantic or sexual relationship with the worker, even if some might have fantasies about this. But when a worker is able to be warm and caring, showing a sense of humour and the idiosyncrasies of their personality, children and young people feel that the relationship is real and that they matter as individuals. Professional use of the personal self in this way requires both emotional availability and robustness. Some workers may try to defend themselves against personal feelings out of self-protection. One practitioner told me, in relation to a six-year-old girl in care proceedings, "I can't afford to really put myself in touch with what she is feeling. I have to go home at the end of the day and be there for my children, and I only have enough emotional space for either her or them, not both". This got in the way of him forming the kind of relationship with this little girl which would have helped him understand the real meaning of the emotional neglect she was experiencing.

Emotional robustness is also needed when workers feel bombarded with children and young people's distress, anger or 'stonewalling' behaviour (putting up 'barriers' and refusing to talk). One young child lucidly described how much she didn't like workers who went around 'huffing and puffing' (Prior et al, 1999); this can be all too easy for adults to do when they find a child's behaviour challenging or frustrating. Summarising the personal qualities needed to form 'real relationships' (itemised in Box 4), one child said that what made a 'helpful' professional depended "on the person more than what they do" (quoted in Farnfield and Kaszap, 1998, p 11).

Box 4: The sort of people social workers should be

- Outgoing, approachable, easy to talk to
- Not stuck up or too formal
- Able to get on with children and young people
- Capable of understanding "the ways and thoughts of kids"
- Able to keep promises

- Good listeners, able to both listen and be bothered
- Having a sense of humour
- Good at calming other people down when they are upset
- Not judging others, but trying to listen and understand

Source: Morgan (2006, p 12)

Trust and safety

The section above described how children and young people are more likely to engage and communicate when they feel able to trust their worker. Practitioners who are kind, supportive, warm, empathic, respectful, accepting and so on will help them feel safe and cared for and can promote the development of their trust (see Box 5). Using the self purposefully in this way demands emotional awareness and flexibility, but also calls on personal qualities in the individual. Many practitioners come in to the profession because they possess a capacity for such qualities already and can use their qualifying training to develop their potential. Others may need to undertake further self-development. Chapter Six will support readers in appraising existing capabilities and identifying areas for self-work.

Consistent, available and reliable behaviour can also help in building trust but may present a real challenge when the demands of the professional role interfere with pre-planned visits, regular time slots and protected space to plan and execute direct work. Young people have described a 'good social worker' as 'someone you can contact easily', but they do not always find they can get hold of their workers by telephone or have their messages returned; visits may also be cancelled, too (Morgan, 2006, p 7). When this happens, they are left feeling that they are simply the lowest priority. Children and young people would prefer practitioners to be open and transparent about such difficulties; they would like workers to telephone and apologise when they will be late and acknowledge when they have let children down. This would feel much more respectful to them and more like a genuine partnership (Morgan, 2006).

Social workers' dependability is also eroded by the culture common to many local authorities of social workers moving or being moved around frequently, through reorganisation, for promotion or through dissatisfaction. This has further eroded children's sense that they can depend on their social workers. Relationships have to be built again from scratch and children and young people are left sometimes thinking, 'why bother?'. Concerns about the impact on children and young people in care of such inconsistency has led to proposals for independent social work 'practices' (DCSF, 2007) as it is thought these may encourage workers to remain in post for longer and build up more enduring professional relationships with children and young people (Le Grand, 2007). The Social Work Task Force recommendation for improving pay and status to encourage social workers to remain in front-line practice, rather than heading into management in order to progress (Gibb, 2009c), may also improve practitioners' capacity to remain working with individuals for much longer periods of time.

Children and young people's perception of social workers' trustworthiness is eroded, too, by social workers who "'do not always do what they promise they will do'" (quoted in Morgan, 2006, p 7). Children and young people would much prefer it if workers did not give assurances in the first place unless they were sure that they could keep them. Children and young people also want professionals' undertakings to be complied with more speedily, for example, when services or interventions have been pledged but are slow appearing.

> ### Box 5: Qualities and behaviours that can help a child or young person feel trusting and safe
>
> - Kindness, supportiveness, a caring attitude and showing personal concern for children
> - Empathy, sympathy, showing understanding
> - Comfortable with, containing of and responsive to what children say, feel or do
> - Openness, genuineness, congruence and honesty
> - Accepting and non-judgemental approach
> - Friendly and warm in manner
> - Respectfulness towards children
> - Accessibility and availability
> - Consistency, trustworthiness and reliability
>
> *See* Munro (2001); Bell (2002); NCB (2004); Hart et al (2005); Thomas (2005); Freake et al (2007).

An anti-oppressive approach

An anti-oppressive approach may also help young people feel safer to communicate with professionals. Many will have experienced prejudicial or oppressive attitudes elsewhere in their lives, perhaps about their sexuality, race, culture, religion or disability, about having a social worker, being in care or living on a particular housing estate. Feeling judged, blamed or criticised by professionals who also seem to hold negative assumptions and stereotypes can mean some young people may never feel safe to talk about the things that really matter or are most private (Freake et al, 2007). Lesbian, gay, bisexual and transgender (LGBT) young people, for example, can feel particularly unsafe and be wary of open communication about their needs, views and experiences where they experience workers to be judgmental, heterosexist and homophobic, rather than accepting (Freed-Kernis, 2008). Practitioners will need to challenge themselves to check that they are not promoting hetero-normativity through their casual and unthinking use of language (Hunt and Jensen, 2006). Black and minority ethnic children and young people have highlighted in research studies the fear and discomfort they feel when misunderstandings arise from culturally different communicative and relational styles; the worker's lack of knowledge about their cultural or religious norms can oppress and silence them (Kohli, 2006).

Confidentiality

A confidential space is important to many children and young people, enabling them to feel safe enough to talk about very private issues or sensitive matters (NCB, 2004). Young people do appreciate that there are times when professionals must breach confidentiality if it is to protect them from serious risk of harm (Freake et al, 2007). However, they would prefer a space where they can safely explore their thoughts and feelings without it all getting written down in the file and shared with strangers, as many have found seems to happen (Munro, 2001). To protect themselves against this some young people will simply not tell the most sensitive information to professionals they do not trust and this may affect their capacity to use supports to help them (Ryan et al, 1995). Policies such as the National Service Framework do require organisations working with young people to have procedures that ensure that their right to confidentiality is respected (DH, 2004; Welsh Assembly Government, 2005), so these structures should now be supporting young people's expressed views on this. There will be further exploration of conflicts in confidentiality in Chapter Eleven.

Being listened to

The importance of really being listened to is emphasised by children and young people in numerous research studies. Those who are homeless (de Winter and Noom, 2003), young carers (Dearden and Becker, 2000), those who have been sexually abused (Prior et al, 1999), children using mental health services (Hart et al, 2005), children in care (McLeod, 2007) and those going through care proceedings (Masson and Oakley, 1999; Ruegger, 2001) have all emphasised the significance of this to them. Some who had been through child protection investigations, for example, highlighted how "careful listening, without trivializing or being dismissive" was among the most valued attributes of their social workers (quoted in Bell, 2002, p 8). Three quarters of children and young people in one study relating to care proceedings considered the 'ability to listen' as their guardian's most important skill (Bourton and McCausland, 2001).

Where children and young people feel they have been listened to and that their contribution to decision making has been taken into account, this has enhanced the likelihood of successful outcomes for interventions (Bell, 2002; Hart et al, 2005). Improved emotional and psychological benefits also accrue when children and young people have been invited to actively participate and feel their views have been taken seriously (Dearden and Becker, 2000; de Winter and Noom, 2003). Such beneficial outcomes led Schofield and Brown (1999, pp 27–8) to conclude that 'developments in contemporary social work practice which are often framed in terms of children's rights and empowerment can be reframed quite usefully as making excellent psychological sense'.

For social workers undertaking statutory roles and tasks, however, 'listening' is not a straightforward process. The complexity is highlighted by young people, who said that:

> A good social worker is one who, while you are still at home with your family, can spot when you are crying out for help, and give that help before you have to be taken into care 6 or 8 months later. (Morgan, 2006, p 7)

In this example, of course, the children are not literally crying out 'help me'. Social work would be much easier, and probably far less necessary, if children could always name exactly what is going wrong and let others know. Unfortunately, children are often too powerless, traumatised, confused or frightened to speak directly about such matters; they may also lack the conceptual understanding or vocabulary to do so. Instead they expect (and rightly so) that trained professionals should be able to listen and observe carefully in order to pick up on emotions and things that are left unsaid. It is in such ways that practitioners should be able to 'hear' children's concerns and act on them accordingly.

McLeod (2007) identified other complexities to 'listening' through observing social workers' communication with children and young people and speaking to them all about the processes involved. The young participants overwhelmingly complained that social workers did not listen to them and that their voices went unheard. This was surprising to McLeod as her observations indicated that the workers had good communication skills and were strongly committed to listening to what the children and young people had to say. It became apparent, however, that the children were feeling that they were not being listened to if the worker did not act in accordance with their wishes; they felt ignored and not heard. This disparity is echoed in Morgan's (2006) consultation with children and young people. They 'wanted social workers not only to ask their views, but really to try to act according to what [they] wanted' (Morgan, 2006, p 19). However, some young people were left feeling that they were only listened to when they said what the social worker already thought best anyway; if they disagreed, their impression was that the social worker had 'selective hearing'!

Assessment frameworks and tools

The process of consulting and listening to children and young people might be expected to be facilitated by assessment frameworks, tools and documentation issued to practitioners to gather information and views from them. However, children and young people have described significant reservations about formalised, pre-structured formats that may be time-consuming, off-putting or stultifying and lack flexibility (Francis, 2002). Their advice is that practitioners need to use such formats flexibly in order to make them relevant to the individual. Pre-structured questions or exercises may not be appropriate for children of all ages or cognitive abilities. Some young people feel patronised by documentation they perceive to be over-simplified or 'childish', while others are put off by finding the language and concepts used to be too complex. If workers treat assessment frameworks and tools as a straightforward 'checklist', going through a sequence of questions, young people may feel like they are being 'put into boxes', with their lives compartmentalised. Instead they want the complexities and nuances of their individual needs and experiences to be recognised and addressed as they might in a freer interaction (Francis, 2002).

Interpersonal skills and building a relationship are often a crucial prerequisite to the successful use of such tools as some young people are reluctant to respond to questions from someone they do not know very well or do not have a good relationship with, particularly where sensitive questions are concerned. As a final word on the subject, Box 6 relates what young people think would be the worst kind of worker to carry out a CAF[3] assessment with them (NCB, 2004).

Box 6: The world's worst CAF assessor

This would be someone who:

- is too official, patronising, or intimidating
- laughs at you and any problems you have
- makes derogatory remarks
- tells you what to do instead of advising you
- has no opinion, sits on the wall too much, rather than finding a balance between giving advice and telling you to do something
- has no manners
- drones on, keeps talking over you
- thinks they are better than you
- has no consideration for you, who you really are as a person
- doesn't give you the attention you need
- has a 'my way or the highway' attitude and does what you don't want them to do
- brands all children and young people with the same brush
- treats you like you are stupid
- has no intention of helping you but is just going through the motions
- doesn't have their heart in their job – it's just a salary
- 'blackmails' you
- isn't like you at all
- gossips about you
- often turns up late and answers their telephone while talking to you
- refers to other people's problems in order to resolve yours

Source: NCB (2004)

Conclusion

Numerous reports and research studies are now available which allow children and young people's voices to be heard about what is important to them in communication. A number of themes have emerged in this chapter. It is clear that children and young people want a child–centred approach, one which goes at their pace and uses modes and methods of communication which are facilitative. They want professionals to consult them about matters that concern them and keep them well informed. This means practitioners must speak[4] directly with them, not just their parents or carers, listen to them and take what they say seriously. Children and young people want to be involved in meetings about them wherever possible and have any decisions or plans carefully explained to them. Being able to explore and explain what is important or worrying to them requires a relationship of trust and an atmosphere of safety. They need to know that workers can make sense and respond to their feelings, too, not just their words.

Children and young people's requirements for effective communication clearly draw on far more than knowledge and techniques in professionals. Instead, as the child in Farnfield and Kaszap's (1998) study which is quoted above indicated, skilfulness depends significantly on the people themselves, not just what they know and what they do. Chapter Five later sets out a model of 'core capability' in communication that is based on this idea. First, however, in Chapter Four, there is a consideration of what communication theory can tell us about skill and effectiveness in this area of practice.

Notes

[1] Wherever practice examples are used in the book, all names and identifying details are changed.

[2] Empathy is the process by which individuals try to acquire a sense of what the other person is thinking, feeling or experiencing by trying to temporarily step into the other person's shoes, to see the world from their point of view and reflect on what this might be like. They then aim to find a sensitive way of conveying to the other person that they have been heard and understood.

[3] CAF is the popular shorthand for an assessment carried out under the common assessment framework in England (CWDC, 2008).

[4] Terms such as 'speak' are used as shorthand in this book to refer to direct forms of dialogue with children that do not have to be verbal, but could also include conversation through sign language, using a communication board or be via an interpreter.

Key questions

1. What do you think are the three most important messages from children and young people about how professionals should communicate with them? Why?
2. How would you define a child-centred approach?
3. What factors can help a child or young person feel safe enough to communicate with a worker?

Further reading and resources

Freake, H., Barley, V. and Kent, G. (2007) 'Adolescents' views of helping professionals: a review of the literature', *Journal of Adolescence*, vol 30, pp 639-53.

Headliners (2009) *Children's professionals: What I really think of my ...* (www.headliners.org/storylibrary/stories/2005/childrensprofessionalswhatireallythinkofmy.htm?id=6787184094961558887).

Hill, M. (1999) 'What's the problem? Who can help? The perspectives of children and young people on their well-being and on helping professionals', *Journal of Social Work Practice*, vol 13, no 2, pp 135-45.

Morgan, R. (2006) *About social workers. A Children's Views report*, Newcastle upon Tyne: Commission for Social Care Inspection (https://www.rights4me.org/content/beheardreports/3/about_social_workers_report.pdf).

Other studies directly reporting children's views on professionals' communication with them in specific contexts which readers may find useful to consult, depending on their role:

- Children and young people who have been assessed under the assessment framework (Cleaver et al, 2004)
- Children and young people who have been through child protection investigations (Bell, 2002)
- Children and young people who have been interviewed (Westcott and Davies, 1996) or received services (Prior et al, 1999) following sexual abuse
- Young people who have had contact with doctors, mental health workers and other 'helping professionals' (Freake et al, 2007)
- Children who have been looked after by the local authority (Munro, 2001; Francis, 2002; Leeson, 2007; McLeod, 2007)
- Children and young people who have had a guardian during care proceedings (Masson and Oakley, 1999; Bourton and McCausland, 2001)
- Children who have been adopted (Thomas et al, 1999)

- Young people in the process of leaving care (Biehal et al, 1995; Gaskell, 2009)
- Homeless young people (de Winter and Noom, 2003)
- Disabled children and young people (Turner, 2003)
- Children who have witnessed or experienced domestic violence (Hague et al, 2002)
- Young carers (Aldridge and Becker, 1993)
- Young people involved with youth offending services (Triseliotis et al, 1998)

4

Some theoretical perspectives on the nature of communication

Introduction

Communication lies at the heart of the social work process; it is the very means by which assessments, planning, interventions and reviews are carried out with children and young people (Trevithick, 2005). 'Communication', however, is a complex term, covering a whole range of behaviours and interpersonal processes. Definitions of what it involves and what makes it work are not necessarily consensual. This chapter reviews some key perspectives on communication, considering their relevance and usefulness for different social work roles and tasks with children and young people. They are illustrated through the practice vignettes of Robbie, Manako and Mandy.

Two-way nature of communication

Practice vignette: Longer-term work with Robbie

Robbie is a 14-year-old white young person who has been in care for six months following a history of neglect and physical abuse by his mother. His social worker, Ben, meets with him regularly to support him in his placement, keep him informed and consult with him about the progression of care proceedings. Ben is also helping Robbie to rebuild his relationship with his father, who has been prevented from seeing Robbie for several years by Robbie's mother as the situation became acrimonious following their separation.

Communication as a transmission of information

The most simple and straightforward way of thinking about communication is that it involves a linear process of exchanging information, or what might be termed *messages*. Each message is thought to have a *basic* content

– something that one person wants or needs to let another know about. This message is then purposely *transmitted* to another person or persons. In relation to the practice vignette above, examples of transmission of messages might include Ben notifying Robbie about his father's request to re-initiate contact, or Robbie telling Ben that he does not like the food his foster carer cooks for him. Howe (1996) refers to such exchanges of basic messages as 'surface interactions'. These primarily involve conscious thoughts and intentions and are conveyed deliberately through formal communication systems, such as verbal language, writing or a sign language such as BSL (British Sign Language). Language needs to be shared as messages might not get through if, for example, Ben were to use jargon that Robbie is not familiar with or concepts that Robbie does not understand.

However, such a definition of communication reveals only part of the complex, multidimensional web of interchanges and interpretations involved (Luckock et al, 2006a). It does not take into account the 'depth interactions' between people that are just as significant in communication (Howe, 1996). Some of these additional layers will now be explored.

Communication as interpersonal and interactional

The first layer to be explored is the *interpersonal* one. The very notion of 'transmission' implies interaction – there needs to be a *receiver* of the message. However, social workers are not blank screens or empty repositories for receiving messages and nor are young people. The nature of the relationship between the two individuals will affect what one person says and how the other hears and makes sense of it (Marsen, 2006). A chain of message exchanges may ensue – what we might call a dialogue. Or the communication may cease, either because the matter is resolved or because one or other person withdraws.

Defining who is the initiator or responder within a dialogue may not be straightforward. A social worker might instigate a conversation by asking a young person questions about their wishes, feelings, experiences, needs or concerns. However, children and young people may also choose spontaneously to confide in a professional who provides the *facilitating conditions* which encourage them to share their thoughts, feelings, ideas and concerns with them. These conditions might be relational (building up a sufficiently trusting relationship with the child so he or she feels safe to talk) or environmental (ensuring there is sufficient time without interruptions, a comfortable space, clarity regarding confidentiality issues and so on).

The role of body language and paralanguage

The next layer to be explored relates to what might additionally be conveyed indirectly and unintentionally between children and their social workers. As well as the basic message that one might intend to put across to the other, both young people and their workers might additionally transmit a whole range of thoughts, feelings and perceptions through non-verbal means. In fact, research by Mehrabian (1971, quoted in Dunhill, 2009) found that only seven per cent of communication involved the direct words spoken between people. Instead it was *paralanguage* that conveyed 38 per cent of the meaning of the message. Paralanguage refers to someone's speed of speaking, their tone of voice, the loudness, pitch and intonation of their speech and so on. Body language, behaviour and other non-verbal signs accounted for the remaining 55 per cent of information transmitted.

This additional information may concur with the basic verbal message. So, for example, a professional's responsive body language, softened eye contact and gentle tone of voice may express their feelings of compassion and help their words seem more authentic to a child or young person. An impatient tone of voice or a foot tapping might alternatively, however, give away a worker's feelings of irritation that they are trying to conceal.

> **Practice vignette: Indirect communication between Robbie and Ben**
>
> Robbie is being driven by Ben to meet his father for the first time in four years. Robbie is anxious and needs reassurance so keeps on asking Ben how he thinks the meeting will go. The traffic is heavy on the road and it is raining so Ben has to concentrate on his driving and feels rather irritated with Robbie. Although he is trying not to show it, traces of annoyance are apparent in his tone of voice, which Robbie picks up on ... and becomes even more insecure and anxious.

Unconscious or disowned feelings and motivations may also be revealed in this way. If Ben generally feels rather negatively towards Robbie, but knows this is unacceptable given the professional role he is in, he might try to repress such feelings. Rather than disappearing, these feelings could operate outside of Ben's awareness and become less subject to his conscious control. They may manifest themselves through his body language and paralanguage, conveying an unwelcome message to Robbie.

Where a child or young person with a speech or language impairment is using a particular communication system such as a picture board or 'touch talker', the process may be similar to that in verbal conversations, that is, the basic message is carried in the sign, picture or written word, with body language or sound adding further layers of meaning. Some children do not use formal language systems, however, and so their gestures, facial expressions and sounds may replace words, signs and symbols. Family members and carers know that these are purposeful and meaningful forms of communication and are able to interpret them once they are familiar with the child (Millar and Scott, 2003):

> "James communicates through body language and facial expression. His sister describes him well. She says that he 'beams all over' when he is happy and 'screams all over' when he is upset. I think that sums him up really. Perhaps I would add that there are many shades of grey between the beam and the scream." (parent, quoted by Murray, 2006, in Marchant, 2008, p 153)

Miscommunication and 'noise'

The next layer to be explored is miscommunication. Individuals need to respond not just to the basic content of a message but also the *meta-messages*. These convey the underpinning meaning of a communication, what the transmitting person thinks and feels and what they intend to convey to someone else (Thompson, 2003). Meta-messages are not carried solely through formal language, but also within body language and paralanguage. Receivers will not necessarily 'hear' the meta-message unless they take in more than just the words. The response they then make in return (verbal or non-verbal) will need to be formulated in such a way that conveys comprehension of the entire meta-message rather than just the basic content.

   In social work, however, as in every day life, there are often misunderstandings or misinterpretations of what has been said, shown, heard or witnessed. These can be defined as *miscommunications*, where 'the message does not reach the receiver in the way it was intended by the sender' (Marsen, 2006, p 32). Children often struggle to convey clearly what is important to them (the meta-message) and workers may not fully understand what it is they are hearing or seeing. The reverse is also true: practitioners are not always able to find intelligible or appropriate ways of explaining difficult or sensitive issues, leaving children unable to make sense of the information presented. This is not just true of conversations, but also when reading another's reports, emails or text messages, viewing their art imagery or communicating via sign language.

   Children and young people will 'read' the body language and paralanguage of their workers to see whether or not they indicate that their confidences or experiences have been understood, accepted and respected. If the workers' responses seem mis-attuned they will not receive the impression that their meta-messages have been received. In the vignette above, Robbie's meta-message might be "I'm anxious, please reassure me!". Because he is busy driving, however, Ben only hears a request for an opinion about the meeting and does not provide the reassurance that Robbie needs. In fact, his mis-attuned response might even give Robbie the message, "I don't care", or even "I think the meeting will go really badly, but I'm not going to tell you that".

By monitoring and evaluating the mood and atmosphere between them, practitioners can work out whether they might need to moderate their tone of voice, facial gestures or body language to alter the nuance of the exchange and help children and young people feel that their meta-messages have been heard and understood.

'Noise' and 'ideal speech'

Many factors might cause miscommunication and get in the way of two people establishing a shared understanding. Complex thoughts and feelings (such as fear, anxiety, mistrust, anger, envy and shame), interpersonal and social dynamics (such as blame, expectations, assumptions, prejudice and oppression) and difficult environmental conditions (such as danger, tiredness, poor lighting, background sounds, needing to undertake a task at the same time) might inhibit, limit, interrupt or distort the communication between two people (Ekman, 2003). Such processes can be thought of as *noise* between people, preventing unconstrained and reciprocal dialogue and derailing the establishment of shared understanding (Shannon and Weaver, 1949). In the practice vignette, the 'noise' between Robbie and Ben included the difficult driving conditions and Robbie's anxiety.

The social theorist Habermas (1984) contended that where 'noise-free dialogue' is enabled to occur between individuals and communities, an emancipated society could emerge; all individuals would be able to fully participate socially and politically through unconstrained, authentic and mutual exchange. Habermas advised that individuals and wider society would need to make an ethical commitment to reducing power differentials, distortions, distractions, muddle, inhibitions, misunderstandings or manipulations if such *ideal speech* conditions were to be created (Outhwaite, 1994). These concepts of 'noise-free dialogue' and 'ideal speech' can usefully be borrowed for social work, setting an aspiration for practitioners and their services to create the kinds of facilitative conditions which can empower children to fully participate in dialogue and consultation in meaningful (rather than tokenistic) ways.

Interpretive nature of communication within context

Encoding and decoding

The discussion above illuminates how meaning cannot always be transmitted between two people in a straightforward manner. Theorists within the discipline of semiotics[1] would suggest that this is in part due to the symbolic nature of language (Barthes, 1972). From this perspective, words are seen as signs and symbols that are combined and *encoded* in systems to form messages to be exchanged. The words 'Happy Birthday', for example, do not represent something in and of themselves. They have merely been arbitrarily selected by people in a particular social and cultural context to encode and represent a set of common feelings, rituals, experiences and expectations. Such encoding needs subsequently to be *decoded* by the receiver of a communication, drawing on cultural knowledge to contextualise and interpret the words (Halliday, 1996).

As words are combined to form sentences, statements, requests and expressions, and are overlaid with body language and paralanguage, decoding becomes ever more complex (Griffin, 2006). So, while a child may describe her experiences in words (the basic message), exactly what these words mean (their meta-messages) may not be properly understood and appreciated by the worker unless and until he or she has decoded or interpreted them.

Children and young people, such as Robbie, often struggle to name or convey their inner thoughts or feelings and experiences in words, and might demonstrate these more through their behaviour, play, body language, tone of voice or way of relating to others. Professionals will consequently require *observational* and *interpretive* skills to enable them to 'listen' and respond appropriately to children and young people. If workers and children have different cultural and social reference points then they may evaluate what has been communicated very differently and misunderstandings are particularly likely (Fiske, 1990). (See Chapter Nine for a further discussion of the role of observation in communication and some of the interpretive processes involved.)

Figure 1 illustrates this interactive and interpretive nature of effective communication. A thought or feeling forms and is encoded into the primary language of the adult or young person initiating an exchange. The basic message is then transmitted to the one receiving it. This may be in speech, writing (such as email or text messaging), sign language or mediated through an augmentative or alternative communication system such as picture board, touch talker or some form of electronic tool (Millar and Scott, 2003). The receiver then listens carefully and tries to make sense of what was meant and intended. To do so, they will have to take account of not just the basic message, but also the meta-message, which may have been encoded into behaviour, body language, play or creative artefacts, such as drawings, rather than just the words. A response can then be provided to indicate what has been understood. Again this may not just be through the words used.

Figure 1: A process of effective communication interchange

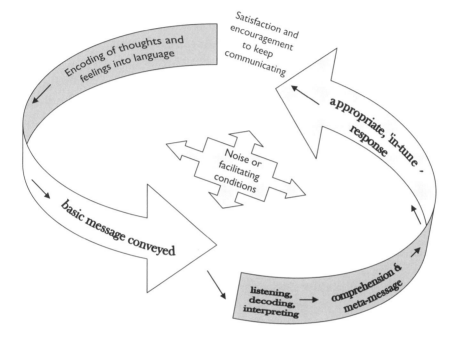

Habitus

Cultural beliefs, values and norms all help people to encode and decode messages. These provide subconscious heuristics, conventions and customs that enable individuals to rapidly appraise and interpret social situations and work out the 'right' or acceptable way to respond. Another social theorist, Bourdieu (1991), named this as *habitus*. Habitus is considered to be historically and socially situated and so only assists interpretation of communications with others who share or value the same conventions, rituals or customs, such as family and friends, neighbours or particular community or ethnic groups (Lovell, 2000). For example, in the British culture, people who do not make eye contact might be perceived as untrustworthy, depressed or lacking in self-esteem. In other parts of the world not making eye contact might be seen as a mark of respect or sexual modesty (Hargie and Dickson, 2004). Social and cultural practices such as offering to shake hands, use of first name or surname/family name, slang, street language and professional jargon are just some examples of practices which can provoke offence or lead to misunderstanding if they are misinterpreted (Maybin, 2001).

Practice vignette: Cultural differences in communication

The Kobayashi family are Japanese and moved to live in the UK four years ago. Their son, Tadami, is terminally ill with leukaemia. The hospital social worker, Roy, has become concerned about their daughter, Manako, as she does not seem to be expressing any emotion about what is happening.

Comment on the vignette

Responses to strong feelings or difficult events are also culturally laden. In this practice vignette, Manako has taken on her family's cultural beliefs and expectations that she should not publicly express feelings such as anger, fear or sadness. The cultural context within which she has been raised has tended to valorise self-restraint and attempts to understate, avoid, ignore or diffuse intense or unpleasant situations (Kitayama et al, 1997). Manako's habitus makes it very hard for her to respond to Roy's attempts to encourage her to express such emotions.

Roy does not share Manako's habitus and is not aware of this particular belief system and set of customs, so he fails to appreciate the cultural reasons behind her reserve. He is wondering (wrongly) whether she is not upset about her brother's condition or does not understand how serious it is. He is also in danger of pathologising her lack of expressed emotion, wondering if it reflects a problematic family life which has not allowed Manako to recognise her feelings or feel safe expressing them (which, again, is not the case).

The concept of habitus highlights how communication 'never happens solely within the confines of a relationship, but in a larger world which affects both the nature of the relationship and the nature of the communication that properly takes place within it' (Koprowska, 2008, p 6). Roy needs to enhance his *cultural competence*, increasing his knowledge of Manako's cultural background and norms to avoid tensions and misunderstandings arising due to any differences in communicative and relational styles (Caple et al, 1995). It is important, however, that he does not make assumptions or over-simplifications about this based on literature, as 'deductions that are made about a culture to which one does not belong can sometimes be over-simplified and lacking in insight' (Ahmed, 1986, p 147). Instead he should try to learn as much as possible from Manako and her family as there are often individual and sub-cultural variations from macro-cultural patterns.

Misunderstandings may be particularly significant where professionals are communicating with children like Manako for whom English is not their primary language or who are bilingual, but whose command of English seems good enough that an interpreter is not required. Much of the nuance of their expression may be lost or misinterpreted. Children like Manako may only be able to give a thin rather than rich account of their lives and intentions in English, as it is often only when speaking in their native or primary language that an individual is able to fully represent and narrate their experiences, thoughts, feelings and wishes.

The concepts of 'high context' and 'low context' cultures are helpful in understanding such intercultural communication norms and values. Asia, Japan, the Middle East and South America have been classified as high context cultures (Manrai and Manrai, 1996, quoted in Robinson, 2007). These are ones in which little of the meta-message is carried in the basic content of the message; most is conveyed through the contextual reading of body language, rituals, paralanguage, and so on. Low context cultures, such as those in Western Europe, appear to place a greater reliance on the verbal part of the message. The unfamiliar nature of others' communication may lead to suspicion and mistrust as well as miscommunication. For example, those from low context cultures perceive those from high context cultures as non-disclosing, sneaky and mysterious, while they are viewed as overly talkative themselves (Anderson, 1990).

Power issues inherent in intercultural communication

Paralanguage, body language, vocabulary, slang, accent, dialect, discourse and so on are a key way in which people express their cultural, sub-cultural and ethnic identities, as the linguistic distinctiveness is shared with others from similar communities or groupings (Keats, 1997). Habitus provides one way of understanding communication and miscommunications between individuals from different groups. What it misses out, however, is the dimension of power. Individuals commonly make value judgements about others' social class, education and ethnicity on the basis of their use of language:

> Generally speaking there is a pecking order among languages that is usually buttressed and supported by the prevailing political order.... Since many Western societies place such a high premium on the use of English, it is a short step to conclude that minorities are inferior, lack awareness or lack conceptual thinking powers. On the other hand, those who speak English are evaluated according to their various accents and dialects. (Robinson, 2007, p 110)

Workers from a dominant racial or ethnic background may deliberately or unthinkingly replicate and perpetuate class-based or ethno-centric norms, further disempowering children and young people. For example, the patois[2] used by young black people has often been seen as a deviant or deficient form of mainstream English by those in positions of authority who focus on what seems to be 'missing' or grammatically incorrect. If, however, patois is viewed alternatively by professionals as a language in its own right, rather than a dialect, its unique and logical syntax, semantic system and grammar are accepted and appreciated. Young black people are then better positioned to use a language that expresses their racial and cultural group identity in an assertive way.

Similarly, while a misreading of black people's emotional expressiveness might be attributed to cultural difference, the power dimension should not be ignored. There are indeed cultural and ethnic variations in what are considered appropriate levels of emotional expression, as the example of Manako, above, illustrated. But social workers need to guard against operating by a set of white Eurocentric norms that risk pathologising children and young people. A fuller exploration of power issues in communication is provided in Chapter Six.

Naming and conveying inner thoughts and feelings: post-structuralist ideas

Inherent in some of the discussion above are assumptions that 'real' or 'authentic' thoughts, wishes, feelings and ideas may exist inside children's minds, waiting to be conveyed to others as a meta-message when the opportunity arises, that is, a belief that children's communications can *reflect* the 'reality' of their inner worlds. The post-structuralist theorist Derrida (1978) suggested, by contrast, that it is the very act of speaking, writing or signing thoughts and feelings that brings them into existence, that is, the process of communication *creates* inner world feelings and experiences, not just reflects them. From this perspective, the context within which dialogue occurs is thought to influence not just how a meta-message is conveyed but actually helps to construct its content (Shotter, 1993).

This viewpoint caused Derrida to believe that written words were superior to conversations as they offered the opportunity for reflection and re-working; a closer approximation of the meta-message could then be developed and conveyed. Derrida contended that the spoken word, being in and of the moment, was more influenced by the social and cultural environment in which it emerges and by the behaviour, presence and response of others; it might, therefore, be less representative of the unalloyed internal thought. The implications are that, while what a person says in the moment may have an enduring representativeness of what is thought and felt over time, it is possible that it may only signify a fleeting perception or passing mood. It may only reflect a stage in a developing narrative or it might be completely misrepresentative of what the person usually thinks or feels, such as an attempt to impress, which is later regretted. Other aspects of the overall picture of what a person thinks or feels may be hidden, forgotten, emphasised, downplayed or changed in the telling.

If Derrida's theory is accepted, it has implications for how professionals attempt to ascertain children's views, wishes and feelings in a given situation. First, it might behove workers to be cautious that what a child says at one point is the whole of what they think or feel. The example of Mandy (a white Scottish child) in the next practice vignette provides a helpful illustration.

Practice vignette: Expressing complex feelings

Mandy lives with her mother, mother's partner and younger siblings. She sees her estranged father most weekends. The relationship between her mother and father, always volatile, has been particularly strained since her mother's partner moved in. During a fracas outside the family home, a neighbour called the police concerned about the children who were watching at the window. A social worker visits and hears from the mother that the fight was because Mandy didn't want to go to a 'contact' visit with her father, and her father did not accept this. The social worker asks Mandy how she feels about seeing her father. Mandy says "Sometimes I wish he would just disappear".

Comment on the vignette

It could be very unhelpful for the social worker to jump to the assumption that this represents the whole of what Mandy feels about her father. While she may, indeed, feel negatively about contact with him on that day, it might be because she wants to avoid any future family rows. She might also be trying to go along with her mother's feelings on the matter, to please or placate her, or out of obedience. Only a fuller assessment, in which Mandy feels safe enough with the worker to begin to explore the complexities of the situation, might enable her to work out what she really does feel and want and then to express this. Considering the whole of the context alongside the words is, then, crucial. Chapter Eight considers how best to do this in an assessment.

Second, workers should be aware of their own influence over what children say. Children tend to be more sensitive to the unexpressed desires and feelings of others than is often appreciated (Jones, 2003). If Mandy feels the worker disapproves of her father, she may express negative feelings about contact to please or appease him. The perceived powerfulness of professionals in decision making, their emotional importance to a child and the child's prior psychosocial experiences will all be influential here.

Third, to promote therapeutic change, children need to be encouraged to process their experiences, thoughts and feelings in order for distress, loss and trauma to be processed and integrated. Their narratives are likely to need to be told and re-told, constructed anew in every encounter with the worker, changing and developing in the telling, without earlier versions of 'truth' and 'reality' necessarily being held on to (Wickham and West, 2002). Mandy's way of thinking and speaking about her father may vary over a period of weeks or months as she struggles to come to terms with the complex family relationships. If the worker allows her a safe, free and non-judgemental space then Mandy will be able to express and reflect on her ambivalent and painful feelings and even resolve some of the complexities.

Dynamic and contextual nature of communication between workers and children

What children bring to the encounter

Children as well as professionals bring assumptions, feelings, qualities and experiences to encounters. As highlighted in Chapter One, every child has a unique developmental trajectory providing them with different kinds of characteristics and capabilities which influence how they 'do' communication. Many of these will vary over time as children mature but other factors, such as their social and cultural capital,[3] experiences of abuse, neglect, trauma and separation, and illness or impairments, will also affect individual children's capacities and ways of communicating.

As noted above, the social, cultural and interpersonal context of communication all affect how children communicate. Factors include the extent to which children want to engage with professionals, have a liking for particular individuals or feel safe or motivated enough to enter a dialogue. Pre-existing perceptions and assumptions of professionals, based on personal experiences, family views or media discourses, can interfere with how workers are seen, regardless of what they actually do. Negative feelings and perceptions may mean children 'going silent' on the worker, not turning up to appointments or hiding important information. Children could seem compliant on the surface but could be just saying what they think the worker wants to hear. Feeling disempowered or disadvantaged in the situation can also interfere with the manner in which children express themselves.

What workers bring to their communication with children

The characteristics, feelings and capabilities of the worker similarly affect the extent to which children are able to express themselves. Practitioners' capacity to engage and form relationships with children and to inspire feelings of trust and safety can contribute to facilitative, 'ideal speech' conditions. Conversely, their inability to do so may erect barriers to communication. Practitioners' feelings about particular children and the situation within which they are communicating are likely to affect how they go about it. The extent to which they have the time or resources for the work or good supervision may enhance or detract from their creativity, clear thinking and emotional engagement with a child. They may find themselves feeling warm and nurturing towards a particular child, irritable with their behaviour or bored by them. These feelings will all be communicated along with any words they say through paralanguage.

The exchanges between social workers and children, as was outlined earlier in the chapter, take place within a particular social and cultural context at a given moment in time. They also occur within a specific professional context and for a *purpose*, such as to promote assessment, participation or therapeutic change. The habitus of both worker and child will influence how they interact and construct meaning within the communication. These processes indicate, then, that effective communication is a function of the interactional dynamics both between workers and children and between them and their environment. Figure 2 reflects some of these dynamic, interactional and contextual aspects.

Figure 2: Modelling the dynamic and contextual nature of communication between children and young people and their workers

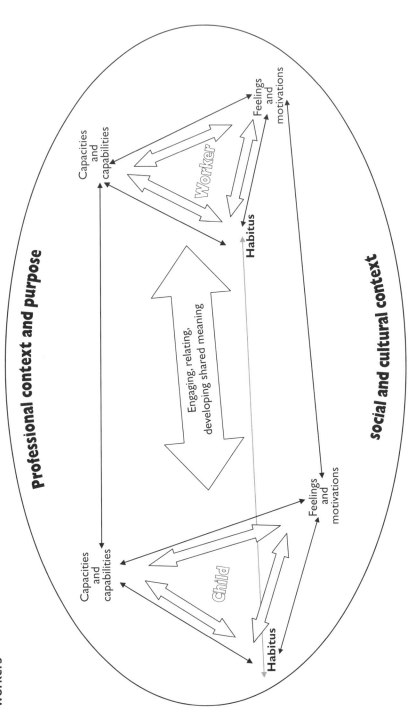

Conclusion

In this chapter communication has been shown to involve a complex set of interactional processes and dynamics that may easily lead to miscommunication and misinterpretation. The 'encoding' of one person's thoughts and feelings into formal language requires that they are subsequently 'decoded' by another. It is not only the overt content of a message which needs to be listened to, but also the paralanguage and non-verbal forms of communication, as these help the deeper and intended meaning or 'meta-message' to be interpreted and responded to appropriately. Emotional and cultural awareness and observational and interpretive skills are all needed if professionals are to do this effectively, particularly when the worker and child have a divergent 'habitus'. In order to overcome the inhibitory effects of the context of their communication, practitioners will also need to provide 'facilitating conditions', free of 'noise', if they are to encourage children to engage and share their thoughts, feelings and views. Workers will need to develop both themselves and their practice in a range of ways if they are to achieve this.

Notes
[1] Semiotics is the theory and study of signs and symbols, especially as elements of language or other systems of communication.
[2] Patois is a Creole language or dialect characteristic of black (African American and African Caribbean) culture. It is also referred to as Black English (Robinson, 2007).
[3] Social and cultural capital are defined and discussed in Chapter Five.

Key questions

1   What is the difference between the basic message and a meta-message?
2.   How does habitus help people to work out how to communicate and interact with each other?
3.   What kinds of factors cause 'noise' between social workers and children?

Further reading and resources

Augmentative Communication in Practice (eds) (2003) *Augmentative communication in practice: An introduction*, Edinburgh: Scottish Executive Education Department (http://callcentre.education.ed.ac.uk/SCN/Intro_SCA/IntroIN_SCB/introin_scb.html).

Hargie, O. and Dickson, D. (2004) *Skilled interpersonal communication* (4th edn), London: Routledge.

Laird, S. (2008) *Anti-oppressive social work: A guide for developing cultural competence*, London: Sage Publications.

Richards, S., Lefevre, M. and Trevithick, P. (2008) *Communication across social and cultural differences*, London: Social Care Institute for Excellence (www.scie.org.uk/publications/elearning/cs/cs10/index.asp) [an interactive e-learning resource, available to use free of charge on the SCIE website].

Thompson, N. (2003) *Communication and language: A handbook of theory and practice*, Basingstoke: Palgrave Macmillan.

Communicative capability and how it might be achieved

5

Introduction

Earlier chapters in this book have considered children and young people's views and preferences about their communication and interactions with social workers and some of the interpersonal and contextual dynamics that facilitate or interfere with their communication. This chapter now further explores what might be encompassed by terms such as 'effectiveness' and 'capabilities' in communication. The analogies of driving a car and playing a musical instrument are used to explore definitions of skill and competence. A framework is presented which may help practitioners develop the kinds of knowledge, approaches, values and personal qualities which they will need if they are to meet their statutory requirements to support children and young people, keep them informed and fully involve them in all matters which concern them. The practice vignettes of Niamh, Ghadi and Kofi illustrate these different aspects of communication and engagement with children and young people.

What might be meant by skill and effectiveness in communication?

A worker who is thought to be effective in his or her communication with children and young people might commonly be described as having a good level of skills in this aspect of practice. But is there a shared understanding of what these skills are or even of what is meant by the term 'skill'? The *Oxford English Dictionary* defines a skill as a 'capability of accomplishing something with precision and certainty', an 'ability to perform a function, acquired or learnt with practice' that might involve 'practical knowledge' or understanding of something 'in combination with ability; cleverness, expertness'. It categorises skill as potentially 'an art or science'.

In order to interrogate this definition of 'skill' further, we will consider how the components relate to carrying out other kinds of task.

Defining 'skill' in driving

Good drivers certainly need to be precise in the way they handle the car on the road. When learning how to drive, they will have to practise their manoeuvres, particularly the most complex ones, such as parallel parking. Drivers need not only practical knowledge (such as about how the car works) and theoretical knowledge (for example, the Highway Code), but also a capacity to apply this knowledge to a given situation (perhaps in line with the dictionary definition of 'cleverness'?). These abilities help them to be definite and clear about the decisions they take, not only in terms of choosing a direction and changing gear, but when there is a split second need for emergency braking or swerving to avoid danger. Being able to appraise the driving conditions, be constantly alert and 'compute' all the variables is what will distinguish a more expert driver from a beginner or someone who is potentially a hazard to other road users.

What the dictionary definition above seems to miss out, however, is the *ethical* component of safe driving. Those who we might define as skilled drivers often seem to act with more consideration and care for other road users. They may avoid drink driving, excessive speeding, 'tail-gating', parking infringements and so on, perhaps not just to avoid legal remonstration, but also because they can see the potential harm such actions may cause to others. Instead they make an individual commitment to considerate and safe driving. This suggests that part of what makes a good driver is something about *who they are*, not just what they know and what they do.

Defining 'skill' in musical performance

If we shift metaphors to the competent playing of a musical instrument, further dimensions of this *use of self* emerge. Like a driver, a musician certainly needs to combine practical understanding (of how the instrument works), theoretical knowledge (for example, how to read musical notation, dynamics, time signatures) and technical skills (such as playing notes quickly and evenly, louder or softer, creating a particular pitch or timbre through the position of the mouth or touch of the fingers). An 'expert' might be thought to be one who is able to bring these aspects together with dazzling displays of virtuosity. However, skill without passion, warmth, playfulness or sensitivity is likely to result in music that feels 'empty', what people describe as having 'no soul'. What might be missing is the capacity in the individual to engage in the emotional realm of the music, to allow their feelings and 'inner world' to enrich their playing (Meyer, 1956).

A musician may also need to be in tune culturally with his or her particular audience in order to play in an idiom that makes sense to them and is acceptable for the occasion, whether that be a rock band playing in a dark pub late at night or a classical orchestra. Audience members will draw on their existing understanding of the musical structures and conventions underlying that style to connect with the music and judge the performer's expertise according to those customs. The concept of habitus, described in Chapter Four, is one way of referring to these shared norms.

Moving towards a definition of 'skill' in communication

Through these two analogies, and drawing on findings from research studies with children and young people, a more coherent understanding of what makes for a capable communicator may begin to be built up. It is someone who is able to draw on both practical and theoretical knowledge (a domain of 'knowing' about communication) to underpin the techniques and micro-skills that are developed (a domain of 'doing' communication). But in order to use these appropriately, safely and creatively, three key aspects of 'use of self' ('being') are also required: an individual commitment to ethical behaviour; ability to draw on a range of personal qualities and emotional capacities; and a well-developed use of habitus.

Figure 3 sets out these domains of 'core capability' in an interactional model with effective communication at the centre. The Venn diagram emphasises how each domain does not exist in isolation but overlaps with and influences the other domains. This model is research-informed, based on a systematic review of the literature on what counts as effectiveness in communication with children and young people (Luckock et al, 2006a).

Figure 3: The knowing-being-doing model

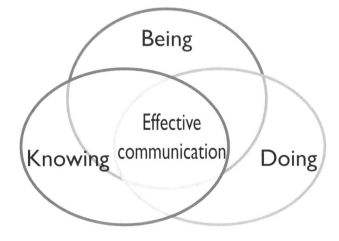

'Knowing': knowledge and understanding

The domain of 'knowing' refers to the knowledge which practitioners require in order to understand how best to communicate with children and young people. Most practitioners would be aware that they might need to know something generally about what kinds of vocabulary and concepts children might be expected to use at particular ages as well as about specific models and methods of communication. Such disparate forms of knowledge cannot be 'applied' simplistically to children, however, but rather inform the understanding which needs to be developed of particular children and how best to communicate with them, such as their unique developmental trajectory and habitus. What workers understand about their role and task within its legal context with a particular young person and how this shapes, frames and may even inhibit the communication is crucial; communication in a child protection investigation or pre-sentence report, say, is likely to be very different from that during life story work, where the pace of the work is slower and the aim more therapeutic.

Different kinds of 'knowing'

Schwandt's (1997) model for distinguishing between different kinds of knowledge is useful here. The first, theoretical knowledge, is termed *knowing about*. This would cover the kinds of theoretical perspectives, informed by research evidence, which help practitioners understand more about young people and childhood. Two aspects of these, the 'hundred languages of childhood' and child development, are discussed in more depth later in this section. How experiences of abuse, trauma, oppression, discrimination and social exclusion affect a young person's readiness and ability to communicate are other examples.

The second might be called *craft* or *skill knowledge*. This would include an understanding of what models, approaches, skills and techniques might be required, such as utilising listening skills, knowing how to do a genogram or being able to converse with a child or young person through puppets, an interpreter or using a communication board. The crafting of communication skills is discussed below in the 'doing' domain. This is illustrated by the overlap between 'knowing' and 'doing' domains shown by the Venn diagram.

The third area referred to by Schwandt is *practical-moral knowledge*. This involves the way in which knowledge is interpreted for particular circumstances. Schwandt suggests that this 'requires not cleverness in application but understanding' (Schwandt, 1997, p 76). In order to communicate for a particular purpose and within a specific role and context, the practitioner would need to think about how theoretical knowledge might be drawn on for it to be made relevant and for the appropriate skills to be employed. The practitioner's values would be involved in this interpretive process. This is explored further below in the 'being' section and illustrates the overlap of 'knowing' and 'being' domains.

Reflective practice (discussed further in Chapter Six) is one model for framing this interpretive process. It enables workers to develop a 'practice wisdom' that is rigorous and reflexive rather than unthinkingly reliant on the often tacit forms of knowledge which have been learned more informally. People are often unaware of the ways in which such knowledge processes are formed or the extent to which they influence our professional actions, recognitions and judgements (Shaw, 2009). Consequently, not all of the knowledge which influences the way practitioners communicate with children and young people may be valid, relevant or appropriate. It may be outdated or based on media, community stereotypes rather than research evidence. Workers may also not be using it in a thought-through manner. By moving towards more mindful, reflective practice such tacit forms of knowledge can be made more explicit and opened up to critical scrutiny.

Three further specific aspects of knowledge are mentioned only briefly here but will be discussed in more depth elsewhere in the book. One is knowledge about the specific child or young person with whom the practitioner is to communicate, which helps them tailor the communication. This will include the child or young person's personality, history, age, developmental trajectory, cultural background and so on. How to develop such an understanding and prepare for working with a specific child or young person is covered in Chapter Seven. Another is about 'knowing the self'. In order for practitioners to develop the kinds of fully engaged working relationships that help children and young people to feel safe, and in which the feelings of both worker and young person can inform rather than disrupt the work, professionals need to develop a significant degree of self-awareness. Chapter Six includes a reflective exercise in which readers will be encouraged to explore 'knowing themselves' further. A third relates to workers' clarity about the purpose of communication within particular professional roles and tasks and how the context, setting and wider environment impact on the communicative encounter. This theme will be returned to many times in the remaining chapters of this book. The different forms of knowledge discussed in this section can be seen in Figure 4.

Figure 4: Knowledge needed to form an understanding of how best to communicate with a child or young person

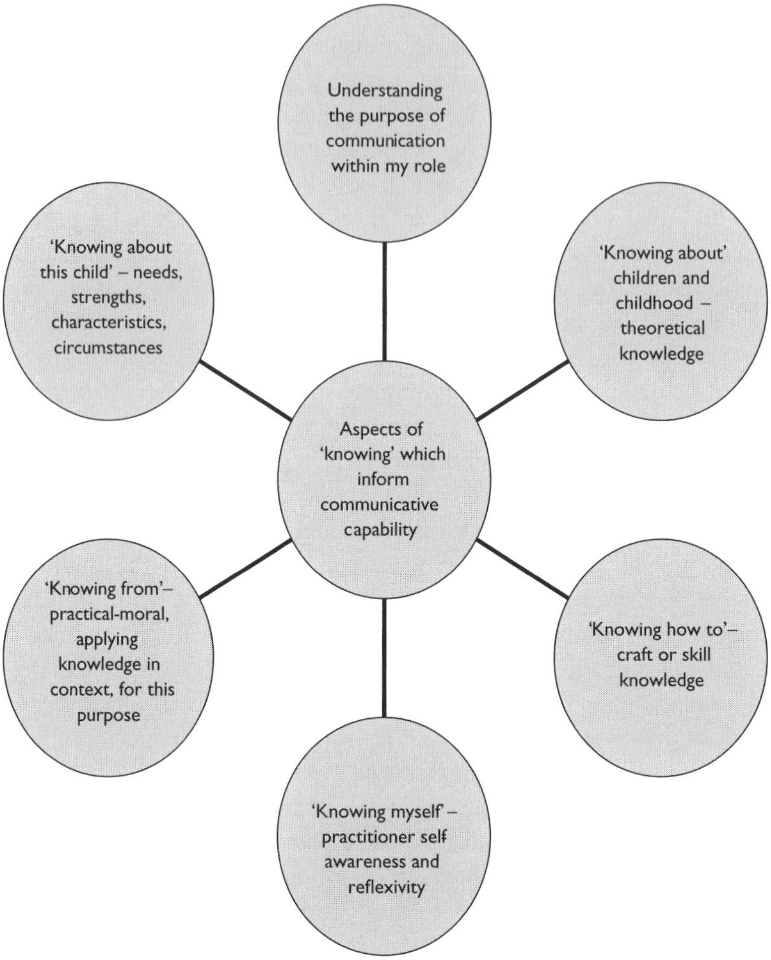

The 'hundred languages of childhood'

A significant aspect of the 'knowing' domain is having knowledge about the manifold ways in which children and young people instinctively communicate. Much of what children think and feel is difficult for them to convey in the ways that more mature people do. They do not always possess the range of words or concepts that many adults can draw on. This does not mean, however, that children should be considered as less competent at communication. In fact, the Italian educationalist Malaguzzi has suggested that there are 'a hundred languages of childhood', a multiplicity of possible modes in which children communicate with the world around them (quoted in Edwards et al, 1993). These might include play, metaphor, drawing, music-making, facial expressions, tone of voice, eye contact, postural movement, moving close to or far away from others, affectionate, loving or fearful responses to others, attachment style and way of dressing. Instead, perhaps we should see professionals as the ones who might be lacking competence, as they are not always as well-versed as they should be at using children's range of possible languages (Thomas and O'Kane, 2000).

Practice vignette: Communication through play

Razia is using play in her work with Niamh, an eight-year-old Irish girl, as part of supporting her in her foster placement. Niamh likes to act out stories with dolls and wants Razia to join in with her. Typical plots involve dolls being left to wander in the woods, starving and getting attacked by wild beasts. Often there is an amazing rescue that results in the doll ending up as a princess where everyone loves her. Razia plays alongside Niamh, 'tuning in' so that her own doll characters can respond appropriately within the story line.

Comment on the vignette

Niamh seems to be engaging in metaphorical play here as a way of helping herself work through some of the abuse and neglect she experienced prior to coming into care. Metaphorical play contains an implied comparison, presenting the real world symbolically through an alternative picture. It can provide an opportunity for children to explore the world from a more lateral perspective or to convey their inner feelings without having to name, acknowledge or own them directly. It would be unsafe for Razia to assume that this play directly reflects Niamh's actual experiences at home and to use it as evidence in an assessment or care proceedings. However, it is likely to reflect how she perceives or feels about those experiences and this will be very important for Razia to appreciate if she is to be able to help Niamh.

The more professionals feel comfortable with the full range of direct and indirect modes of communication, the more effectively and accurately they will be able to observe, hear and make sense of what children are experiencing and conveying. They will also find ways of putting things across to children in ways that have meaning to them. To do so, they will need to develop a whole range of knowledges and forms of understanding about the different needs, stages and experiences of children, the social work role and task, appropriate theories, approaches, and methods, research findings on effectiveness, and so on (Clark and Statham, 2005).

Knowledge about developmental trajectory and the impact of different experiences on communication

Practitioners generally find they need to use different words, concepts and sentence structures when finding out information or explaining things to children at different ages or levels of maturity (DH et al, 2000). For example, younger children such as Niamh and those with learning difficulties will generally require clearer and simpler language than young people like Robbie who was discussed in Chapter Four. Research literature provides helpful guidance on child development norms that are useful for workers to bear in mind as they begin to plan their work with a child or young person (see, for example, Aldgate et al, 2006; Sheridan, 2008).

What child development frameworks cannot do, however, is provide hard and fast rules that can consistently be applied to every child or young person. Abuse or neglect, traumatic experiences such as experience of war or genocide, separation from carers and socioeconomic deprivation can all have a significant effect on whether children are fulfilling their physical, emotional and educational potential and, consequently, whether workers' expectations are realistic. Instead, workers should aim for their practice to be informed rather than overwhelmed by such abstract or 'received' knowledge. Otherwise there is a danger that it can restrict and compartmentalise workers' views of individual children or young people, not allowing them to be seen in their own right and failing to recognise their particular competences or requirements. In fact, some developmental research has indicated that the variations between children of the same age are just as significant as differences between the age-related averages (Davis, 1998).

Getting to know a range of children and young people of different ages, cultures, social classes and abilities can really help 'flesh out the bones' of developmental charts, as the uniqueness and disparity between them cannot then fail to be seen. It also needs to be remembered that knowing only children who are in receipt of services can also be very misleading; workers' sense of baselines may become skewed by familiarity only with children who have been unable to develop to their full potential due to environmental issues or life experiences.

It is also worth bearing in mind that some writers have queried the validity of research findings on developmental 'norms' on the grounds that they are socially, culturally and politically located, and hence may marginalise or discriminate against particular groups of children or young people (Taylor, 2004). Robinson (2007) and Goldstein (2002) accuse researchers of unknowingly incorporating considerable cultural bias; they argue that current models of child development have been arrived at almost entirely through the study of white children and young people, with the result that they focus on the deficits rather than the strengths of black children and ignore the impact of racism on developing black identity.

Disabled children

There is also a lack of information on what norms might be considered appropriate for disabled children and young people as developmental charts and expectations for particular ages and stages may be entirely inappropriate (Oosterhoorn and Kendrick, 2001). Some disabled children have impairments that affect either their receptive communication (the way they perceive and understand others) and/or their expressive communication (the way they send messages and information to others) (Marchant, 2008). What can be equally significant, however, are the ways their communication may be disabled by others: being talked about as if they are not there, being ignored, being misunderstood, not being taken seriously, not being seen as competent communicators, not having others use their communication systems.

With all children and young people, the key to planning the work is to find out as much as possible in advance about how they communicate, from the parent, health visitor, school, and so on. Marchant's advice regarding disabled children is clearly relevant for all:

> If you are seeking information about a child's communication, the way you approach this is important. Generally, "does he talk?" and "does she communicate?" are unhelpful questions. A more useful starting point is an assumption that all children communicate, and thus the question is "how does he communicate?". If the response is that the child doesn't communicate, try asking "how do you know if he's hungry or tired?", "how can you tell if she is relaxed or distressed?". Another useful question is "Can I communicate with this child? And if not, then who can, or who can help me to do so?".
>
> Similarly, written requests for information about a child's communication need to be clear and explicit, for example, "Please list all the ways s/he communicates (eg responds to people; makes requests; shows that s/he wants or doesn't want something; shows his/her feelings)". Whatever you are told about a child's communication, keep a very open mind and remember that all children use a combination of methods. (Marchant, 2008, p 155)

The other person to find out as much as possible from is, of course, the child or young person themselves! Most are unlikely to be able to tell you directly exactly what they want from your style of communication, but if you pay close attention to their interactions and responses to you, it is possible to build up a better understanding of what works for them. A period of non-directive play or other activity at the beginning of an assessment or piece of work with a child or young person is invaluable in being able to build up this kind of picture.

Box 7: A summary of aspects of the 'knowing' domain

- Theory, conceptual perspectives, research findings
- Models, methods, approaches and frameworks
- Law, social policy and practice guidance
- Child development norms and pathways
- The hundred languages of childhood
- The impact on children and their communication of adverse experiences and circumstances, including oppression
- How this child relates and communicates
- The purpose of communication within the professional role and task
- How to draw on knowledge critically and reflexively

'Being': what kind of person you are

Values and individual ethical commitments

> "My worker's made a difference to my life by helping me be good. I trust her because she's good at keeping a secret and I believe she would keep confidential any information on me." (Jamie, aged 10, quoted in Headliners, 2009)

In the car-driving analogy above it was suggested that part of what makes a skilled driver was being ethically committed to safe and considerate driving and that this quality was something to do with the *self* of drivers, rather than just being about what they knew about the Highway Code, or the car's functions, and so on. That is similar for social work. The research findings reporting children's views and concerns, discussed in Chapter Three, indicate clearly that they want workers who see ethical, child-centred, anti-oppressive practice as important. These approaches are embedded within professional codes of practice and national occupational standards, but, ultimately, workers need to make an individual and personal commitment to developing and adhering to values which underpin them, as success in communicating with children seems directly linked to the strength of workers' personal beliefs that achieving mutual communication is their responsibility (Thomas and O'Kane, 2000).

A key tenet of child-centred practice is the commitment to meeting children's rights as well as their needs, including the right to have a voice in decisions that affect them. This means recognising children's competence and intentionality, facilitating their self-expression and listening carefully to what they convey. This requires a real commitment on the part of the worker as fully involving them in assessment, decision making and planning entails providing them with information and explanations in an appropriate way such as simple summaries of decisions, with pictures or symbols to illustrate, or using diagrams or props to explain to a child what a court or a judge is. The 'doing' section below provides examples of how to do this, and the subject is discussed in more depth in Chapters Ten and Eleven. Here we can see the overlap of the 'being' and 'doing' domains of this core capabilities model.

An anti-oppressive approach to child-centred communication encompasses the commitment to sharing power appropriately with children and young people. Research studies referred to above highlighted how important it was to young people that they and their wishes were respected, for example, with regards to confidentiality, transparency, honesty, openness and reliability. Practice that recognises the impact on children of racism, discrimination and socioeconomic disadvantage and deprivation, and seeks to ameliorate this where possible, rather than buying into preconceptions and stereotypes, will also promote children's participation (Graham and Bruce, 2006).

Personal qualities and emotional capacity

> "The only thing that's not good about my social worker is sometimes she's grumpy and she could be a bit more interesting."
> (Jamie, aged 10, quoted in Headliners, 2009)

The musical analogy used above highlighted the other aspect of the self that is seen to be important: emotional capacity and real engagement at a human-to-human level. Research studies with children emphasise again and again how important a real relationship with their key worker is to many children in receipt of services. For those who are in care this has been increasingly recognised as important, with the *Care matters* White Paper (DCSF, 2007) proposing a reconstruction of services to enable the statutory social work tasks to be enacted through a core, consistent relationship between children and their social workers. The social work role with children in care has been conceptualised as a *bridge* for the child – between the family and the substitute placement, between the past, present and future, between internal world feelings and perceptions and external word experiences and interactions (Winnicott, 1986). Luckock (2008), however, writing in association with two young men who had been in care, contends strongly that the social worker should in fact be seen more as a *companion and ally*. He contrasts this with the more distanced image implicit elsewhere in social policy of social workers as some kind of 'travel guide' or 'tour operator' who help to steer children through their contact with services.

Relationship-based practice requires workers to have the emotional capacity to be able to bear, contain and respond in an attuned fashion to the wide range of feelings children have. Clare Winnicott advises they should be able to 'live through the experience with the child as fully as possible, without denying the pain and accepting the sadness, anger and depression' of what they are going through, 'right down to the painful sad bit in the middle' (Winnicott, 1986, pp 40-1). The feelings of both young person and worker may be enacted in complex ways through the relationship. Psychodynamic theories such as transference, counter-transference and projection and attachment theory can be a helpful way of unpicking some of what is going on. These will be explored further in Chapters Six and Nine but are also illustrated through the practice vignette of Kofi, a black British toddler.

Practice vignette: Communication through touch

Kofi tended to be indiscriminately affectionate with strangers. The first time he met social worker Razia he got on her lap and clung to her, crying, when she needed to leave. When his mother tried to take him from her to comfort him, Kofi cried even harder, pushing away from his mother. Razia felt disconcerted by this. She did not want to leave Kofi feeling rejected but knew it was important to ensure their physical contact was appropriate. She gave him lots of eye contact and smiles to reassure him while lifting him back on to the sofa next to her. Instead of providing physical affection to him to develop a relationship, which would not have been appropriate, she engaged him in games such as peek-a-boo and rolling a ball back and forth between them. This communicated to him that she was interested in him and responded to the insecurity of attachment that his behaviour appeared to be conveying.

Coming back to the analogies used above, for many areas of skill, such as playing music, an individual might have a 'born' potential which means that they 'naturally' or 'intuitively' are much better than others at such aspects. Some people, for example, are able to play music 'by ear', without needing to read music. There is something of this, too, in communication skills. Some individuals do seem instinctively to have a warm, playful, friendly, open and engaging manner which invites children and young people to communicate with them, or a general potential to be empathic, good humoured, caring, emotionally available and resilient in their interactions with children and young people. This is not to say others cannot learn to communicate better, just that they may have more predispositional difficulties to overcome and will have to work harder to develop their emotional capability in communication. 'Capability' here is defined as 'honed competence, a development of the underlying capacity so that it can be used in a constructive and informed manner within interventions with a range of children' (Lefevre et al, 2008a, p 171). Trevithick (2005) encourages social workers to familiarise themselves with their own strengths and limitations in communication, for example looking at what kind of facial expression they have in repose. Those whose faces seem 'naturally' to look more anxious, unfriendly or miserable will, she suggests, need to work harder to look friendly and at ease if they are not to seem off-putting to children and young people. What kind of atmosphere they put across from how they sit or move will also be important.

Habitus

The concept of habitus (Bourdieu, 1991) was introduced in Chapter Four. It refers to the cultural structures, patterns and rules that enable people to negotiate around social interactions and decode someone else's meta-messages through interpreting words, body language, paralanguage and other behaviour. Habitus is thought to lie mainly outside of an individual's conscious awareness, with people only becoming aware of it when miscommunications illuminate how their beliefs, attitudes and perceptions are different from someone else's (Pinker, 1999). In this way habitus could be construed as a dimension of the worker's 'being' domain, an aspect of the 'way that they are' in the world, which is influenced by what they culturally 'know' and affects what they 'do'. Again we can see where these different domains of the core capabilities model overlap.

This hidden nature of habitus could make it harder for social workers to know how to develop better communication skills. From a child or young person's response or reaction they might be aware *when* they have communicated well or badly but not always what they did wrong. So, they struggle to know how they might do it better, what alternative or additional rules or structures they might need to adopt in the future. Even when they have worked out what needs to change, adopting new and different patterns often feels alien and workers will need to practise until they become habitual (Koprowska, 2008). Conceivably, then, self-awareness, reflexivity, commitment and persistence should all be considered as core capabilities of communicative competence.

Box 8: A summary of aspects of the 'being' domain

- Ethical commitments to core social work values, including:
  - > anti-oppressive, culturally sensitive practice
  - > respectful, honest, transparent and accountable practice
  - > inclusive, collaborative, rights-based and child-centred practice
  - > principles of reliability, availability and confidentiality
- Ability to draw on personal qualities and emotional capacities appropriate to a situation, including:
  - > sincerity, genuineness, congruence, and openness
  - > warmth, caring, friendliness, humanity, empathy and patience
  - > enthusiasm, a sense of humour, and playfulness
  - > a capacity and willingness to form real relationships within appropriate professional boundaries
  - > emotional robustness, sensitivity and a capacity to understand, contain and respond to children's strong feelings and interpersonal dynamics
- Self-awareness and reflexivity

'Doing': communication in action

The domain of 'doing' refers to the skills, techniques and approaches that are required for effective communication within the full range of professional roles. Different tasks will require different methods:

- Keeping children and young people informed about matters which concern them, such as the progress of care proceedings, needs to be done not only verbally but also in writing, or using diagrams, pictures, stories or dolls to illustrate where these might be helpful (see Chapter Ten).
- When finding out from children and young people about significant information or events, perhaps during an assessment or a child protection investigation, interviewing techniques and questions are one approach (see Chapter Eight), but observation (Chapter Nine) and creative exercises (Chapter Ten) can also be useful.
- Consulting with children and young people to promote their participation, such as seeking their views on what they would want from a new placement, needs to happen in a way that allows young people to play an equal part in shaping the dialogue. Workers might then find out

not just what they think they want to know, but what the child most wants to express. Methods discussed in Chapters Eight and Eleven will be helpful here.

- Helping children and young people make sense of their present, past and future should happen not only within more formalised life story work, but through dialogue and exploration at any opportunity which arises (see Chapter Seven).

- Working to support children and young people therapeutically in the aftermath of abuse or trauma will require a safe place to be provided within which their thoughts and feelings can be expressed and contained (see Chapter Eleven).

The learning and deployment of disembodied micro-skills and techniques will not be enough for the effective 'doing' of communication but need to be integrated with the knowledge and understanding, personal qualities and ethical commitments that have been developed in the worker; their response can then be attuned and fitting for that specific situation and child or young person. For example, it would not be enough for a practitioner to try to learn 'listening skills'. How they should listen to a young person might need to be different depending on a whole range of factors relating to the particular child (their cognitive capacity, primary language, previous experiences, any disability), the task (such as finding out their views, wishes and feelings, talking with them about a placement move) and the context (child protection investigation, care proceedings, pre-sentence report).

Box 9: A summary of aspects of the 'doing' domain

Capability in skills, techniques and approaches, such as:

- going at the child's pace
- creating a safe space for the child to communicate
- using child-centred forms of language and modes of communication which make sense to children and facilitate their participation
- using play, creative artwork and activities to help children explore and express their thoughts and feelings
- using vocabulary and concepts that the child will understand
- using visual methods and metaphors to help clarify complex matters
- reading and interpreting non-verbal communication
- using listening skills and interviewing techniques, such as summarising, clarifying and prompting, which enable young people to convey their views and experiences in formal language

- flexible, confident and creative use of tools and frameworks (for example, ecomaps and genograms, the assessment framework questionnaires, common assessment framework [CAF])

Interaction between the knowing, being and doing domains

TheVenn diagram in Figure 3 showed how the different domains of knowing, being and doing within the core capabilities model each overlapped and were interdependent.The following practice vignette of Ghadi and his social worker Eric helps to illustrate this interaction.

Practice vignette: Explaining matters to young people

Eric's task is to explain to Ghadi what happened at the child protection conference that had been held that morning. Ghadi is a 13-year-old young person from Somalia who has been classed as an unaccompanied asylum seeker and has been placed in foster care. Eric is a white social worker.

Comment on the vignette

Eric needs to explain matters to Ghadi in a way that he can make sense of (a task in the 'doing' domain).To carry out this task effectively Eric will need to draw on knowledge and understanding about a range of matters ('knowing' domain).This will include ascertaining Ghadi's level of written and spoken English, his cognitive development and his intellectual capabilities, and learning how Ghadi's traumatic experiences may have affected his capacity to make sense of his current situation and to relate to Eric. These points demonstrate how 'doing' overlaps with 'knowing'.

Recognising that, at the very least, Ghadi is likely to be fearful and anxious ('knowing' domain), Eric will need to manage his own feelings of anxiety and convey warmth, sensitivity, care and trustworthiness ('being') if he is to engage Ghadi and communicate to him that he is able to bear Ghadi's distress and can help him ('doing'). Careful and considered use of self will be crucial. The whole person of the worker needs to be fully involved here to be congruent, but this will also need careful attention to personal boundaries to get the level just right for each individual.

Eric needs to consider the impact on Ghadi of living in another country in a mainly white area, where people speak a different language, and having to interact with a white professional ('knowing'). Eric might assume that Ghadi is likely to feel mistrustful, disempowered and wary about the implications of anything he says. Ghadi and Eric do not share a common first language and their habitus is likely to be very different ('being'), so Eric will need to be wary of miscommunications and misinterpretations. While Ghadi speaks some English, it is not his first language; he may speak enough to communicate about superficial matters, but not to convey more nuanced thoughts and feelings about his situation or to understand the complexities of the UK welfare system. Eric, then, will need to consider involving an interpreter. These points illustrate how anti-discriminatory practice ('doing') draws on core social work values and ethical commitments ('being').

Conclusion

A model for effective communication has been set out in this chapter which requires workers to integrate and underpin their skills, techniques and approaches (ways of 'doing' communication) with a range of knowledges about children and their context ('knowing'), with individual commitments to ethical, anti-oppressive, reflexive practice, and with personal and emotional qualities and self-awareness (aspects of 'being'). The kind of child-centred, inclusive, relationship-based approach presented here clearly demands time, patience, preparation, individual effort and personal commitment. It is not enough for workers to have a set of 'off-the-shelf' techniques and methods to draw on when the situation demands. Instead a more 'bespoke' or 'made-to-measure' approach is required, which is tailored to the needs of the particular child and situation. Workers will need to develop both themselves and their practice in a range of ways if they are to achieve this.

Key questions

1. How would you define 'skill'?
2. What personal qualities are considered important in working with children?
3. Name as many as you can of the 'hundred languages of childhood'.

Further reading and resources

Luckock, B., Lefevre, M. and Orr, D. (2006) 'What counts as effective communication with children in social work practice?', *Teaching, learning and assessing communication skills with children and young people in social work education*, Knowledge Review, London: Social Care Institute for Excellence, pp 11-31.

Prior, V. and Glaser, D (2006) *Understanding attachment and attachment disorders: Theory, evidence and practice*, London: Jessica Kingsley Publishers.

Scarlett, W., Naudeau, S., Salonius-Pasternak, D. and Ponte, I. (2005) *Children's play*, Thousand Oaks, CA: Sage Publications.

Sheridan, M. (2008) *From birth to five years: Children's developmental progress* (3rd edn, revised and updated by A. Sharma and H. Cockerill), New York, NY: Routledge.

Trevithick, P., Lefevre, M. and Richards, S. (2008) *Overview of communication skills in social work*, London: Social Care Institute for Excellence (www.scie.org.uk/publications/elearning/cs/cs10/index.asp) [this is an interactive e-learning resource, available to use free of charge on the SCIE website].

Appraising capabilities and learning needs in communication with children and young people

6

Introduction

The preceding chapters have emphasised that how practitioners communicate with children and young people is as much about who they are themselves, their ethics and beliefs, and what they understand about children and childhood, as it is about the methods and techniques they have learned. These qualities have been termed 'knowing', 'being' and 'doing' domains of 'core capability' in communication. Acquiring these will require professionals to develop their knowledge, values, skills and 'use of self' in a range of ways.

Some readers will have sought out this book because they are just beginning to work professionally with children and young people, while others may be experienced practitioners who are wanting to further develop their skills, perhaps because they are in a new role or because their work with a particular young person is especially challenging. Whichever of these is the case, an essential place to begin is by forming a realistic appraisal of both strengths and areas of struggle in order to identify transferable skills and future learning and development needs. Reflective exercises in this chapter facilitate this process. The practice vignettes of Millie, a social work student, and Edwin, an experienced practitioner, are threaded throughout, enabling the kinds of issues under discussion to be explored and illustrated.

Reflective appraisal of skills and capabilities

Categorising existing strengths

Determining your existing strengths will help you build on what you are already good at and identify where these skills and capabilities may be transferable to other situations. A good place to start is to reflect in some depth on those children you have worked with where you were able to engage and communicate with them well. An example of doing this is provided in the following practice vignette with Millie.

Practice vignette: Millie, the social work student

Millie is a white British woman, aged 20, who is to undertake a practice learning opportunity in a women's refuge. A key focus of the placement will involve Millie running an after-school activity for children who are aged 5-11. Millie has never knowingly encountered children before who have witnessed domestic abuse. Consequently she is feeling rather under-confident and confesses this to her practice assessor, Kim.

Kim asks Millie to tell her a bit about her life experiences and learns that Millie has had a lot of contact with children. When leading the Children's Meeting for worship back home as part of her Quaker spiritual practice, Millie was able to identify that she had developed quite a few skills through this, including confidence in designing and leading activities for children of a range of ages, abilities and backgrounds, not being fazed by needing to adapt to changing circumstances or needs, and creating a safe, reflective space. When asked how the children at the Meeting might describe her, Millie realises that they might value her warm and approachable manner, her calmness in a crisis, her sense of fun and her clear way of putting things across.

Through this exercise Millie started to recognise that she had quite a lot of existing expertise to bring to the placement that provided a solid foundation to build on.

Exercise 1

On a big piece of paper sketch out the knowing, being and doing diagram of the core capabilities model (Figure 3 in Chapter Five). Identify situations in your personal and professional life where you have communicated successfully with children and young people. Jot down not only the techniques and approaches you used (the 'doing' domain of the model) but also whether you developed a particular understanding of the children, their needs and what they were thinking and feeling (the 'knowing' domain) and whether you formed a trusted relationship with them, attended to ethical issues and worked anti-oppressively (the 'being' domain). Summarise your areas of strength and confidence.

Comment on Exercise 1

A range of capabilities may now become apparent from your diagram. You may have noted down, for example, that you have a solid knowledge base about child development that helps you select the most appropriate kinds of vocabulary, concepts and sentence structures to use with children. Perhaps you have identified a capacity to draw on your warmth, friendliness, humour or empathy when relating to children. This exercise will help you consider how the skills and capabilities that you have identified might be transferable to work with children or young people in other situations.

Identifying gaps in capability and confidence that require further learning and development

The next exercise enables you to consider some of the reasons for your lack of confidence in particular aspects of work with children and young people and identify areas of knowledge, personal qualities, values or skills you might need to develop.

Exercise 2

What kinds of children and young people and what kinds of situation do you feel least confident in working with? Include:

- the full range of ages, from 0 to 18
- girls and boys
- those who are different from you (perhaps in terms of ethnicity, religion, culture, social class, sexual orientation or primary language)
- disabled children and young people, including those with learning difficulties, complex healthcare needs and speech or language impairments
- different presentations of emotions and behaviour, such as rude and abusive, withdrawn and passive, or vulnerable and clingy
- children who have been abused, neglected, traumatised, bereaved or displaced
- a variety of practice frameworks, methods and approaches

Comment on Exercise 2

This exercise will have helped you identify where you lack confidence, experience or expertise. If you noted that you lack confidence in using certain methods and tools as a way of gathering information or assessing children or young people, try some of these out on yourself or with a trusted colleague or fellow student. It is not ideal to use tools or approaches that you have not experimented with previously, as you will be less aware of how emotive they can be or how hard it might be to get the dynamics just right. You could try setting up peer reciprocal arrangements to undertake ecomaps, life rivers or the kinds of arts-based activities that will be discussed more fully in Chapter Ten. Setting careful boundaries around such peer-paired work is essential, however. Ensure that you have created a safe and confidential space to 'hold' the work and allowed plenty of time to debrief. Work out in advance how you will manage things if one of you becomes particularly angry, unsettled or distressed through the work.

If your lack of confidence is because you have had minimal contact with certain kinds of children, you would probably benefit from creating opportunities to spend time with children and young people from a range of backgrounds and with different attributes and experiences to see how they interact and communicate. Millie's experience of Children's Meetings was invaluable here. Undertaking formal child observations can be particularly informative (see Chapter Nine), but even reading children's books or watching youth programmes can help adults become more familiar with ways in which young people think and interact. Shadowing is another way of gaining experience of work with children in different contexts, as illustrated by the following practice vignette of Edwin.

Practice vignette: Edwin, the experienced social worker

Edwin, a 47-year-old black British social worker, has worked in child protection for the past 10 years. Becoming disillusioned and de-skilled from the lack of opportunity for more in-depth work with children and their families, Edwin had started to feel that all he was doing was 'ticking boxes'. Consequently, when a job came up with a placement support project he decided to apply as it would offer him more opportunities for direct work. Edwin's role will be to work intensively with young people aged 12-16 and their foster carers where there is a risk of foster placement breakdown.

Now he has accepted the new job, Edwin is worried that his rusty direct work skills will not be up to the task of engaging and communicating with young people whose behaviour foster carers have been finding very challenging. He feels rather middle-aged and out of touch with the language, culture, interests and music of younger teenagers. To increase his confidence, as part of his induction period for his new job, Edwin negotiates opportunities to shadow a number of other workers in the organisation to see how they deal with challenges presented by the work.

Edwin provides a good example here of the importance of *self-awareness*. Recognising and owning your areas of struggle means you are then in a much better position to identify appropriate learning opportunities for yourself. Many organisations support shadowing experiences such as that organised by Edwin as they provide a creative mechanism for sharing expertise.

Most practitioners will become aware through Exercise 2 that they feel less comfortable working with certain kinds of life issues, experiences or behaviour. The reasons for this are important to clarify. If it is because you lack understanding of the impact on children of their needs and experiences, you might consider reading more about how abuse, racism, homophobia, insecurity of attachment, and so on, can inhibit or affect children's ways of engaging and communicating with others. This doesn't just have to be through academic texts, however, as novels and films may provide a very vivid way to understand and empathise with such experiences. Mark Haddon's novel, *The curious incident of the dog in the night-time* (2003), for example, is narrated by a 15-year-old boy with Asperger's syndrome. His way of interpreting and engaging with the world is conveyed vividly through the structure and prose style of 'his' own words.

It will also be important for workers to identify whether any discomfort in working with children who have had particular experiences relates to their own unresolved emotional or psychological issues. Self-exploration work, such as genograms, life path exercises, life story work or counselling/therapy can be helpful in working these through. This is discussed further below.

Capacity to play, engage in activities and facilitate creative work by children and young people

Play, creative work and activities are just a few of the 'hundred languages of childhood' referred to earlier in this book. Chapter Ten provides some ideas about the kinds of activities suitable for different purposes and provides suggestions for props and tools. However, as the 'knowing, being and doing' model emphasises, successful use of play and activities in communication does not just depend on skills and techniques but requires a real engagement by the human self of the practitioner. Being able to feel comfortable playing or supporting children in creative work will require workers to readily 'decentre' from an adult to a child perspective (Colton et al, 2001). A worker who is able to do this will feel more comfortable to engage in a puppet-to-puppet conversation with a six-year-old or kick a football around with a 15-year-old without feeling unduly silly or self-conscious.

Exercise 3

Reflect on how comfortable you would feel with playing alongside children using dolls, puppets, games or stories. How ready would you feel to facilitate children and young people in expressive artwork, such as drawing, painting, using clay, writing poetry or making music? How relaxed and congruent would you be in undertaking activities with young people, such as playing football, darts or pool, going window shopping or going for a coffee?

Comment on Exercise 3

Children and young people readily intuit when adults are embarrassed or awkward with such activities and can become self-conscious themselves in turn. This is likely to be particularly so for those who have received limited encouragement to play and express themselves and who need professionals to help them to 'come into a state of being able to play' (Winnicott, 1971). They need a worker who is not subdued by inner critical voices and instead is able to display enthusiasm for, say, painting, without being worried that they lack any natural talent or expertise in this. In the next practice vignette, Millie's capacity to play and 'use her self' helps her as she begins group work with the children in her placement.

Practice vignette: Experimenting with 'ice-breakers'

A warm-up exercise Millie used previously at the Quaker Children's Meeting was 'show and tell'. Everyone would bring an object to the meeting that symbolised an aspect of what they were thinking or feeling or had been experiencing. They would show this to everyone and say as much or as little as they wanted. The purpose of this was to help everyone settle into the group and to be able to say something about their week and/or how they were feeling that day. The group would listen carefully and aim to respect and 'hold' what had been said.

While preparing for her first after-school group at the refuge, Millie reflected on her successful prior use of 'show and tell' with her supervisor and decided to use it with this new group of children as it was something she knew could work and she felt comfortable with. Millie considered that she was part of the group as well as the leader of it and decided that she would participate in the 'show and tell'. She selected a little toy dog with a wagging tail and big excited eyes and, leading off the exercise, spoke to the children of how much she had been looking forward to meeting them. This seemed to break the ice, and all the children found something to say, expressing a range of emotions about how things were for them at the moment.

Comment on the vignette

Millie was able to draw on her previous experiences with children to construct helpful activities in the professional setting. The success of the exercise resulted from the personal qualities Millie brought to the activity, including her 'use of self' to create a safe and relaxed environment and her willingness to be playful. Practitioners will, however, need to guard against becoming too 'native' in a child perspective and losing their 'adult self', as this can be unsettling to children and unsafe if any risks emerge. Instead they need to be able to move readily back and forth between adult and child 'ego states' (Clarkson, 1990). Keeping a foot in both 'adult' and 'child' camps enables workers to contain and manage the interaction, keeping it safe, and to make helpful interventions or explorations, even while being playful.

Power dynamics

Central to a better understanding of what it might be like for a child or young person to have a social worker is an appreciation of some of the power relations and dynamics inherent in the situation.

Exercise 4

Reflect on how aware you feel of what it may feel like for children to have a social worker. If you have never had contact with a social worker yourself, it may be useful to try to get in touch with this by reflecting on situations where similar kinds of dynamics might be found. You might cast your mind back to times as a child when professionals around you, such as teachers or nurses, were responsible for making decisions about you or looking after you. Try to identify both a positive and a negative occasion of having been in that situation. You could also reflect on times as an adult when this has happened, for example, being a student or visiting a GP.

Comment on Exercise 4

Recalling which aspects of those professionals' communication with you were helpful may help you identify what you might want to replicate in your own practice. For example, you may remember clear and helpful explanations, gestures of kindness, body language expressing warmth and comfort, humour used to defuse tension, words of reassurance or feedback indicating your concerns had been understood. This might have caused you to feel safe and cared for, or helped you to off-load distressing feelings.

Similarly, more negative experiences which stopped you articulating what you needed, caused you to feel embarrassed about sharing intimate or personal details or left you feeling misunderstood can help indicate approaches to be avoided. Remembering the emotions evoked at such times, such as feeling vulnerable, frightened, disempowered, controlled or even oppressed, provides an insight into how children you are working with might feel in their contact with professionals. Your reflections, too, may provide examples of how, as a child or young person, you raised your emotional and psychological defences to try and protect yourself. Young people will all vary in their responses. Some might become withdrawn or passive, others adaptive and pleasing, or truculent and defensive when feeling under threat. The capacity of professionals to comprehend the feelings underlying this behaviour and to respond sensitively will be key to whether children can start to lower their barriers and feel safe enough to engage and confide.

Different perspectives on power

A significant dynamic between children and their social workers, and one that may affect communication between them, is power. There are different ways of conceptualising power relations between social workers and young people. A structuralist perspective would start from the premise that certain individuals possess more power on the basis of particular individual or social characteristics which confer status, authority, rights or capacity, such as gender, age, profession, ethnicity or wealth (Thompson, 2002). Such a hierarchical analysis would consider that power in our society is located with adults more than with children due to the latter's social and legal status as 'juveniles' or 'minors'. Children and young people may consequently be disempowered, even oppressed, because parents, guardians and other adults make numerous decisions on their behalf, such as where they go to school, what medical treatments they should receive, whether they should do their homework, what diet they will follow, whether they practise a particular religion and so on. Adults' powerfulness may reassure children ("I don't know what to do and grown-ups generally do, so he may be able to sort it out"). But it may equally result in fear ("I have to do what grown-ups say or I'll be in trouble"), resentment ("Here's yet another adult telling me what to do; I'm not listening") or disenfranchisement ("Maybe this adult knows better than me, so I ought to defer to him, even though it's not really what I believe"). Children and young people are likely, then, to feel the full weight of adult powerfulness added to the positional power and status of the social worker (Cooper, 1994).

The impact of the social worker's powerfulness

Communication has been described as a two-way street (Triangle, 2001), but children and young people are not always willing participants in this. Involvement with social workers may be imposed or mandated in some way, perhaps by parents who are eager for a particular intervention to take place, by the interprofessional system that has directed this as part of a child protection plan, or from the court that is concerned about offending behaviour. Such compelled involvement can leave children and young people feeling particularly disenfranchised in the interaction, and may result in fear or suspicion of, or hostility towards the social worker even when he or she is attempting to work in a supportive or constructive way (McLeod, 2007).

Disempowering prior experiences in relationships or upbringing, such as familial abuse, may have particularly eroded children and young people's capacity to feel safe around adults (Ryan et al, 1995). While a social worker may see it as essential that they speak to young people on their own to ascertain what has happened, this will be counter-productive if the powerlessness of the abuse situation is re-evoked and a child is too frightened or traumatised to speak. Instead, it may be better to work out whether there is another person whom the child or young person trusts who could also be present. Of course, it will be essential to ascertain that this other person does not him or herself pose a danger to the child nor might find a way of preventing him or her from disclosing abuse (Jones, 2003).

Children and young people's fear or wariness of social workers may have been influenced by their own earlier experiences of professional intervention or by having imbibed the negative views of others (Bell, 2002). Some parents may warn or threaten children not to speak to 'the social'. The media also influences children and young people as well as adults, with its polarised lambasting of social workers as either useless 'do-nothings' or interfering 'do-gooders' who are able to 'snatch' children from safe and loving homes. By doing so they negate the role of the courts in making care and protection orders and perhaps leave children with an over-inflated view of social workers' authority to take draconian action. This can further reinforce their sense of powerlessness and fear within interactions.

Difference and oppression

Where there are differences between the social worker and child or young person, for example of gender, sexual orientation, ethnicity, culture, class or language, this may well leave the young person feeling more vulnerable or oppressed and less able to communicate freely. Personal assumptions and beliefs on both sides, often reinforced by dominant social views, will affect the way each relates and interprets the other's communication, but it is the responsibility of the social worker to mitigate the effects of these. Chapter Five discussed the practice vignette of Ghadi, a 13-year-old unaccompanied asylum seeker from Somalia who has been placed in foster care. Ghadi was wary of communicating with his social worker, Eric, for a whole range of reasons that related to power. These included: uncertainty about whether what he said to Eric might result in bad things happening; not always understanding what Eric or the interpreter said but being too nervous to keep asking for clarification; and worrying that Eric, who is white and English, might have racist views and or mistaken cultural beliefs about him. A commitment by Eric to anti-oppressive ways of working, including developing his appreciation of how living in a white-dominated, perhaps institutionally racist, society will affect Ghadi's interaction with him, could begin to create a safer space for Gahdi to communicate in (Robinson, 2007).

Power from cultural capital

Social workers are also likely to have more of what the social theorist Bourdieu terms 'cultural capital' than the children and young people with whom they are working. By this Bourdieu meant that some people have 'greater cultural resources to draw upon in terms of influencing others' and can exercise their power more readily (quoted in Thompson, 2003, p 23). Cultural capital is acquired through maturation, education, reflection and other privileged experiences which social workers are more likely to have had than many families who are in receipt of services. Consequently social workers are in a better position to influence children and young people both subtly and overtly through being more articulate, socially skilled and confident, better able to read paralanguage and more able to use words and body language to create the desired effect.

How workers may also feel disempowered

A solely structural analysis of power may be inadequate, however, for illuminating why workers may sometimes feel disempowered, deskilled, helpless and useless when faced with a child or young person who stares impassively at them, berates them or hides under their 'hoodie' rather than answering questions. While children and young people have a capacity, and arguably also a right, not to listen to or communicate with professionals, social workers generally have to keep attempting to communicate them despite their unenthusiastic, unreceptive, antagonistic, even violent responses. Because of their statutory responsibilities, they have to keep trying to consult with, inform, listen to and intervene with children and young people. Practitioners might, then, feel at times as if the power advantages are not all on their side.

A post-structuralist analysis of discursive power provides an additional window of understanding (Thompson, 2003). This concept of 'discourse', based on the work of Michel Foucault, posits that the ways in which humans speak, listen, read, writes and so on, are 'performative micro-practices', which not only reflect but also construct and reinforce our personal and social worlds, our ways of seeing, thinking, feeling and being (White, 2009). Language and communication are understood as actions by us, with us and for us. They change, create and influence others, not just through the content of what has been said or written, but through the manner of communication and the ideas, beliefs, feelings, cultural practices, and so on, which are embedded within them.

Practice vignette: Edwin's struggles in his new job

Very quickly into his new job, Edwin is finding that his confidence is further dented by the way some of the young people are acting towards him. While he is able to form positive engagements with some, others seem to him to be determined to avoid him, ignore him, 'wind him up' or upset him. One taunts him about being overweight and unfit, running off when Edwin tries to talk to him. Another shakes his head at Edwin's choice of music in his car, telling him he is 'well past it', and laughs at Edwin when he doesn't understand the street jargon he uses.

A discursive analysis of communication between children and their social workers recognises how the power of children's silence, hostility, withdrawal or ridicule can leave a worker like Edwin feeling old, stupid, 'uncool' and rather unnerved by being around teenagers who seem to him to be hip, lively, sharp and critical. This analysis does not mean that power is now conceived as being located all with the young person, as they may also concurrently feel fearful, coerced, out of control or manipulated; indeed this may be the source of their behaviour. Edwin, too, does not lose all of his social and cultural capital just through feeling undermined by the young people's behaviour.

Instead power may be seen as interactive, flowing through the 'capillaries' linking individuals, rather than being one-way, top-down. These power dynamics may be analysed from the forms of language used between worker and child, including body language and paralanguage, such as the withering looks from the young person that 'tell' Edwin he is hopeless and useless. How Edwin feels and acts in response to this communication will co-construct this as more or less powerful. So workers' capacity to withstand attack, recognise and manage their feelings and feel resilient within themselves will be crucial here.

Working with the feelings evoked by contact with children and young people

Working with distressed, angry and vulnerable children and young people can evoke very strong reactions in professionals and, when the organisation and supervisory system surrounding them does not support and contain this, there is a real danger that workers may retreat into a defensive state (Rustin, 2005). Rather than engaging with children's very real emotional pain, workers may distance themselves or 'cut off'. This leaves children without a space where their inner thoughts and feelings can emerge and be understood – important both for assessing risk and for helping them heal psychologically. Practitioners need to know themselves very well if they are to truly engage with children at an emotional level:

> To understand a child's fear, sadness, loss, trauma, joy for instance, workers have to be able to understand how they themselves experience these emotions so they can understand how their feelings influence their understanding of and contribute to their interactions with children. (Krueger, 1997, p 155)

Exercise 5

Reflect on what kinds of strong or difficult feelings working with certain children or young people with particular experiences or characteristics brings up in you. Consider how able you are to manage and contain your feelings and the extent to which you have a safe space to reflect on them and learn from them.

Comment on Exercise 5

Most workers will find that certain children or young people make them feel unusually riled, irritable, frightened, upset or over-protective. They might end up wanting to attack, control, love or rescue them. Thinking of such feelings as a 'reactive counter-transference' (Mackewn, 1997) can be useful. This is a term from psychodynamic theory which refers to the emotional and psychological responses professionals sometimes feel have been 'conjured out of them' by their interactions with particular service users and carers. For example, children who are very vulnerable, distressed, traumatised, angry or neglected may send out very strong 'rescue me, take me home' messages which are hard to resist. Other young people seem able to alienate almost any professional with surly, disengaged, rude and defensive behaviour, evoking what transactional analysts might term a 'critical parent' response, where there is a desire in the professional to punish or control rather than understand or care (Clarkson, 1993).

Enhanced awareness of their own reactions can give professionals an important insight into children's experiences and needs. Conversely, not recognising and containing their own feelings can be unhelpful and even dangerous. Not only might what children are really thinking and feeling be misunderstood, but also practitioners may 'act out' their counter-transference response rather than make an appropriate professional intervention. The next practice vignette discusses how Edwin was able to reflect on his counter-transference so he could use it to better understand and respond to a young person, rather than 'act it out' himself.

Practice vignette: Reflective practice

Edwin is finding that negative feelings are being invoked in him by Robbie, aged 14, who is on the verge of a further placement breakdown. His carers tell Edwin that they are at the end of their tether with Robbie's surly and rude behaviour. As soon as he meets Robbie, Edwin very quickly gains an insight into the carers' frustration, himself feeling irritated and wanting not to bother with Robbie. Reading Robbie's file, however, helps Edwin recognise and contain his reactive counter-transference feelings. He recognises how Robbie's behaviour is likely to stem from his earlier difficult experiences in his birth family. Robbie had been constantly humiliated and berated by his parents when growing up and they had then ejected him from the family. Edwin considers Robbie's behaviour as a form of indirect communication: it lets him know how Robbie sees others (punitive or neglectful) and what he expects from them (abuse or abandonment). Edwin uses his reflective practice to prevent him acting out the counter-transference and reinforcing this early message from childhood

▶

back to Robbie. He talks to Robbie in a firm but kindly way about the impact his behaviour has on others. In this way he manages to provide a different response to Robbie than his internal unconscious self might be expecting.

Practitioners also need to consider whether their emotional responses say more about themselves than they do about the children. If you notice that you are regularly having the same kinds of reactions to different children and young people, this might be better thought of as 'proactive countertransference', that is, material from your own history and internal world which has been evoked by the work (Mackewn, 1997). For example, if your motivation for working with vulnerable children is that becoming a significant person to them makes you feel liked or needed, powerful, important or special in some way, then this may be because it is meeting unmet psychological or emotional needs for you. This can be very risky as you can then become over-involved and lose the personal/professional boundary that enables you to take a critical overview of children's needs and entitlements. Instead, you should seek to ensure your personal life adequately fulfils your needs for validation and affection and deal with any earlier unresolved issues from childhood through counselling/therapy or other self-exploration. Enhancing your self-awareness and dealing with personal 'baggage' in this way should help you maintain appropriate boundaries, expand your range of interpersonal responses and improve your capacity to assess the nature of other people's relationships.

Supervision can be a helpful place to begin reflecting on such processes, not to try to make your supervisor into a therapist for you, but rather because supervision can provide the kind of thinking and feeling containment that reflexive practice requires (Ruch, 2007). To maintain boundaries in this environment, the following guidance can help:

> The basic boundary in this area is that supervision sessions should always start by exploring issues from work and should end with looking at what the supervisee does next with the work that has been explored. (Hawkins and Shohet, 2000, p 55)

Developing a personal approach to practice

This final section considers the different aspects that make up professionals' individual approaches to their practice. Questions to help readers determine their own general approach, how they conceptualise their communication with children and young people and how they might review and evaluate their work are summarised in Table 1.

Table 1: Identifying your personal approach to your work

	Ontology	Epistemology	Theoretical base	Values and beliefs	Ethics and codes of conduct	Personal qualities and capabilities	Skills and techniques	Professional practice context
Questions to help you clarify your general approach to practice	What is your personal philosophy? How do you view the world and individual or social needs?	What kinds of knowledge do you base your approach on? What is your learning style?	What experiences, research and theoretical frameworks inform your practice?	How do you think that you (and other people) should behave?	How does your professional body think practitioners should behave?	What are the key personal qualities that you bring to your work?	What models, skills and techniques are you already proficient in?	What resources, policy, practice guidance and law, shape your practice?
Questions to help clarify how you approach your communication with children and young people	How do you view children and the helping role?	What do you know about how to communicate with children and young people and how did you learn this?	How does this knowledge help you to communicate with this child or young person?	What do you believe is the right thing to do with this child?	What would be classed as ethical behaviour in this situation?	Do you possess the qualities and capacity to relate that children and young people value?	What tools and practice approaches are needed for you and the child to communicate together?	What is your role and task with this child?
Questions to assist with evaluating your work with children and reviewing your approach	Did your view of the situation help you in your work? Do you need to revise the way you see the world?	What did you learn from this encounter? What else do you need to know to work with this child or other children?	What are the gaps in your knowledge? How might they be filled?	Were your values and beliefs a guide and support or did they interfere with or constrict the work?	Did you act according to professional ethics or were there conflicts with your personal values?	Are there any areas in which you need to undertake personal development?	What did you do well or struggle with in a particular situation? What further skills are needed?	Did the context support or constrain your practice?

Ontology

Professionals tend to have their own idiosyncratic ways of approaching and undertaking their work that is based on a range of influences. Their personal philosophy and way of 'being in' and understanding the world (what might be called their *ontology*) is at the bedrock of everything they are and do (therefore a key aspect of the 'being' domain of the core capabilities model). Ontology is like a lens through which everything is seen, categorised and interpreted and influences people's intentions, perceptions, feelings and responses to what they encounter. It can affect, for example, whether a practitioner sees children and young people as vulnerable, developmentally incomplete and needing protection from distressing matters, or as citizens and social actors with rights to information and to be consulted. Questions that practitioners might need to ask themselves to determine their ontological underpinnings include: how do I view children and childhood and the nature of the professional role?

Epistemology

The way we see the world directly affects the ways in which we seek to learn about it and know it; this may be termed our *epistemology*. It shapes the ways that practitioners build up the kinds of *knowing what* and *knowing how* knowledges discussed in Chapter Five. Learning within the 'knowing what' dimension provides practitioners with the information and critical capacity which they require to make sense of their professional role and the children and young people they encounter. This might include research findings, such as how neglect can affect the development of children's brains and slow down the acquisition of language, or formal theoretical frameworks, such as attachment theory, which shed light on what children's behaviour might be saying about their experiences.

Knowing how knowledge is a more practical understanding that informs the way in which practitioners go about their roles and tasks, such as how to draw a genogram with a child or interview a young person. Both 'knowing how' and 'knowing what' dimensions of knowledge might be acquired through 'top-down' or *deductive* approaches to learning, where information is taken in from outside, such as theoretical frameworks or research findings about effective practice, to inform practice. Knowledge may also be built up through 'bottom-up' or *inductive* processes, where an understanding is formed through reflecting on and evaluating personal and professional experiences.

In order to clarify their epistemology, practitioners might ask themselves more generally, 'what do I know about how to communicate with children and how did I learn this?'. They should also reflect on their specific encounters with children to consider whether their approach had been effective and what else might need to be learned or developed to improve practice. It is in this way that a more reflexive approach to practice is established.

Values, beliefs and ethics

Professional codes of practice, such as the British Association of Social Workers (BASW) code of ethics and the General Social Care Council (GSCC) code of practice (GSCC, 2002) set an ethical baseline for communication with children and young people. The GSCC code, for example, requires social workers to protect children (and others) from harm, establish their trust and confidence and promote their interests, rights and independence. Professionals' personal values and beliefs about how people should behave will lie at the heart of their 'being', however, and are likely to be as much or even more influential on their practice. While practitioners might accept an externally determined principle of promoting young people's participation, for example, it is likely to be their personal recognition of the importance of this that will cause them to prioritise a young person's involvement and try especially hard when they might be tempted to give up. In fact, it is precisely this personal ethical commitment that is particularly associated with success in achieving communication in difficult circumstances (Thomas and O'Kane, 2000). To clarify their values and ethics, practitioners might ask themselves not only 'what might my professional body think would be the correct ethical approach in this situation?' but also 'what do I believe is the right thing to do with this child?'. These might converge, but there might, at times, be conflicts between the two, such as around confidentiality. Such ethical dilemmas will be discussed in more depth in Chapter Eleven.

Personal qualities and capabilities

The 'being' domain of the core capabilities model also includes the personal qualities and emotional capacities that professionals bring to their work. Some workers will instinctively be able to draw on their warmth, friendliness or openness to help children feel comfortable. Their capacity to emotionally 'tune in' and create a safe space will help them support children who are distressed, frightened or tearful. Others, through their emotional robustness and capacity to combine authoritativeness and assertiveness with sensitivity and humour, will manage particularly well with children who are behaving irritatingly, angrily or aggressively. This chapter has encouraged readers to identify and value their existing qualities so that they can be used more mindfully, as well as identifying areas where some personal development might be needed. Self-reflective questions to facilitate this include:

- What are the most significant personal qualities that I bring to my work?
- Do I have the personal qualities that children value?
- Are there areas of relating to children or working with feelings that I need to develop further?

Professional practice context

As has already been observed, professionals' practice might be either facilitated or constrained by the practice context. The social work role and task with an individual child or family is determined by contemporary government policy, legislation, practice guidance and local convention as much as by the assessed needs and explicit preferences of that children and family, so workers must be aware of national agendas and legislation that circumscribe their role. Environmental constraints may influence the amount of time and resources practitioners have to prepare and carry out their work and how much support and supervision they receive. This means that individuals and teams will need to reflect on how best to map a pathway to effective practice which takes into account the sometimes conflicting dynamics of personal skills, policy agendas, legal requirements, family needs and resource constraints.

Practice vignette: Millie's approach to practice

Millie believes there is something good ('of God'[1]) in everyone and is committed to promoting human rights, social justice and respect and care for others. She finds herself drawn to humanistic philosophies, theoretical frameworks and models such as the person-centred approach (Rogers, 1951), which emphasises the importance of creating the right 'conditions' within which service users and carers can grow and change. This includes practitioners using themselves in a genuine way (congruence) to get alongside service users, form an understanding of their world (empathy) and to create a safe non-judgemental space (through unconditional positive regard) within which service users can 'actualise' and develop.

Comment on the vignette

In this example, it can be seen how Millie's spiritual values underpin her approach to other human beings. As with many other people, it is important to her to find an approach to practice that is congruent with who she is and how she sees the world. She is then able to further her knowledge and understanding of research findings and theoretical frameworks that are consistent with this.

A framework for identifying practitioners' personal approaches to their work

Drawing on earlier work by Watson and West (2006), and illustrated in this last section of the chapter, a framework has been developed which summarises the different influences on practitioners' personal styles. Set out in Table 1, it outlines questions to help individuals map out their own approach. It is anticipated that this exercise will consolidate readers' reflexivity in this and the surrounding chapters regarding the dimensions of their existing capability and future learning and developmental needs.

Conclusion

Self-awareness has been identified as a key quality running through the 'core capability' domains of 'knowing, being and doing'. It helps practitioners to be honest with themselves and to develop a realistic appraisal of their current knowledge, qualities and capabilities so that they can identify transferable skills and future learning and development needs. This is an essential step towards more competent and reflexive communicative practice.

Identifying how their own approach has emerged and influences their work can be helpful, too, as, by so doing, workers are likely to be more able to see where further development or modifications are needed. They are also then less likely to rely on a 'practice wisdom' that is based on unarticulated, non-codified and undocumented knowledge from professional or life experience or half-forgotten, out-of-date prior learning (Macdonald, 2000). Instead, transparency about how credible knowledge from a range of various sources is obtained, processed and used will support their ability to make sound judgements and interventions based on a range of experiences and understanding in complex situations.

Note
[1] See *Quaker faith and practice*, the authorised collection of writings that express Quaker theology.

Key questions

1. What are your greatest strengths in each of the domains of knowing, being and doing?
2. How would you summarise your individual approach to practice?
3. What three key areas of professional learning and professional development will you now prioritise?

Further reading and resources

Howe, D. (2008) *The emotionally intelligent social worker*, Basingstoke: Palgrave Macmillan.

Ruch, G. (2005) 'Relationship-based practice and reflective practice: holistic approaches to contemporary child care social work', *Child & Family Social Work*, vol 10, pp 111-23.

Schofield, G. (1998) 'Inner and outer worlds: a psychosocial framework for child and family social work', *Child & Family Social Work*, vol 3, no 1, pp 57-67.

Getting the context right for communication

7

Introduction

It can be difficult to second guess in advance exactly how children and young people might respond to contact with a new worker. Many will be unclear about who the practitioner is and the purpose of the contact and will need this explaining carefully. While some might be desperate to off-load significant information or to receive help, others could be dreading the first meeting with a worker. A number will have been influenced in advance by their parents' and carers' feelings about professional involvement, even primed to respond in a particular way. Such dynamics can interfere with the engagement the worker is trying to form with children and young people and can cause 'noise'[1] or miscommunications.

This chapter covers how to prepare for the first meeting with a particular child, young person or sibling group, attending to these kinds of issues. Ensuring that the right kind of context is put in place can make a real difference as to how all family members feel about future contact with the worker and with the professional system as a whole (Jones, 2003). As many initial contacts take place in the presence of a parent, carer or other professional, the complexities of three-way communications will also be discussed. A vignette of a fictional, but common, situation is used to illustrate the kinds of issues that arise for a social worker in planning to meet with a family for the first time.

Preparing for initial contact with children

In an ideal world, practitioners should always have enough time to learn as much as possible in advance about a child or young person and the way he or she communicates. This helps the work with them to be planned carefully and thoroughly. The danger may be, however, that in either urgent circumstances or where there is under-staffing and too high workloads, how best to engage and communicate with a child or young person can become one of a number of competing considerations. For example, where a referral has been received by a duty team that expresses concern for a child's safety or well-being, the social work role will include:

- determining whether a threshold is reached for safeguarding procedures;
- how best to communicate with the parents;
- who else should be involved (for example, the police);
- what intervention, if any, is needed to keep a child or young person safe and how swift if needs to be;
- whether there should be a medical examination or formal forensic interview of the child or young person; and
- whether a legal order is needed to safeguard the child.

While these are clearly very important considerations, workers must also prioritise their planning regarding how best to communicate with the young person. Honing their core capabilities (Chapter Five) and enhancing their self-awareness regarding strengths and limitations (Chapter Six) will be of assistance in working rapidly, reflexively and competently in such challenging contexts.

Practitioners may conversely be planning to meet with a child or young person who has been in contact with other professionals for some time, for example, taking over as keyworker for a child in care. Such young people could be approaching the forthcoming contact with a new person with a range of feelings, some of which will relate to their prior experiences of professionals. The previous worker may have been valued or even idealised, with their loss felt keenly. The new worker may have to bear with the denigrating comparisons for some time before they, and what they bring, can be accepted. Conversely, previous negative experiences of professionals may mean young people are poorly motivated and ambivalent about the next worker, perhaps rebuffing them (de Winter and Noom, 2003).

If children have been abused or neglected, are insecurely attached or have suffered significant losses, trauma or displacement, their experiences are likely to affect their responses to new workers and the degree to which they are able to engage with them and trust them. Practitioners will need to be sensitive to this and not expect too much too soon. Neither, however, should they give up trying when they are met with coolness, rebuff or 'testing out' behaviours, as this is an opportunity to help repair children and young people's perception that adults cannot be relied on or do not really care about them.

The following questions can help practitioners plan and prepare to meet and make an initial intervention with a child or young person. Each is explored in depth throughout this chapter:

- Why?
- What?
- Who?
- Who with?
- How?
- What with?
- Where?
- When?
- How long?
- What support?
- What next?

The practice vignette of the Doyle family is used to explore and illustrate key considerations in beginning working with a sibling group. The vignette also continues through the remaining chapters of this book, illustrating the developing nature and changing practice roles common in such situations.

Practice vignette: A referral regarding the Doyle family

A family support team in a small town in the East Midlands area of England receives a referral from the headteacher at the local primary school regarding help that they feel is needed for the Doyle family. They are concerned that the situation is bordering on neglect. Jack Doyle, aged six, is disruptive in class and is often caught fighting with the other children during the break-times. His attendance is poor. The headteacher had invited Jack's mother, Theresa Doyle, in to meet with him and Jack a few weeks ago to talk about this. Theresa had reluctantly agreed to the school completing a CAF[2] assessment at that time and a plan had been made which included Theresa attempting to improve Jack's attendance, the school monitoring his punctuality and Jack agreeing to try to respond better to the boundaries set by the class teacher.

The school's concerns have now increased since the initial CAF form was completed. Jack's appearance has become more unkempt and he has been caught stealing food from the other children's lunchboxes. His behaviour has become so disruptive that school exclusion has started to be considered. The class teacher is worried that Theresa seems depressed as her appearance, too, has deteriorated and she seems 'flat' in her presentation. The school are aware Jack has a baby sister, Isabella, and a teenage sister, Caz. Nothing is known about Jack's and Caz's fathers but it is known that Isabella's father, Janek Kowalik, is no longer living in the UK. He was an economic migrant who returned to his native Poland in the economic downturn. He does not have parental responsibility for Isabella and has remained in only sporadic contact with Theresa.

A review of the earlier plan was due at the end of the school day today but Theresa said she was too tired to come. When asked by the headteacher if she agreed to him making a referral to Family Support, she said, "It's up to you". He took this as consent. After some discussion with the health visitor and reading the CAF form, the Family Support team leader decides that a home visit should be made the next day by social worker Tanya.

'Why?' questions

- Why are you going to be involved with a particular child or family?
  - ☐ What is the purpose of your professional role and the task you have to do?
  - ☐ What are you, the child and other people aiming to achieve, convey or find out from each other?
  - ☐ Is your involvement something the child wants or has it been imposed by the professional system, their parents or the court?
  - ☐ How do the parents or carers feel about your involvement?
  - ☐ Do you have similar or conflicting aspirations and intentions to the child and/or their parents/carers?
  - ☐ If so, what difference might this make?

Purpose of communication

These are fundamental questions about the *purpose* of the communication. It is essential for workers to be clear about what they are intending to achieve and why, as the social work role and task fundamentally shapes the nature of the communication between professionals and children. Where there is pressure for the social worker to provide the young person's view to others within externally imposed deadlines, such as those set by the assessment framework, the court or the Integrated Children's System (ICS), these can be counter-productive. Not only might this result in limited planning time (Broadhurst et al, 2010), but children and young people do not always work to adults' timescales. They often need a relaxed time in an unpressured environment with a trusted worker to make sense of what they have been told and to begin to formulate and convey what they need to express (Howe, 2005). Where this is not possible, professionals should be aware that a child or young person's lack of disclosure of important information does not necessarily mean that nothing has occurred (Jones, 2003).

Where the purpose is advocacy, practitioners need to appreciate that, regardless of their own opinion, their role is to elicit and convey the child or young person's views to the professional system. Colton et al (2001, pp 56-7) give the example of a child who tells an advocate she wishes to return to live with a father who has sexually abused her, believing that the fact that she has told others and he has said sorry will be enough to protect her. The advocate's role in such a situation is simply to convey this view, as much as possible in the child's own words. The investigating social worker, while hearing and taking her wishes into account, may well think that the child remains at risk nonetheless and take protective action that contradicts her view. Such situations can sometimes leave children and young people feeling that they are not being listened to; it may turn them off from sharing their views in the future (McLeod, 2008). Consequently, it is essential that, where there are clashing perspectives and agendas, professionals work sensitively and transparently, explaining diplomatically and clearly to children and young people why they are contradicting their wishes.

Comment on the vignette

The purpose of the initial visit is for Tanya to form an impression of what is happening in the family. It is often unclear at initial referral whether a family are just going through a period of additional stress that requires some further support or whether more serious difficulties are emerging. There is not just the welfare of Jack to consider but also his siblings, one of whom, Isabella, is only six months old. Tanya will need to ascertain whether Theresa will agree to engage in some support services and judge, if not, whether the situation should be referred on to the child protection team for investigation.[3]

It will not be sufficient for Tanya to speak only with Theresa. If at all possible, she will want to gain an initial impression of how the children are experiencing the situation and speak to Jack and Caz on their own. Consideration also needs to be given to engaging with the children's fathers, which can be especially challenging where there has been little recent family contact with them.

'What?' questions

- What is it that you or the child want or need to say to each other? What kinds of information or views are you seeking?
- What might your manner communicate to the young person? Is it the same message as your words?

- What might get in the way of important things being expressed, conveyed or understood?

Content of communication

These are questions about the *content* of the communication. Social workers may have a clear idea in advance about what the focus should be. This may include: providing children with information about services or events that have occurred; consulting with them about future plans, such as hearing what a young person wants from future adopters; learning about the child's experiences at home or in foster care; communicating as part of a focused intervention such as parenting work; or simply keeping in touch with a young person for whom they are a keyworker.

What is to be talked about will shape the nature of the dialogue, including who might be present and where it takes place. If the worker has too prescribed an idea of what needs to be discussed, however, they may gear the conversation and any questions too narrowly to what they are anticipating hearing about. The danger is that unexpected, unanticipated or even unwelcome content is not then sought or heard. Practitioners should always aim to keep an open mind and provide opportunities for children to contribute to the agenda of a visit or meeting. Listening also to children's indirect communications (for example, body language, paralanguage, behaviour) may also help them identify what has not yet been said.

Communicating during child protection investigations

Where the communication relates to child protection concerns, it needs to be framed by local safeguarding procedures and statutory guidance. Informed consent to a social worker speaking with a child or young person would normally be gained from both the parent and young person unless the urgency and seriousness of the matter would mean a child would be placed at significant harm unless this is dispensed with (DfES, 2006a). A legal order[4] might be necessary if there is parental refusal to see a child alone and there is some urgency. Where a joint interview with a police officer is required,[5] this will be carried out by social workers who have received specialist training. However, other social workers may be involved in preparing young people and their family for an interview, supporting them through it, debriefing them afterwards and dealing with any implications that then arise (including for protection, ongoing support or therapy).

Where an initial disclosure of abuse has been made, care needs to be taken not to contaminate the evidence through biased or leading questions (see

Chapter Eight and also Jones, 2003, for a fuller discussion). Children and young people will be extremely susceptible to others' reactions to their disclosure, often being fearful, embarrassed or worried they are not believed, so professionals need to be sensitive and able to manage their own feelings of shock or horror at what has happened. They should convey the impression that they are there to listen, are interested in what children and young people have to say and will do their best to manage the situation appropriately and helpfully. Children and young people have stated in a number of research studies how helpful such a demeanour has been to them (for example, Wade and Westcott, 1997; Prior et al, 1999). The worker's approach should, where possible, be 'open-ended and consist of an invitation to talk if the child so wishes' (Jones, 2003, p 98). Any conversations should be carefully recorded, including as much as possible of what has been said verbatim by both child and worker, and the child's body language and demeanour. This may then be used as evidence in any subsequent court proceedings.

Comment on the vignette

A number of possible scenarios might arise during Tanya's initial visit to the family. Theresa might refuse to allow Tanya to see or speak to her children or even to enter the house at all. Conversely, Tanya may be given the opportunity to observe the family interacting and even to speak with Jack and Caz. Ideally social workers need to get some time alone with children to hear from them in their own words what they might be worrying about and what their views are about their situation. For the Doyle family, however, this is not a safeguarding investigation so it is not strictly essential that Tanya speaks to Jack and Caz alone today if that cannot readily be achieved. It may be better to wait to do so until some initial trust has been built up with the family that will facilitate the situation. Otherwise Tanya may simply find herself with a child or young person who cannot or will not talk, influenced by their mother's negative or fearful feelings about the situation. Tanya's key aim in the initial visit will be, then, to introduce herself to the family, to see if an initial rapport can be established which can be built on later and to see what she can learn about the children and the situation.

'Who?' questions

- Who is the child or children with whom the worker is aiming to communicate?

☐ What is known already about them? For example, their age and maturity; primary language and way of communicating; cultural and racial background; previous experiences; any disability.

☐ What is known about how the child normally communicates? What augmentative or alternative forms of communication might need to be used?

☐ How might the child feel about meeting the worker and how might this affect their communication with them?

☐ What is not known about a particular child or situation?

Understanding the child or young person

These questions relate to forming an understanding of the particular child or young person with whom the worker is to engage. 'Who children are' relates not just to their innate characteristics but who they have become through their experiences (Gerhardt, 2004). Attachment theory, for example, would suggest that children who have developed an insecure–avoidant attachment style because of pervasive neglect and constantly negative messages about who they are, are likely (usually unconsciously) to downplay their own affect and needs and expect to be dismissed or ignored by others (Howe, 2005). Workers may thus encounter a child who seems flat or unresponsive and says "I don't mind" or "It doesn't matter" when they are asked their views.

Disabled children and young people

Some disabled young people, such as those with sensory impairments, communicate differently from other children. Professionals may find that establishing a shared understanding is more challenging than usual or that they are required to employ techniques they are not used to. One risk of this may be that they see the child as the one with the communication 'problem'. Instead, practitioners should operate in line with the social model of disability, which means locating the skill gap with themselves rather than with the child. Building up their own skills and making additional effort is what is most linked with achieving success in communication (Stalker and Connors, 2003). Workers should also avoid having low expectations, stereotypical views and assumptions about disabled children's capacity to communicate as these can limit their own efforts and discourage children (Hindley and Brown, 1994).

Augmentative systems may be the primary form of communication with some disabled children and young people; these can include picture boards, 'touch talkers' and computerised tools (Millar and Scott, 2003). Workers may be able to learn in time how to communicate directly with a young person using their communication system, but a parent or support worker may be required to help or translate in the first instance or where contact is to be transitory. Extra time should always be made available both for planning (to learn as much as possible about how best to communicate) and for meeting with disabled children (to provide extended lead-ins to any subsequent discussion and to allow time for interpreting). Careful consideration of the child's unique developmental trajectory is a necessary part of this. Children who are deaf or hard of hearing, for example, may take longer to acquire formal language and become capable in employing abstract concepts and a visual spatial system of communication (such as a specific sign language) (Kennedy, 1992). Box 10 provides some guidance for working with children and young people who are deaf or hard of hearing.

Box 10: Top tips to help you communicate with children and young people who are deaf or hard of hearing

1. Find out if the child prefers to communicate via sign language and use an interpreter if needed.

2. If the young person is going to lip-read, make sure you don't put your hands in front of your mouth and ensure the light is good.

3. If the child is using a hearing aid, speak clearly but do not shout.

4. Use visual means of communication as much as possible, including words and pictures.

5. Avoid unnecessary noise and distractions.

6. Avoid complex sentences and jargon.

7. Maintain face-to-face contact with the young person, not shifting to look at their carers, other professionals or the interpreter.

8. Be patient and ensure there is plenty of time without rushing.

9. Check out if you and the child are understanding each other.

10. If they haven't understood what you have said, think of different ways to convey the message.

Source: Based on RNID (2004)

Culture and oppression

As discussed in Chapter Four, tensions and misunderstandings may arise when workers and young people have culturally different styles of communicating and relating. It is the worker's responsibility to learn about how a child's cultural, religious or linguistic norms might influence their habitus and to find appropriate ways of engaging with and responding to them. Reflecting cultural patterns in spoken, written or body language may be helpful where this is possible and appropriate (Stevens, 1998). This could be extended to demonstrating an awareness of and interest in young people's sub-culture or music. However, workers should avoid seeming patronising or appropriating of young people's culture and particularly beware of making over-simplified or stereotypical suppositions (Tyson, 2003).

There can be a danger, too, of focusing too heavily on cultural factors and ignoring the impact on young people of oppression and discrimination, such as experiences of racism and homophobia (Thompson, 2006). Black and minority ethnic children may feel effectively silenced by white indigenous workers, particularly when they indicate through their language or practices that they lack understanding of the effects of racism on black identity development and emotional and psychological health, or have no social and structural analysis of black people's history and status (Ahmed, 1994). Professionals must challenge their own underlying racist belief systems and values, for example, stereotypes that black children are either problems or victims, if they are to engage young people in the kind of empowering 'ideal speech' dialogue discussed in Chapter Four.

Similarly, lesbian, gay, bisexual and transgender (LGBT) young people will also only feel safe if they intuit that they are accepted rather than judged by their social workers (Trotter, 2000). Acceptance may be conveyed through social workers avoiding oppressive language in their verbal and written communications, having LGBT literature available and demonstrating their knowledge of the impact of heterosexism and homophobia on young people; this includes comprehending the effects of oppression and the discriminatory legal framework on identity development and 'coming out' (Freed-Kernis, 2008). Professionals need to understand how and why children might be wary of open communication and to offer meaningful responses that take their experiences into account. As with anti–racist practice, this requires both self-knowledge and self-challenge regarding workers' own attitudes and behaviour.

Comment on the vignette

There are a number of things Tanya needs to find out about the Doyle children if she is to tailor the communication to their needs and way of being. She might first want to consider the complexities of culture, ethnicity and habitus. Jack, for example, is of dual heritage with a white Irish mother and black British father. So Jack's primary language is English, as is Tanya's, but there may be cultural practices and interpretations that Tanya is not yet aware of that influence the way Jack communicates. She may not be able to take her 'habitus' for granted, as cultural and linguistic differences may lead to miscommunication. Neither Jack's father nor any of his paternal relatives have had contact with him for some years, and Jack's mother and half siblings are white. Tanya might wonder how his sense of racial and cultural identity is developing, for example whether he is receiving the necessary positive messages about his ethnicity and having contact with other adults and children who are black or dual heritage (Robinson, 2007). She should also consider how he might perceive and respond to her, as a white worker. These issues could be different for Caz but little should be taken for granted in a family with a rich diversity of cultural heritage (Goldstein, 2002).

The children's mode of communication and cognitive and intellectual capacities should be taken into account. Isabella is six months old. While she will not use words to convey her thoughts and feelings, her demeanour and behaviour might reveal a great deal about her state of mind and the quality of parenting she has received (McMahon, 2009), so Tanya's observation skills will be to the fore here.[6] Caz seems to be progressing in the normative range at school so Tanya might reasonably guided by developmental norms regarding the vocabulary and concepts she might be expected to know and use. As the initial concerns have not been about Caz, it might be most helpful to aim for a more relaxed conversation to unfold with her. Jack's cognitive abilities, however, are in the low-average range and his school have advised that he finds it hard to sit still, does not concentrate and often seems to struggle to take things in. Tanya would need to consider more child-friendly ways of explaining her presence and intentions to Jack in a way he can understand and help him to convey his world and experiences.

'Who with?' questions

- Who might need or prefer to be there with the child or young person to support or assist or as part of the wider assessment or intervention? How might both the adults' and young people's needs and voices be elicited and balanced so that each are heard?

■ Might it be essential to see the children on their own to establish whether there are safeguarding concerns or to gain a narrative from them untainted by parental influence?

Seeing a child or young person alone

These questions help workers determine when it is most helpful or appropriate to see a child or young person with someone else, such as a parent, foster carer, support worker or interpreter, or whether it is essential that a child is seen alone. Such decisions will relate to the context and purpose of the communication as well as the needs and preference of the child and their carers. As a result of safeguarding concerns, for example, it may be vital to speak with children alone to determine the risks posed to them – parents or carers might influence what they say or even be the source of the risk.

Having time alone with their social worker is very important to young people; it provides an opportunity for them to have a chat and a laugh together in order to get to know each other, and also to have private conversations about important matters such as contact with family members, their education and medical problems (Morgan, 2006). Young people feel they do not always get the opportunity for this as social workers do not automatically suggest it and it can be awkward for them to ask in front of parents or carers. Some have suggested that social workers establish a system for them to be able to flag up whenever they need a private talk, such as a code word or signal that they can use in front of others (Morgan, 2006).

Seeing a child or young person with another professional

Often social workers do not meet with children alone but in the presence of another family member, carer or professional. Communication here moves from being just two-way in nature, to a 'three-way street' (Triangle, 2009). Sometimes another professional who is already involved with the family can provide more information or support in a meeting with a child and/or family. In a school setting, for example, a teacher might support a young person in their first meeting with an education social worker or Connexions adviser. The other professional may have a different but equally important role as the social worker, such as a police officer in a child protection investigation. As serious misunderstandings can occur where workers share no common language with children, an interpreter might be needed where the child's first language is not English. Alternatively a specialist practitioner might be required as a co-worker to help the social worker understand how best to communicate with young people who use some form of sign language or other augmentative or alternative means of communication (Kennedy, 1992). In all cases, it is essential that each worker is clear about the boundaries and overlaps of their complementary roles and works to a joint purpose so as not to confuse children and young people. It might be useful for the workers to meet in advance to plan this carefully.

Seeing a child or young person in the presence of parents

While parents might be the key facilitators of communication between a child and professionals, they could alternatively be a source of complexity or difficulty, such as when their relationship with the child or young person is problematic or where there are issues of abuse and neglect (Reder et al, 1993). If the purpose is to see a child with a parent as part of an assessment or explanatory process, the practitioner will need to contain and manage any painful or antagonistic feelings that are evoked for the parents in order to keep the situation safe for the child. Where there is a fraught relationship between a young person and their foster carers, seeing them together may be similarly tricky. The worker needs to ensure that space is given to the child or young person's voice without intensifying parents' and carers' distress or anger about their difficult or dangerous behaviour.

Where an interpreter is required (such as where the child does not speak English or has a sensory impairment) parents should not generally be asked to fill this role as they could influence or shape the meaning of what the child is saying; they may even be the source of the difficulty which the dialogue is intending to address.

Children and young people are used to being ignored and marginalised when adults come together, so if professionals start speaking to parents, children may end up feeling they are in the way or are less important (Triangle, 2009). Workers should check that they are always giving eye contact to both children and their parents or carers so that children know they are being included in the discussion. This also stops parents from trying to take over the dialogue. What both the child and the parents or carers have said must be responded to. The vocabulary and concepts used should always be simple and clear enough for the child to understand, even if it feels too basic for the adults. The way the room is laid out should also be inclusive for the child, for example, smaller, lower chairs or cushions on the floor.

Comment on the vignette

Parents in Theresa's position may often be frightened or feel disempowered and show this through distressed or antagonistic behaviour towards professionals. If this happens in front of the children when a social worker visits, this could seriously impact on how they relate to him or her. Jack might be wary of Tanya and Caz openly hostile, for example. Either could be cautious about saying anything that they think might make matters worse. Practitioners will need to invest time and effort in trying to engage parents as well as their children in such situations if they are to create the kind of environment in which children and young people feel able to speak.

'How?' questions

- How should you introduce yourself to a child or young person?
- What kind of vocabulary, language and concepts should you use?
- How should you conduct the conversation?
- Is face-to-face talking the best form of communication in this situation?
- How should your manner and demeanour be?
- How will you use your skills, resources and any additional or alternative methods or approaches towards the identified purpose?

Introducing yourself to a child

Right from the first moment of contact, professionals create a particular impression for better or worse, so they should remember that, although this might be the hundredth child or young person they have visited, this is the first time for that child with them. Children might be uncertain or nervous or find it hard to retain information about who the worker is. A letter in advance with the worker's picture on and a succinct explanation can be a useful way for a young person to start to familiarise themselves with who the worker is (Marchant, 2008). This can help convey the impression that the worker is interested in meeting with *them* rather than just with their parents/carers. It also means an explanation of who the worker is can be given in advance which is less subject to any inaccurate or pejorative explanations given by other people.

Exercise

Write down how you might introduce yourself to a child or young person. Show how you would explain what your professional role is and the reason why you are meeting together. Clarify what will happen, how long you will meet for, how frequently, where the meetings will be and what you will do. Explain how issues of confidentiality will be managed. Make sure your explanation is appropriate for the particular child and situation.

Comment on the vignette

Preparing something in advance to explain your presence to children can be very helpful. Tanya might introduce herself to Jack, for example, by saying, "My name is Tanya. I come to see children and their parents when things aren't going very well. I've come today because your school thinks you and your family might need some help". This introduction has the advantage of ensuring Jack is aware both that she knows how difficult things have become at school and that she and the other professionals will be working together. Of course, mentioning school might be a double-edged sword as Jack's negative feelings about school may be transferred to her.

Caz, at 14, is likely to have more awareness of what social workers are and what they do, so it could be useful to ask what she already knows about social workers and where she learned this. This could clarify any assumptions she has formed through characters in soap operas, films and books, or through experiences a friend has had. Doing so enables Tanya to build on Caz's initial understanding (or to correct any misunderstanding) while also offering an opportunity to engage Caz in wider conversations about her life and experiences.

Selecting the most appropriate approach

As discussed in Chapter Six, practitioners' individual approaches will influence their understanding of children and how best to work with them. Workers should consider how suitable their general approach is for a particular child and any relevant evidence regarding effective practice. From the first moment of face-to-face contact, attention needs to be paid to building rapport through 'tuning in' to children and young people's ways of being, providing a reliable and non-judgemental space and being warm, open and friendly. Consideration then needs to be given to whether a directive or non-directive approach is needed. Directive work focuses on a specific purpose which then shapes the method and pace; for example, informing a young person about the outcome of an interim care order hearing. Non-directive work, by contrast, presents a child with open-ended time and space so that what they need to express or convey can surface in their own way and at their own pace. While the latter is often more associated with the work of a therapist than a social worker, it can be extremely effective in informing assessment work as a deeper understanding of what is significant to the child or young person can emerge (Thomas and O'Kane, 2000).

Communicating with disabled children and young people

The worker's beliefs about and commitment to effective communication are often what make the difference, particularly with children who have learning disabilities or speech and language impairments.

> If adults expect to get little or nothing from communicating with these children, that is probably exactly what they will get. (Stalker and Connors, 2003, p 27)

Facilitating communication with disabled children and young people should draw on the same general principles as with any others. It should be 'in an age-appropriate manner, combining fun with a more serious aspect, as appropriate, so as to engage but not patronise the child' (Stalker and Connors, 2003, p 33). Young people's primary mode of communication should be used and any assistance needed with this should be sought from those who know them well. This may include using specific communication systems such as Makaton, Rebus or Blissymbolics (Oosterhoorn and Kendrick, 2001). Careful observations of children will help practitioners to make sense of their more indirect communications (Atkins-Burnett and Allen-Meares, 2000). Visual, creative and play-based methods may be particularly facilitative (Harvey, 1996). Rather than focusing on their own feelings of struggle or being de-skilled, workers should always appreciate children's frustrations at the challenges of mutual communication and respect their needs, wishes and rights at all times.

'What with?' questions

■ What tools, props or resources might be needed to facilitate dialogue with a child?

Tools and pro formas

A range of tools and pro formas might be used in direct practice with children and young people. Some are mandatory within statutory roles, such as ASSET,[7] CAF assessments or personal education plans.[8] Others constitute official guidance when doing such work, like the tools and checklists within the *Framework for the assessment of children in need and their families* (DH et al, 2000). A whole host of supplementary and facilitative resources are additionally available, however, to help social workers complete the full spectrum of assessment, planning, intervention and review tasks. Examples are given at the end of this chapter and in Chapter Ten.

Younger children and those with learning difficulties often find it hard to grasp and remember complex or important things that have been said to them, so diagrams, drawings, puppets or figurines might be useful to help illustrate explanations or clarify matters. A well-stocked playroom is a boon to any worker, but is not available to most. So for the worker on the move, it is useful to have a bag containing a few props. This can be fairly basic with just crayons and paper. If possible, however, workers could expand this to include finger puppets, play dough, small figures or animals (including families and monsters) and worksheets such as happy/sad faces to encourage children into dialogue about their feelings. Where workers have laptops, purpose-designed interactive computer-based tools can be included. But a whole range of the computer's usual functions might also be useful, such as WordArt for drawing, listening to music, playing video clips or using Google Earth to explore the social environment (Ahmad et al, 2008). More will be said about play and activity-based work for children and young people of different ages and abilities in Chapter Ten.

Comment on the vignette

Practitioners need to work reflexively in their communication, reviewing the situation as they go and modifying their approach accordingly. Tanya might begin offering Jack some open prompts to see how he responds to them, such as, "Tell me about how things are at school". If Jack cannot engage with such focused conversations, she might then try some activities to explore the situation, such as getting Jack to draw what someone might see if they were looking through the window of his home. Such activities might not only give Tanya an impression of how Jack views family life, but also help her learn more about his way of engaging in tasks and communicating his inner world. This would help her in future work with him. If this, too, is unsuccessful, Tanya might content herself with observing the interactions between Jack, his sisters and mother and seeing if she can engage with Jack by 'mirroring' or 'tracking' his play.

'Where?' questions

- Where is the best place for the communication to take place?
- Where will the child feel most comfortable?

Determining where to meet with children and young people

The best setting for an interaction with a child or young person will vary depending on the focus and purpose of the involvement. Many children and young people find formal settings for meetings and interviews off-putting or intimidating, so careful attention needs to be given to location if their participation is to be facilitated. Where a review is to be in an office meeting room, attention should be given by the agency to making this more comfortable and welcoming for children. For some, the best place to talk may be at home, foster home or school while, for others, this would not work due to a lack of privacy or because this is where the problems are (Jones, 2003). A more neutral venue may be a cafe or snack bar. Some practitioners work within a setting where a dedicated play or interview room is available and this can be set up for the particular focus of the interaction. Where workers are to meet with a child or young person without their parents/carers for a number of times in such a setting, it is then advisable to introduce them to the space first, inviting the parent or carer where appropriate to come and view the room with them in advance. Some children may also feel more comfortable where the parent/carer remains in the building during the session.

Where dedicated spaces appropriate for play- or activity-focused interventions with children are not available, it is worth seeing if a room can be booked in a local family centre or child and adolescent mental health centre for assessment, therapeutic or family work. At other times it becomes a case of making the best of available resources. Ward (2008) discusses the value of work led by opportunity, describing important conversations that can occur on the doorstep or on a car journey where the worker seizes the moment, tackling issues as they arise during a crisis or when a young person allows their defences to drop momentarily. Any venue, any opportunity, can thus provide a therapeutic space. This is not always led by the worker's intention as children and young people, too, take the opportunity of car journeys and other informal meetings, where an intimacy or bond is forged for the moment, to talk about what is important to them. Disclosures of abuse may even be made at such times when they take advantage of a worker partially concentrating on their driving to talk about difficult things without their gaze being entirely on them.

Where the conversations need to be with a group of siblings or with the family as a whole, the family home might be a suitable place for all to talk together, particularly where the focus of an assessment or parenting work would benefit from the professional seeing the family in their natural environment. The practitioner may need to negotiate a boundaried space on such occasions; this may include asking for the television, music or computer to be switched off, requesting that everyone stay in the room during the work and agreeing time boundaries. It is important to recognise and respect the reasonable defences of both adults and children, however, as either may use the television, music, computer, and so on, as a way of diffusing the intensity of the interaction. Removing this safeguard from them may mean the situation feels too challenging and result in running away, either literally (some children will even climb out of the window if they feel too cornered) or figuratively (going silent or becoming attacking).

Wherever or whatever the setting, the crucial issue is to help children and young people feel as relaxed and comfortable as possible. For younger children, 'getting alongside' them at a physical as well as an emotional level helps (Winnicott, 1964) as professionals will usually be bigger than them and this adds to the other power differentials. 'Coming down to their level', literally as well as figuratively, might involve the professional sitting on a lower chair than the child to even up the height difference. A relaxed and comfortable atmosphere may be created by a worker and child sitting or lounging together on the floor. Surrounding themselves by crayons, paper or toys gives both a 'third thing' to focus on rather than unremitting eye contact that may be too intense or feel intrusive at times (Winnicott, 1964).

A note of caution

Talking with a child or young person in his or her bedroom may offer a real insight into their lives and offer a private, uninterrupted space. Indeed, it is often part of an assessment for the worker to view a child's bedroom so that the living conditions can be ascertained. However, workers should be cautious about spending time alone with children and young people in their bedrooms. First, this is their personal space and workers should not normally intrude on it unless invited. Second, some children and young people might feel vulnerable alone with an adult in a bedroom, particularly if there have been issues of sexual abuse. A child could misconstrue the worker's intentions or behaviour in this environment and feel very unsafe. Some young people, too, might misinterpret the boundaries if they have romanticised or sexual feelings towards the worker. Third, parents or carers might question the appropriateness of private contact in such an environment and misconstrue it. It is advisable for workers to discuss plans to meet alone with children and young people with their supervisors in advance and gain parental permission where possible. It may be safer or more appropriate to take young people out for a coffee, a car ride or a walk in the park to talk with them, depending on the purpose of the meeting and the degree of confidentiality that is required.

'When?' questions

- When is the best time to meet with a child?
- When might a child feel freshest and most relaxed?
- When might it be appropriate to bring a child out of school for professional contact?

Planning the timing of visits and meetings

Most children and young people do not want school or other activities to be disrupted by visits by and meetings with professionals as this makes them stand out from their peers. It also interferes with their learning and social development, so should be avoided unless the situation demands it. However, younger children in particular may be very tired after a day at school and this should be taken into account if important discussions are required. Some will revive with a rest and refreshments so these should be made available by the worker if not by the parents/carers. Children's dietary requirements and parental preferences should be checked out regarding these as not all parents are happy for children to be offered, say, squash, caffeinated drinks or biscuits. If children are being involved in distressing or unsettling conversations parents and carers should be pre-warned wherever possible as children might need additional support and comfort afterwards.

Practice vignette: The first home visit

When Tanya visits, Jack is laying on his front playing a noisy computer game that involves lots of shooting. He scarcely notices Tanya's presence, but she calls over to him, "Hello, Jack!" anyway as she is introducing herself. When the conversation moves on to how difficult Theresa is finding it to manage Jack, he looks round briefly, his eyes seeming 'hooded'. Isabella is fast asleep in the carrycot when Tanya arrives, but becomes quite grizzly when Theresa talks crossly about Jack. Theresa picks her up, ostensibly to comfort her, but handles her quite roughly, with the result that Isabella descends into inconsolable sobbing. Caz saunters by the doorway and sticks her head in to say "I'm going out". Her hair is round her face and she gives no one any eye contact.

Comment on the vignette

Tanya chooses to visit the family home in the after-school period as this can provide an opportunity for her to see the family in their usual context with as little disruption as possible. By doing so, she gets to see some of the family's usual interactions played out in front of her. Even with minimal direct dialogue, and little said on her part, Tanya feels a lot has already been communicated to her.

'How long?' questions

- How long should individual encounters or meetings last?
- How should endings be dealt with?

Length of meetings

Children and young people's concentration span needs to be taken into account during individual encounters, so advice should be sought from those who know them best about the length of meetings. Generally, the more complex, unsettling or distressing the subject matter, the longer children may need to process it. This does not imply that meetings should be lengthened to allow for this! Rather it means that children should not be bombarded with too many questions or too much information. Instead the time allocated should allow pauses for recovery and reflection between chunks of more focused conversation. This is particularly so for younger children who may need to get up and run around, go to the toilet or have some refreshment between snatches of dialogue. But teenagers, too, may find the subject under discussion emotionally, psychologically or cognitively taxing, so will need sufficient processing time too.

Workers' anxiety about success in consultation can be counter-productive. Persisting ad infinitum when young people are clearly conveying with their body language that they need to stop is a good example of *not* listening to children. If a child runs off or changes the subject, this may not be unnecessary deflection or avoidance, but the child clearly conveying the message, 'Hang on, I need a bit of time before I come back to this'.

It is also important to remember that communication can take almost double the length of time when augmentative and alternative methods, including interpreters, are used.

Talking with a child or young person while they are drawing or undertaking an activity can be a good strategy as the focus can move between the dialogue and the activity to give children 'time out'. It helps young people, too, to have more control over the pace of the conversation. Reiterating to children and young people the main points of any discussion held, confirming any decisions made and clarifying actions to be taken, including those expected of the child, provides the containment needed to help them 'close down' and make sense of what has occurred (Bannister, 2001).

Working with endings

A professional's interaction with a child may be a one-off contact or part of a longer intervention. Whichever, it will be temporary and time-limited, even where the involvement is longer term. McLeod (2008, p 123) advises that 'the key to negotiating the end of a piece of work is to bear it in mind and bring the child's attention to it from the beginning'. Workers should explain how long they are spending with a child or young person on each occasion and, wherever this is ascertainable, how many more times they are to meet and how often. Even in one-off encounters children may develop a significant rapport with a worker which needs to be honoured, as they can feel quite upset when a professional just departs without a special leave-taking (Westcott and Davies, 1996). Practitioners need to put aside their own reticence or any feelings of 'not mattering' to be able to acknowledge the real impact they may have on vulnerable children. They need emotional resilience, too, for when they are dismissed by some young people who have been abandoned or let down too many times to connect with or openly acknowledge where their feelings have been engaged.

Where a professional relationship becomes longer term, the preparation for ending needs to be given particular attention. Children may have formed quite a significant degree of affection for, or dependency on, a practitioner. The loss of the worker may re-evoke other significant life issues, particularly for young people who have insecure attachments, have been bereaved, are separated from their birth families or who are refugees or have been displaced. When talking to young people in care, Bell (2002, p 4) learned how many felt 'bereft, forgotten and confused' when the relationship with the social worker ended. These feelings might be conveyed in disparate ways, including sadness, disappointment, clinging, frustration, disengagement or anger. Elbow (1987) suggests that the worker and child might complete together a 'memory book' as a way to enhance their dialogue about the ending (see Chapter Eleven for more on endings).

What support is needed to carry out this work effectively?

Preparation, resources, containment and supervision

In order to communicate effectively practitioners need sufficient time to prepare for it adequately, to carry it out and to reflect on it afterwards, even where the encounter is relatively brief. As discussed in Chapter Six, direct work can evoke powerful feelings in both children and their workers, with 'primitive' emotions such as fear, anger, loss and envy creating anxiety. It is the worker's role to recognise, hold and manage this anxiety for the young person, but professionals, in turn, also need their anxiety containing. Without this they are likely to engage in defensive behaviours such as detachment and depersonalisation, focusing on bureaucratic tasks to the detriment of the interpersonal relationship (Menzies-Lyth, 1988).

The employing organisation and/or supervisor can and should be a key source of the resources, support and containment practitioners require to think about their work, relate to children and young people, be creative and reflective and be emotionally intelligent and resilient. Just as practitioners should provide a safe, non-judging space within which young people may be able to trust them enough to feel, think and talk about the most difficult material, supervision should provide a mirroring potential space where workers are able to acknowledge their professional vulnerability rather than just be about workload management and quality assurance (Ruch, 2007). The organisational climate should validate and enhance the direct work needed through a manageable workload, provision of planning time, suitable space and resources, forums for sharing best practice and skilled guidance from supervisors or other specialists.

However, the wider context of social work practice in the UK often militates against this. Many practitioners experience overwhelming workloads, bureaucratic and time-consuming computerised recording systems, a lack of resources and validation for direct work and inadequate supervision, lacking the space for reflection (Garrett, 2009). These create barriers between children and their social workers, who lack the time for planning and to be consistent, available and reliable in the way that children want and need. The anxiety in workers that would be naturally provoked by the work can then become overwhelming. The result can be, often understandably, that workers feel undermined, de-skilled and overwhelmed and give up. They cut off from children and young people's emotional experience or even avoid spending much time with them.

While this may be understandable, it is neither ethical nor professional for this state of affairs to continue. As noted in Chapters One and Two, the reports of the Social Work Task Force (Gibb, 2009a, 2009b, 2009c) and the subsequent government commitments to meeting recommendations for more manageable workloads and improved supervision (Burnham and Balls, 2009) provide new impetus for employers to provide the support which direct work requires. Practitioners, too, can contribute to the development of a new organisational culture, in line with their code of practice requirements for them to be accountable for the quality of their own work. A first step is for workers to negotiate the kind of supervision they need, providing feedback on what works/does not work for them and what additional input they require for their role and task. Second, radical social work approaches, which have traditionally sought to build alliances among like-minded people to create wider change, might be drawn on. Practitioners could attempt to build communities of practice within their agencies by sharing effective approaches through peer supervision and co-working which help to provide the organisational, emotional and epistemological containment suggested by Ruch (2007). Third, and interrelatedly, practitioners, either singly or working together, might re-present to their employers the research evidence, policy, statute and practice guidance which underpins the imperative for their direct work with children and the necessity for this to be supported and contained in the ways suggested here. It is in such ways that direct work may be re-claimed and can make a difference to children and young people's lives and futures.

What next?

■ What further work now needs to be done?

Planning future work

An analysis of what has been learned at the initial meeting with children, young people and their families helps determine what should happen next. Sometimes, the encounter will help clarify, as with the Doyle family, that more needs to be known and some kind of assessment will be embarked on. This will need to fully reflect the views and experiences of any children in the family. While there might then be no need for further action, it may become clear exactly what intervention is necessary and the worker's communication skills will be called on to maximise its likely success.

Practice vignette: Next steps with the Doyle family

During her initial visit to the family, Tanya has learned from Theresa about how depressed she has been feeling since Isabella's father, Janek, returned to Poland. He left following an escalation of arguments between them, which were primarily about the unplanned birth of Isabella and him not wanting to stay somewhere where he could no longer find work. He has cut off from the family completely and Theresa feels devastated. It has become apparent that Theresa is now not coping well with the children and Jack's well-being and development is already suffering. More yet needs to be learned about the impact of the situation on Caz and Isabella. Tanya secures Theresa's agreement to a core assessment[9] to see how the family might best be helped. Tanya's suggestion, which Theresa accepts, is that this should include observations of all the children with their mother, some focused discussions with Jack and Theresa about the school difficulties and some separate time with Jack and Caz on their own to hear about any difficulties they are experiencing, their views on the situation and possible solutions.

Conclusion

Getting the initial contact with children and young people right is crucial as it can determine whether they are able to engage with the professional, understand what is being said and feel safe and motivated enough to communicate their thoughts, feelings and intentions. This chapter has covered a number of key questions practitioners should be asking themselves to inform their planning for communication with children, including about the purpose of their involvement, what needs to be talked about and how, who needs to be present, where the contact should take place and for how long and what supports or resources they need. Such planning is as essential for urgent situations and one-off assessments as for longer pieces of direct work.

While management objectives, performance indicators, excessive workloads, poor supervision and time pressures may adversely affect individual workers' autonomy to practise effectively, where workers have made a personal ethical commitment to engaging with, consulting and informing children they are much more likely to have developed the core capabilities which promote this even when time is short (Thomas and O'Kane, 2000). They can also play their part in influencing the cultural context of their team towards one which does not see direct engagement and communication with children as an unnecessary luxury or optional extra, but rather as at the very heart of making a difference for children.

Notes

[1] The concept of 'noise' in communication is discussed in Chapter Four.

[2] CAF is the common abbreviation for an assessment under the common assessment framework (CWDC, 2008). This brief assessment is to be completed by professionals working with children and/or their families in England where there are concerns about progress, where needs are unclear or the support of more than one agency is needed. It covers issues to do with parents and carers, family and environmental factors and the child's development. (At the time of writing, CAF is also being piloted in Wales.)

[3] As the vignette is set in England, this would be under Section 47 of the 1989 Children Act.

[4] For England this is most likely to be an Emergency Protection Order or Interim Care Order as Child Assessment Orders are rarely used for this purpose.

[5] In England and Wales this would be under *Achieving best evidence* guidelines (Home Office, 2007).

[6] There will be a fuller discussion of the role of observation in communication in Chapter Nine.

[7] ASSET assessments contribute to pre-sentence reports in England and Wales when a young person has offended. They cover what social, environmental, developmental and family factors might have contributed to the offending behaviour.

[8] Personal education plans are a tool for planning how to help children and young people in care in England and Wales reach their full academic and life potential. They are put together through discussion between the child, their carers, the key social worker and the designated teacher at school.

[9] This is an assessment carried out in England and Wales under the *Framework for the assessment of children in need and their families* (DH et al, 2000) that must be completed within 35 working days.

Key questions

1. In what kinds of locations and environments are you likely to meet with children and young people? What difference might these make to your work together and what should you bear in mind?
2. How might you introduce yourself the first time you meet a child or young person? Write down an introduction for a five-year-old, for a teenager and for an 11-year-old with learning difficulties.
3. Give one example of when you might use non-directive work with a child and another when you would use more directive work. What would be some of the key aspects of your approach with each of these?

Further reading and resources

Dalzell, D. and Chamberlain, C. (2006) *Communicating with children: A two-way process*, London: NCB (www.ncb.org.uk/resources/free_resources/communicating_with_children.aspx) [a pack of free resources and tools to use with children and young people].

Hutton, A. and Partridge, K. (2006) *'Say it your own way': Children's participation in assessment: A guide and resources*, Ilford: Barnardo's Publications.

RNID (2004) *Communication tips: If you're deaf or hard of hearing*, London: RNID (www.rnid.org.uk/information_resources/factsheets/communication/factsheets_leaflets/communication_tips.htm).

Romaine, M. with Turley, T. and Tuckey, N. (2007) *Preparing children for permanence: A guide to undertaking direct work for social workers, foster carers and adoptive parents*, London: BAAF.

Triangle (2009) *Three-way street: Putting children at the centre of three-way communication*, Hove: Triangle [a training dvd].

8

Communication skills for assessment

"Put the questions a bit smaller!" (advice of a six-year-old to interviewers, quoted in Westcott and Davies, 1996, p 465)

Introduction

Communication with children and young people themselves, not just their parents and carers, should lie at the heart of assessment and decision making. Social workers and other professionals in children's services are required by policy, legislation and practice guidance to seek out and listen to children's thoughts and feelings about their lives and experiences and, while balancing them with assessment of their needs and any risks, take their opinions and preferences into account. This means that methods and frameworks will need to be tailored to the individual young person and the assessment context. This chapter focuses on how to set up assessment work with children and what kinds of approaches might be most appropriate. The vignette of Tanya and the Doyle family, first encountered in Chapter Seven, will be further developed to explore and illustrate issues.

Practice vignette: The Doyle family

Social worker Tanya will be undertaking a core assessment[1] with the Doyle family to better understand their needs. The first priority is carry out some parent–child work with Jack (age 6) and his mother, Theresa, and observe how they interact with each other during the intervention. Tanya will undertake some direct work sessions with Jack on his own and will observe Theresa and baby Isabella together. She will then seek to include Caz (age 14) in the assessment, too, aiming to find an opportunity to speak to her on her own about how things are at home.

Core capabilities for assessment with children

Why and how practitioners undertake assessments with children, young people, their families and carers varies not only in relation to the needs of each family but also according to the legislation and policy in different parts of the UK which determine professional roles and tasks. Sometimes workers may need to use statutory frameworks and 'tools' to assess what needs children have, whether they are at risk of harm and/or whether they pose any risks to others. For example:

- Social workers in England and Wales must ascertain children's wishes and views when assessing those considered as in need under the 1989 Children Act and when they are carrying out initial or core assessments under the assessment framework (DH et al, 2000).
- Practitioners across children's services in England need to seek children's permission for a CAF assessment and involve them fully in it.
- Connexions personal advisers in England should work closely with young people who require intensive support to develop a full assessment profile using the assessment, planning, implementation and review framework (APIR).
- Youth offending service workers in England and Wales undertaking ASSET assessments[2] need to interview young people and record their views using the 'What do you think?' form.
- Those involved in assessing and preparing a child for adoption and undertaking the matching process must use appropriate forms to record not just information about the child and the views of professionals, parents and carers, but also the carefully ascertained wishes and feelings of the child.[3]

Whatever the structure or formats of these assessments, there are a number of similarities in the ways that social workers and other professionals must approach the assessment role and task. Any or all of the core capabilities underpinning effective communication, which were set out in the 'knowing, being and doing' model in Chapter Five, will be drawn on to enable practitioners to carefully, sensitively and effectively consult with children to find out more about their experiences and learn what they know, think, feel and want. Box 11 summarises some of the qualities and skills needed when assessing children and young people who are thought to be vulnerable.

The 'knowing' domain

In terms of *knowing*, practitioners will require: knowledge and awareness of: statutory frameworks for assessment and the legal and policy context within which the work with a child is situated; theoretical models and research findings which help them make sense of what children are saying and doing; effective approaches with children who are different ages and who have different abilities and ways of communicating, including disabled children and those for whom English is not their primary language; and 'tools' and activities which are an alternative or adjunct to direct discussions.

The 'being' domain

The *being* core capabilities require practitioners to develop interpersonal skills such as warmth, friendliness, humorousness, openness, empathy, non-judgementalism and a caring manner. These help children and young people feel motivated and safe enough to engage and open up, particularly when the context surrounding the assessment sessions is frightening, irritating, distressing or unsettling. Ethically, practitioners will need to commit to transparency, collaborativeness and inclusivity. On occasion workers will have to weigh children's views against their needs and any risk of harm to them; this might require them to break confidentiality or act against young people's expressed wishes and they will need both emotional and ethical robustness to manage this as well as the capacity to sensitively and carefully explain the reasons for doing so. Self-awareness will also be needed, enabling workers to reflect in the moment and use their 'habitus' to communicate in socially and culturally appropriate ways.

The 'doing' domain

The *doing* domain of communicative competence comprises all of the skills and techniques practitioners require to competently use models, frameworks, methods and approaches. The ethics, values and personal qualities of the 'being' domain will be operationalised to enable workers to act in respectful, collaborative and child-centred ways, enhancing young people's participation and mitigating the effects of oppression. Particular techniques and counselling skills might well be needed for assessment, such as questioning, summarising, clarifying (all of which will be discussed below), but the aim is to go at children's pace wherever possible, using their preferred way of communicating.

Box 11: Core qualities and skills professionals need when assessing vulnerable children and young people

- Listening to the child
- Conveying genuine interest
- Empathic concern
- Understanding
- Emotional warmth
- Respect for the child
- Capacity to manage and contain the assessment
- Awareness of the entire transaction between interviewer and child
- Self-management
- Technique

Source: Jones (2003, p 65)

Involving children in assessment work

The *assessment framework* used in England and Wales emphasises the importance of child–centred direct work at the heart of assessments:

> This means that the child is seen and kept in focus throughout the assessment and that account is always taken of the child's perspective. (DH et al, 2000, p 10)

Communicating directly, seeking children and young people's views and listening to their experiences is essential not just for moral and ethical reasons but also practical ones (Hutton and Partridge, 2006). Where decision making and planning reflects their views and perspectives, young people are more likely to be 'signed up' to proposed interventions or changes, such as a new foster placement or a reduction in contact. Children are likely, too, to have a great deal of information about their situations and insight into what might help. It makes no sense for the knowledge and experience of the 'insiders' to a situation to be ignored, because workers are too busy filling in forms in the office to spend time getting to know them – and, as the Social Work Task Force in England has found, this does seem to be happening more often than it ought (Gibb, 2009a).

Ensuring the participation of some disabled children and young people and those for whom English is not their primary language is likely to require additional preparation and planning by workers. Advice and assistance might need to be sought from specialist workers, parents or carers, and augmentative or alternative communication methods might be required (see Chapter

Seven). Interpreters should be used where necessary to ensure children fully understand what is happening and for them to share their views and concerns. It is important to remember that meetings where an interpreter is used can take much longer than usual. Workers should ensure that they are directing their body language towards the young person (for example, looking at them) even when the words are mediated through an interpreter.

Involving children and young people in assessments clearly poses challenges to professionals. An evaluation of the *assessment framework* carried out shortly after its inception (Cleaver et al, 2004) found that, while communication with parents and carers had improved and assessments were providing a more holistic picture of children's needs, insufficient progress was being made regarding the level of children's inclusion in assessments. There was limited evidence of social workers seeing, observing, engaging, talking to and playing with children and young people. Professionals interviewed for this study attributed this to limited time, resources and skills. It also seemed that direct contact with children was viewed as a lesser priority than talking to parents and carers and undertaking the more administrative elements of their role.

As part of Cleaver et al's study, eight young people over the age of 10 were interviewed about their experience of being assessed. Only two remembered the social worker explaining to them why an assessment was being carried out and what would happen during it. Just four felt the social worker had involved them in the assessment process. These young people provide helpful guidance for professionals: assessments would improve, they think, if social workers were to listen to children, respect their views, believe what they say, explain what is going on during an assessment and give them some written information to remind them of what had happened and explain what is likely to happen in the future.

A child-centred approach

Practice vignette: Setting up assessment sessions with Jack Doyle

Tanya wants to acquire Jack's informed consent to the assessment and to fully engage him in it. She has provided him with a simple explanation of the reason for the assessment and what will happen. She attempts to motivate him to participate by suggesting that by meeting with him and his family she might be able to find out what is going wrong and help sort this out his problems at school and the difficulties these are causing at home. Tanya explains where and how she would like to meet with him, and the boundaries to the work. Taking Jack's level of maturity, concentration and cognitive functioning into account,

Tanya uses short, clear sentences, uncomplicated concepts and a simple vocabulary, regularly checking out that he understands what she has said.

The school has agreed to make their counselling room available for Tanya to meet with Jack for their regular direct work sessions. Unfortunately they do not have any space for this at the end of the school day and Tanya is initially reluctant to take Jack out of class as this will disrupt his education. After discussion between Tanya, the school and Theresa, the consensus is that the priority at this point should be the assessment work as Jack is at risk of being excluded for his difficult behaviour. Many other children also regularly leave the classroom situation for additional input such as counselling, learning support or health interventions so his appointments will not be particularly noticeable or disruptive. While Jack agrees to meet with Tanya for these sessions in school, Tanya rather suspects this was more so that he could avoid being in class.

How to secure Jack's attention and manage any difficult behaviour during sessions will be a key challenge, given accounts of his poor concentration and what the school have described as 'disruptive behaviour'. Tanya intends to begin her individual sessions with him free play while she gets to know him better. The sessions with Theresa and Jack will be held after school in the family home, with a neighbour providing childcare for Isabella to minimise distractions.

Engaging a child or young person in an assessment may be complex and challenging. In the practice vignette, Tanya attempts to secure Jack's involvement in and agreement to the assessment through a child-centred explanation. She will begin the work with free play sessions, which can be more child-centred. Free play may allow a worker to make sense of a child's way of exploring, relating and conveying their 'inner world experiences' (their subjective thoughts, feelings, fantasies, fears and perceptions) as well as how they talk about what is going on in their 'outer worlds' (the daily life of events, facts and other observable phenomena) (Schofield, 1998). Play draws on the 'hundred languages of childhood' rather than 'just sitting around talking' and having professionals 'asking questions' which many children find off-putting (Thomas and O'Kane, 2000, p 828). In fact, a question-and-answer style with teenagers may leave workers 'doing most of the talking' and not finding very much out at all (Corcoran, 1997, p 278). Free play is more child-led, going more at the pace of the child than the adults (Clark and Statham, 2005). Even though the externally set timescales of the court, assessment framework or ICS do not always seem to take this into account, one social worker emphasised how important this is: "'You do have to wait for them. You can't go and expect them to perform"' (quoted in Ruch, 1998, p 41).

Play-based work can enable a relationship to be built up where a child feels relaxed and safe enough to convey their world in the way that makes sense to them, rather than responding to a professional agenda circumscribed by questions and checklists. Bell (2002, p 3) found from talking to young people who had been through child protection investigations that it is only through such trusting relationships that 'children can assimilate information, make informed choices as to what their views are and how they are best represented and be enabled to exercise their rights to participation and service provision'.

Setting the frame for an assessment

Professionals need to explain clearly to children and young people what is going on and what is to happen during assessments in a way that makes sense to them. Explanations could be made through diagrams, drawings or using small figures as well as in words, particularly for very young or learning disabled children, who find such concrete illustrations more easy to make sense of (Wake, 2009). Explanations should fit the nature and approach to assessment work. Where the sessions are solely to comprise child-led free play, children might be told "This time is for you to use in any way you want because I want to get to know you better", or "...because some difficult and upsetting things have happened and having a safe place to play and express yourself might help". Where an initial period of free play sessions will move on to some more focused work, this, too, should be clearly explained so children know what to expect. Giving young people simple leaflets with diagrams to take away or writing to them after an initial visit may help the explanation to stick in their mind and provides them with a focus for further exploration with their parents or carers.

Drawing up agreements with children and young people

In the vignette, Tanya has attempted to explain about the assessment to Jack in a child-centred way but is left with some reservations about how genuine his agreement is. Not only may his motivation come from the wish to avoid lessons rather than to positively participate, but he may feel he has little choice but to attend anyway as he is used to coming up against rules and structures and being told off when he does not comply. Collaborative and participative working practices mean professionals are now used to drawing up contracts and written agreements with parents and teenagers for assessments and interventions. Many, however, do not routinely do the same with younger children such as Jack but there is no reason why this should not happen. Tanya may find that Jack exhibits disruptive behaviour in her sessions with him, such as that demonstrated in school, which will make their work more challenging. Being clear about the boundaries from the start will be important and written agreements can formalise this. Box 12 provides an example of this that could be made more visually appealing by use of coloured paper and fonts and the addition of 'clip art' pictures to illustrate.

Box 12: Sample contract for use with children and young people

What Jack and Tanya agree to do

Jack will come to see Tanya every Wednesday in the blue room just after lunch. Tanya wants to get to know him better to see if she can help him and his family.

Tanya will listen carefully to everything Jack says. She will also come and see Jack with his mum at home after school a few times.

Jack is allowed to play with anything in this room and to decide what to play. Sometimes Tanya might have ideas about games, stories and drawing, too.

There are just a few rules in the blue room:

- The meetings always have to end after three quarters of an hour and Tanya and Jack will start clearing up five minutes before the end.
- Jack should stay in the room until it is time for the session to end.
- Nobody in the room should get hurt, and the room and the toys shouldn't get hurt either, so Jack needs to listen and do what Tanya says if she asks him to stop doing something.

Signed Jack: .... Tanya: .... Date: ....

Involving younger children in assessments

Isabella, at six months old, is genuinely too young for her permission to be sought regarding involvement in the assessment, so Tanya must try to put herself in Isabella's shoes to ensure the assessment is not distressing for her and disrupts her routine as little as possible. Getting to know Isabella's wishes and feelings and understanding more about her inner world cannot be gained through words: it will require careful observation and 'sense making'. This is covered in Chapter Nine.

Assessment work with teenagers

Practice vignette: Engaging Caz Doyle in the assessment

Caz (age 14) tends to go where she wants when she wants – Theresa just throws her hands up in the air and says she has no control over her daughter. Unless Caz wants to meet with her, Tanya may have real difficulty in even seeing Caz, let alone conversing with her. Tanya determines that she will have to negotiate an appointment time with Caz herself, and recognises that she will have to seize any opportunity she can for this initial conversation.

Comment on the vignette

The referral concerns have related to Jack primarily, but that does not mean his older sister, Caz, should be excluded from the assessment. She may have much to contribute in terms of her perceptions about family dynamics and her memories of when things were more positive in the family. Securing the involvement of a teenager such as Caz in assessment or intervention can be equally tricky as young people can and do 'vote with their feet' on occasion – as they are more in control of their time and activities they can simply avoid the situation. Trying to arrange a formal meeting with her through Theresa may be pointless as Caz may simply not turn up. It may even be counter-productive if Caz gets put off Tanya through her mother ordering her to come and meet with someone she does not know.

Ward's (2008) advice about 'opportunity-led work', discussed in Chapter Seven, may be helpful here. Tanya will be visiting the family home quite regularly and may be able to gradually get to know Caz, finding ways of drawing her into conversation and building a rapport. Caz might then respond positively to an invitation to join the family work sessions or to going out for a coffee to have a one-to-one conversation.

Conversations with children and young people in assessments

Listening to children

> Tools and resources are no substitute for an attentive and culturally sensitive listener. (Hutton and Partridge, 2006, p 1)

Practice vignette: Beginning to engage with Jack Doyle

Tanya carries out her first assessment session with Jack and his mother. During the meeting she says to them, "I'd really like to hear from you both about how Jack is getting on at school". Both Jack and Theresa immediately start speaking over each other, becoming agitated that neither is listening to the other and arguing about the causes of Jack's school-based troubles. Tanya sits quietly for a while trying to take in all of what she is hearing. When Jack swears at his mother and goes to lay down in front of the television, she says to them, "You've both told me quite a lot and I've been listening very hard. I hope I understood it all. I'm going to say back what I heard and you can tell me if I got it right. I'll do it in turns and start with you, Jack".

Comment on the vignette

Professionals often do not meet with children on their own but are seeing them in a family situation. This provides the added challenge of how to elicit and hear their voices among those of their parents or siblings. Each family member may want to be heard first and the adults and children may not be able to find constructive ways of going forward with this. In the vignette, as this is the first session, Tanya wanted to find out what the pattern of listening was within the family. She quickly discovered that reciprocal dialogue was not always the norm and shouting might be the main way of each person trying to be heard.

This observation already provides Tanya with useful information for her assessment. Rather than interrupting mother and son, Tanya finds she can 'open up both ears' to try to get an overview of what is being said and how. She might well have missed some things as it is common for humans to mis-hear and mis-remember (Munro, 1999). Consequently, she feeds back to them what she thinks she has heard and checks whether this is accurate with each of them in turn. She starts with Jack to model the importance she is placing on his contribution and because she guesses his concentration would wane quickly otherwise. She can then do the same with Theresa.

As well as listening to the words, workers also need to listen 'with the third ear', that is, to what is not being said, to what may be being thought and felt and to the wider social and cultural context of the communication (Trevithick, 2005). Tanya may not have understood the meta-message behind the basic content of the words.[4] Listening to the body language and the paralanguage, the 'music behind the words' (Malekoff, 1994) can help her to gain a fuller understanding of feelings, thoughts and perceptions which may expand on, or differ from, what has been said. It will also be important for Tanya to check out similarities and differences in habitus as this governs how she interprets what she hears. Tanya's heritage (white, English, agnostic and middle class with considerable cultural and social capital coming from her university education and social status) is very different to Theresa's, who is white, working class, Catholic, born and raised in Southern Ireland, having left school with no qualifications and feeling intimidated by professionalised language and jargon. Jack will probably have taken on much of his mother's habitus but, being dual heritage, he may well have developed alternative or additional cultural understandings and self-identity.

Creating a listening space in assessments also means making sure it is safe enough for children and young people to talk. Children may need to explore and discuss negative perceptions and feelings about home and family life or about particular people. It may be difficult or unsafe for them to do so in front of parents or carers. As one child warned, "'Don't ask me how home is in front of my parents'" (quoted in Triangle, 2009). This is one reason why it is so important to try to see children and young people on their own wherever possible, getting a court order to do so if the situation is sufficiently worrying to suggest that there is a risk of significant harm. Sometimes children may talk more freely in the presence of siblings, where they are able to jointly present a view of their environment. In other situations, however, the presence of siblings may be a deterrent if they might tell their parents what one of them has said, or if they are the source of concern themselves (as with abusive or bullying siblings).

Telling a trusted worker about their experiences can really help children and young people contain and transform their trauma and distress. Listening to such painful material may be very stressful personally and emotionally for practitioners, however. It might re-evoke thoughts and feelings stemming from their own difficult earlier experiences; this may cause them to stop listening or be too much for their current level of emotional capacity or resilience. Schofield and Brown found from their study that, in such situations,

> Listening to [young people] required from the worker a great deal of time and patience and a capacity to hear the nature of the emotional communications as well as paying attention to the reality

of their current and past experiences.… [It required] having a space to think. (Schofield and Brown, 1999, p 29)

The suggestions made in Chapters Six and Seven about the importance of self-awareness, self-reflection and self-development and of receiving emotionally containing and thoughtful supervision are very relevant to such situations.

Importance of direct conversations

While play and activities can be an extremely helpful way of building rapport and gathering information more creatively, this does not mean there is no place for direct dialogue, particularly with older children and young people. Indeed, Shelley, a young care leaver now in her twenties and with a child of her own, was quite derogatory about the way a professional had avoided directly discussing matters with her:

> "I mean if she understood me and had spoken to me about it, talked to me as a person instead of getting me to write things down and play with play dough and do finger painting and things like that.… I really didn't feel it was appropriate in trying to help me understand why I had first gone into care. Apparently it was supposed to make me understand, I don't see how they expected it to, really." (Shelley, quoted in Lefevre, 2008a, p 24)

Talking directly about difficult matters such as abuse and neglect can be distressing and destabilising for some children and young people, particularly when they are not ready for it or it is not discussed in a sensitive, child-centred way (Holoday and Maher, 1996; Moroz, 1996), but this does not have to be the case. Most of those interviewed in Prior et al's (1999) study of young people who had received social work input following reporting of sexual abuse said that direct conversations about what had happened had provided emotional support and reassurance. Power and control may be a key dynamic here, as one nine-year-old particularly expressed her appreciation that she was not "'forced to talk'" by the social worker (quoted in Prior et al, 1999, p 141). This is particularly important in sexual abuse situations, where feeling compelled to talk or being asked intrusive questions may recreate some of the dynamics of abuse and be re-traumatising (Jones, 2003). Where conversations are thoughtfully and sensitively held, this can be an important way of finding out what has happened to young people and what they think.

Talking about abuse

This book does not discuss the formal forensic interviewing of children who have experienced or witnessed a crime, such as those who have been physically or sexually abused. Such interviews are carried out by specially trained police officers and social workers who follow official guidance such as that in *Achieving best evidence* (Home Office, 2007) in order to obtain a videoed account from a child which may be used as their 'evidence-in-chief' in any criminal prosecution. However, a social worker or other professional may be the first person a child discloses their abuse to and it is important that they find a way of discussing this with the child without it disrupting future criminal investigation. Practitioners must always follow the safeguarding guidance within their own organisations and act in accordance with their designated role (DfES, 2006). Social workers may be involved in the primary investigation whereas others will be passing this role on to social work duty teams and the police. Useful resources for these roles may be found in the 'Further reading' section at the end of this chapter.

Dealing with disclosures

Children and young people are mostly likely to disclose abuse to people they know and feel secure with. This may be a parent, carer or family member who they trust will listen to them, protect, support and help them, but could be a worker that they feel safe with. The allegation may come in response to assessment work regarding their fears and concerns or it may emerge through more open-ended contact, such as on a car journey. Whichever, it is often unexpected for the worker and the first thing they may need to do is manage their own emotional response to the disclosure. It may be upsetting, unsettling, even frightening, to hear an allegation of abuse but it is essential that such feelings are not communicated to the child or young person. They need to receive the impression that the worker is robust enough to hear even the most appalling details, will help sort matters out and will be kind and caring with them in doing so.

Second, it is essential for workers to listen carefully and to convey to children and young people that what they have said has been heard and taken seriously. This is best done through body language and paralanguage, rather than saying "I believe you". At a later stage, workers will have to record accurately what they have heard the young person say. They may be interviewed about it by the police and need to repeat it in court. So it is important they have understood what was said. Repeating back to the child or young person what they heard is one way of checking this out, but they should try to use the child's own words in doing this to be sure they are not 'leading' the child or 'putting words in their mouths'. Direct questioning for further information should be avoided as, again, this could be later construed as 'leading'.

Third, workers should provide children and young people with information. Knowing the safeguarding procedures for their agency will help them explain what will happen next and how. If the young person is worried about who will be told, this needs to be explored to check out their immediate safety and their worries about the future. Information about procedures should be provided in a way appropriate to their age and capabilities (for example, using shorter sentences and simpler concepts for younger children or those with learning difficulties). Information should also be realistic – workers must avoid making promises they cannot keep, such as about keeping disclosures secret.

Fourth, practitioners should provide emotional support and reassurance for children and young people. Even though workers cannot directly question children in such situations, they can encourage them to express their feelings about what has happened and validate these. Children can be reassured that they have done the right thing to tell and that it is not okay for someone else to have done these things to them. Feelings of guilt should be directed away from the child and reattributed to the abuser.

Some disabled children and young people may find it harder to recognise or disclose abuse. For some young people with complex healthcare needs, for example, this is because they are dependent on a wide range of carers, often for very intimate care, and it can be difficult for both them and other carers to identify when legitimate touching by a potential abuser masks grooming and crosses over into abuse (Westcott and Jones, 1999). Learning disabled children might find it harder to comprehend, name and convey what is happening to them because they lack conceptual understanding. Young people with speech and language impairments, who communicate via a touch talker or communication board, might find there are limitations in the language system available to them. It is essential to ensure that any communication system used has a section on sexuality and, if not, consider how additional materials might be provided to ensure young people have the vocabulary they need to discuss what has happened to them (Oosterhoorn and Kendrick, 2001). Professionals should beware of forming judgements about a child's ability to communicate which are based on inaccurate information. Specialist advice, interpreting or facilitation should be sought where necessary (Murray and Osborne, 2009).

Children and young people themselves may have a whole range of questions for the worker about what has happened and what will happen next. Thinking through in advance answers to the questions in Box 13 will help prepare professionals for when such situations arise.

Box 13: Questions children and young people may have for professionals following disclosure of abuse

- What happens now I have told?
- Can you make it all okay?
- Can you keep this a secret?
- Is this my fault?
- Will I be in trouble?
- Will I be believed?
- Can people tell what has happened to me?
- Am I still ok as a person? Have I been damaged?
- Will I have problems in the future, like with getting pregnant?
- Will my family still want me?
- Does the perpetrator hate me/want to hurt me/still love me?
- Why have I got to see the doctor/be interviewed/go to court?
- Should I not have caused all this trouble?

Truth and lies

Children and young people are generally truthful about serious matters so professionals should always attempt to listen to what they say and take it seriously (Jones, 2003). However, research indicates that children can and do lie on occasion (Vrij, 2002). They may hide information, mis-represent it slightly or even fabricate complete untruths on occasion. This may be for a range of reasons, such as:

- to avoid negative consequences such as punishment (most common with younger children);
- to gain a reward;
- to protect their self-esteem;
- to maintain relationships (such as through social lies which are designed not to hurt or upset someone else);
- to protect people they love;
- to conform to norms and conventions (most likely with adolescents) (Vrij, 2002).

Children and young people who come into contact with social workers may have additional reasons for not being fully truthful with them. Young carers may want the extent of their caring responsibilities to remain hidden, even at their own expense, so that family life can be maintained. Children may be attempting to protect themselves in response to threats, such as with a child who has been told they will be beaten if they talk to the social worker. Emotional ties and the need for security can mean that the fear of the family being split asunder if negative aspects of family life are revealed is too terrifying for some children. Young people might hide or deny abuse to protect their non-abusing parents from the distress of learning that their father, friend, new partner, and so on, has been touching them. Children who have been sexually abused are particularly susceptible to feelings of shame or fear, due to the grooming process, and may lie to avoid anyone finding out (Wattam and Woodward, 1996).

Very occasionally children may make false allegations of abuse. Jones (2003) suggests a methodical and careful assessment should be made where there are concerns about this, distinguishing between situations where a child has gone along with what an adult has said, or is trying to give the professional what they think is expected, and those where a child fabricates the allegation him or herself. Younger children, for example, might make up information in an interview if they feel pressurised to say something (Faller, 2003). Professionals can help by explaining that it is fine for children to say they 'don't know' or 'don't understand' in response to questions.

There is, however, no reliable test for ascertaining whether children and young people are telling the truth and workers' clinical judgement in such matters may well be wrong. Substantiation or repudiation of allegations is likely to be through a thorough interprofessional assessment of the contextual factors. While taking what children and young people say seriously, Jones (2003) advises that practitioners should, at the same time, keep an open mind while they draw together what has been said in the light of other information available. Workers should strive to avoid bias by not relying on presumptions or hypotheses but by considering the full range of meanings and possibilities. At the same time, practitioners should be very careful that the child does not pick up disbelief in their manner as this can be extremely distressing and damaging where abuse has occurred (Faller, 2003).

Building up a trusted relationship and listening with the 'third ear' will be particularly important in such situations. Practitioners should consider what feelings may not be being expressed by children and young people or what facts could be being hidden. They should also look for congruence or dissonance between a child's words and their body language and paralanguage.

Questioning techniques for assessments

Closed questions

The most obvious and immediate way of finding out information from children and young people can be through asking them 'closed' or 'focused' questions. Closed questions ask for the very specific kinds of information that are often contained in one-word answers like 'yes' or 'no'. They are helpful when workers want some specific information, such as, "Did your mum give you any breakfast this morning?".

Closed questions need to be used carefully, however. They may steer the conversation away from what the child really wants to talk about but doesn't know how to begin or whether it is okay to interrupt the professional. They can also close a conversation down, particularly with young people who are not that keen on talking with a professional in the first place (Malekoff, 1994), as in this example:

> Worker: "How is school?"
> Young person: "Alright."
> Worker: "Are you getting on okay with your foster carer?"
> Young person: "Yep."

Focused questions

Questions that are *focused* but a bit more *open* enable the worker to follow a particular line of enquiry and gain more detail. They encourage the child or young person to talk about things in their own words as much as possible. Questions beginning with 'how', 'what' or when' are often more helpful than 'why', which can feel both accusatory and overly authoritarian (Seden, 2005). Also, children often do not know the reasons why things happen or why they or other people behave in a certain way; indeed, it is precisely that which might need to be explored. Focused questions may not always feel straightforward to the young person on the receiving end. They may be unsure of what to reply or may find the questions intrusive if the worker is asking for information that is private or personal. Consider the following focused questions that might feel quite 'loaded':

■ Can you tell me about the test at school today?
■ What kinds of food would you like the foster carer to make you?
■ How often do you want to see your mum?

With the first question, young people may feel they should give a particular kind of answer ("It was fine") so they are not in trouble or nobody worries about them, regardless of how it really went. All kinds of feelings may come up with the second question, such as distress about not being at home, missing the kind of food they are used to, feeling alien and strange. This can be particularly so for young people who are placed in a very different environment. One young unaccompanied asylum seeker from West Africa described how the food cooked by her white Scottish foster carer felt unfamiliar and off-putting. It was completely different from what she was used to and she couldn't begin to explain how the carer might shop for and cook the traditional foods that she missed. The third question might be very difficult where children feel unsure, confused or ambivalent. They may be wary about giving the 'wrong' answer or saying something that will hurt their mother or someone else.

Questions may also be too long and complex. One six-year-old who talked about her experience of being interviewed about sexual abuse found that interviewers "'kept talking longer than small, so I couldn't keep up with it, and they kept talking a question then a different question before I answered'" (quoted in Westcott and Davies, 1996, p 465). As a result of their difficulties with closed or focused questions, children may end up saying nothing of any value. They may give a limited response or even give false information. Consequently workers will not find out what they need to know to make a thorough assessment.

Leading questions

As was discussed in respect of allegations of abuse, closed questions can take children and young people in a certain direction. Children are used to taking their lead from adults in authority and may wait for them to signal what the permitted topics of conversation are. Workers may end up finding out about only what it is their questions are designed to elicit rather than what it is they really need to learn about the child. Assessments may then end up reflecting professionals' own bias and presuppositions and the reliability of what children have said is reduced (Ceci and Friedman, 2000). Leading questions should be particularly guarded against. These are phrased in a way that suggests some kind of answer and can run the risk of 'putting words in children's mouths' (Seden, 2005).

Comment on the vignette

For example, with the Doyle family, if Tanya asks Jack what he would like to change about life at home (because she assumes that things might well be problematic), she signals to Jack that she expects that he wants to change something. This might mean Jack could falsely give the impression he wants things to change even if he doesn't, just because he feels that responses about this are expected from him. Tanya is also more likely to hear only about difficulties rather than any things that are going well, which may or may not reflect reality. To aim for a more balanced assessment, Tanya could ask

Jack to tell her about both the things he would like to change at home and the things he would like to keep the same. She could also encourage him to grade the relative importance of these.

Open-ended questions and prompts

Closed and focused questions, then, may be most helpful to check out information already under discussion and leading questions avoided wherever possible. To get the fullest and most accurate picture, it might be helpful to facilitate children and young people to communicate their views, thoughts and feelings in their own words using open questions and prompts.

Open questions require more than a one-word answer and provide an opportunity for children to describe their stories, feelings and concerns in their own way; for example:

- Can you tell me in your own words what happened that day?
- I'd really like to hear about how you are finding your new school. Can you tell me all about it?

These kinds of invitations and cues can be much more effective at eliciting information than focused questions (Thomas and O'Kane, 2000). Where accounts are given in young people's own words, with contextual and peripheral detail, it is also possible to rely more on what has been said, particularly with younger or disabled children (Jones, 2003).

Sometimes children and young people will struggle with open questions, particularly if they are feeling overwhelmed and do not know where to start, or if they are not used to formulating their thoughts and feelings. Where they are particularly distressed or traumatised, forming a coherent narrative on their own becomes particularly difficult and *prompts* may be needed. These are empathic words, phrases and non-verbal communications that workers can use to encourage children to notice, name, reflect on and talk about issues of importance to them. They encourage the other person to keep talking and can really help when children are struggling to put things into words or if they have worries about how what they are saying may be received or acted on. Where prompts are used, longer, more detailed and more accurate accounts can generally be obtained from children of all ages and abilities (Faller, 2003). Prompts may be verbal; for example:

- "That sounds really hard/upsetting/fun."
- "Mmmm.... Uh-huh...."

But non-verbal prompts can be equally powerful or encouraging, where the worker stays silent but shows interest, care and empathy through body language and sounds, such as:

- having an attentive bodily position
- leaning forward slightly when something important is being said
- nodding gently
- giving appropriate (but not intrusive) eye contact.

Scaling questions

Scaling questions are a technique borrowed from solution-focused therapy. They can be particularly useful with older children and young people like Caz as the collaborative nature of the exercises and the attitude of 'respectful uncertainty' can give young people more of a sense of partnership and sharing control (Sharry, 2004). This has been found to be particularly facilitative with young people who are feeling disempowered or oppressed in their lives, such as those from black or minority ethnic groups who have experienced racism or social marginalisation (Stevens, 1998). Scaling questions can help make children and young people's confused or abstract feelings, goals and concerns clearer and more concrete. They may help, too, with disaffected young people's perceived 'aversion to talking about "feelings", "the past"' and other difficult topics, as Corcoran found in his work with young offenders (1997, p 287).

Practice vignette: Using scaling questions with Caz Doyle

Caz had been talking about how bad things were at home now "compared to before" but her rather depressed manner seemed to make it hard for her to be clearer or more specific about what was wrong. Tanya drew a scale showing 1-10 and said, "Let's imagine '1' is the worst you ever imagine it could possibly ever be and '10' is what it would be like in an ideal world. What number is it at the moment?". When Caz replied "2", Tanya said "Okay, if I was asking you last year, what would you have said then?". Caz thought for a bit and said "5". Tanya was then able to help Caz explore the differences between 2 and 5 and what might need to change in her life or at home to nudge the numbers higher up the scale again.

Conclusion

Assessment decisions and plans need to fully reflect children and young people's views, concerns, experiences and expertise. Some key considerations for facilitating this include:

- explaining the purpose, focus and process of the assessment, gaining young people's consent and conveying its outcome in a way which makes sense to them;
- conducting assessments in a child-centred way, going at the child's pace wherever possible and using more of the 'hundred languages of childhood' to ensure children and young people fully understand what is happening and can communicate about issues of importance in ways that are meaningful for them;
- ensuring children's primary language is used, drawing on interpreters, augmentative communication systems and the expertise of the people who know the child best;
- using different kinds of questions and prompts according to the situation;
- listening not just to what has been expressed directly and verbally but also listening with the 'third ear' to gain a broader impression of children's thoughts and feelings.

This chapter has mainly focused on more direct and verbal methods of assessment. Chapter Nine goes on to look at observation as a way of making sense of children's inner worlds and unexpressed thoughts and feelings, which is particularly important with very young children and those with more complex needs. Chapter Ten then considers the use of play and activities in assessment.

Notes
[1] A core assessment is defined in the notes for Chapter Seven.
[2] ASSET assessments are defined in the notes for Chapter Seven.
[3] In England this will be a CPR (Child's Permanence Report), in Wales a CAAR (Child's Adoption Assessment Report) and in Scotland and Northern Ireland a Form E.
[4] It may be useful at this point to refer back to Chapter Four, which explains these processes in communication.

Key questions

1. Give examples of some focused and open questions that Tanya might want to ask Caz about the situation.
2. What might get in the way of Jack being able to respond to direct questions about his home life or the difficulties in school?
3. Think of some scaling questions to ask Jack and Theresa together.

Further reading and resources

Hutton, A. and Partridge, K. (2006) *'Say it your own way': Children's participation in assessment: A guide and resources*, Ilford: Barnado's Publications (www.barnardos.org.uk/sayityourownway).

Horwath, J. (ed) (2009) *The child's world: The comprehensive guide to assessing children in need* (2nd edn), London: Jessica Kingsley Publishers.

Jones, D. (2003) *Communicating with vulnerable children: A guide for practitioners*, London: Gaskell.

Lefevre, M., Richards, S. and Trevithick, P. (2008) *Gathering information*, London: Social Care Institute for Excellence (www.scie.org.uk/publications/elearning/cs/cs04/index.asp) [this is an interactive e-learning resource, available to use free of charge on the SCIE website].

9

Observing children and young people and making sense of their play and behaviour

Introduction

Children and young people are not always able to clearly explain what they think or feel, want or need, hope or fear in a way that social workers and other adults can readily understand. They may not have the words and concepts to name inner thoughts, feelings and complex experiences. Some may be too caught up in what is happening to them to see things clearly. Others could be trying to hide things because of either imaginary or very real fear of the consequences if they tell.

Observing children and young people in their environment is an important alternative way of gathering information and making sense of their worlds in such circumstances. It can shed light on how they are thinking and feeling, the dynamics and relationships between family members and children's experience of being parented, as well as confirm or contradict what has been said verbally. This chapter considers some different approaches to observation and helps readers develop their observational skills. The practice vignette of the Doyle family is continued as the social worker, Tanya, begins to observe Jack (age 6) and Isabella (age 6 months) as part of her core assessment.

Nature of observation

Readers might assume that observation is one of the least challenging of the communication skills discussed in this book. After all, being aware of and observing our environment is something humans (and other animals) do instinctively. However, expertise in observing is not so readily acquired; the German philosopher, playwright and poet, Goethe, noted more than a century ago, 'The hardest thing to see is that which is before our own eyes' (quoted in Fawcett, 1996, p 74). Becoming skilled in observing, however, can help practitioners to understand children and their range of behaviour better and to reassess their own preconceptions about these. The following exercise is designed to help readers appraise their existing observational skills and determine how they might need to develop them further.

Observational exercise

Watch a child, young person or sibling group that you don't know with their parents/carers in the community (perhaps in the park, on the bus or in a shopping centre) for at least five minutes. Try to do this in as an unobtrusive manner as possible, so that you don't disconcert the children or their carers, or disrupt their activity. Do something else for at least half an hour then return to the following questions:

- *Appearance:* what were the children wearing? Did they seem clean or dirty in their clothes or face and body? Were they dressed appropriately for the weather?
- *Dialogue:* how much dialogue was there and how much of it can you remember? Try to write down as much of it as you can verbatim. Who spoke most/least?
- *Interactions:* what kinds of interactions were there between the children and their parents/carers? What can you remember about the body language and paralanguage (for example, tone of voice)? Who initiated most interactions and who tended to be the one to respond?
- *Interpreting what is seen:* what hypotheses and assumptions have you formed about the quality of relationship between the children and their carers and about the kinds of parenting the children have received? How confident are you in these assumptions? How much are they based on research evidence, intuition, practice-wisdom or stereotyping?

Comment on the observational exercise

Some of these questions were straightforward, with right and wrong answers about what has been noticed, such as those regarding what the children and young people were wearing and who said what to whom. However, you may have found that you struggled to perceive and remember as much as you would have liked because you were trying to take in a range of information and stimuli and, subconsciously, work out what was most important to remember. You will have being trying to hold onto an awareness of the surroundings, actions and events, the different ways in which people converse and interact, and the body language and paralanguage. The result may be that you noticed and retained only what was most vivid, unusual or interesting, or the first and last things that happened. Such challenges to memory are one of the reasons assessments and plans are often based on incomplete or inaccurate information (Munro, 1999). Had you answered the questions immediately you might have remembered much more detail, as even a half-hour gap allows much to leach away. Taking notes either during or immediately after an observation can facilitate remembering; even just odd words may be enough to prompt fuller recall.

A number of the questions in the exercise were more complex as they moved from *noticing* to *interpreting*, that is, making sense of what the interactions might indicate. The skills required for this move beyond perception and memory into an ability to sift information so as to work out what may be important and to identify patterns. An awareness of and sensitivity to people's non-verbal communications and a capacity to *analyse* what has occurred is required, not just an ability to recall factual details. For example, a social worker needs to become aware of a child's body language and what it might be conveying about the child's inner thoughts and feelings. This interpretive, analytical process needs to be underpinned by research and other knowledge (such as attachment or systemic theories) so that workers are not simply basing these on biased assumptions (Munro, 1999).

What to observe

Practice vignette: Observing the Doyle family

The social worker, Tanya, will be observing Jack and Isabella with their mother to see what their demeanour, behaviour and interactions might tell her. Neither child's father is available or involved with the children currently, otherwise Tanya would have included them in the observations, too. Tanya will observe Jack at the same time as she is working with him directly in the assessment sessions at the school and with his mother in the family home. This means heightening her awareness to his body language and paralanguage, how he responds to activities and boundaries, his moods and how he relates interpersonally. She needs to ensure that she creates enough reflective space inside her so that her 'seeing' is not detracted from by concurrently 'doing' the direct work.

Isabella is too young to communicate verbally, so Tanya will be particularly reliant on seeing how Isabella responds and interacts. She will observe Isabella in the presence of her mother without interacting or intervening at all to build up a picture of Isabella's world. This will include attending to how content Isabella seems, whether she is thriving developmentally and how her affectional bonds and attachment behaviours are forming. She will be looking to see what eye contact Isabella gives, how she behaves when she has a wet nappy or is tired or hungry, whether she plays happily alone and demonstrates excitement and joy when she is played with and how easily she can be calmed and soothed by her mother.

As can be seen from the example with Isabella Doyle, observation offers an opportunity to attend in detail to the whole of children's experience, development and ways of being in the world. The extent to which children are meeting their developmental 'milestones' can inform assessment of whether there is some physical condition or cognitive delay which has not yet been picked up or whether there is a failure to thrive, through lack of nutrition, nurture or stimulation. Observing children's moods, forms of play and interactions with others over time, at home, nursery, school and so on, may clarify what relates more to the child's general disposition and what might be a reaction to the environment and caretaking experiences.

With older children and young people, such as Jack and Caz, what they convey through their choice of dress, social behaviour, activities, use of slang, and so on, provides insight into their social identity, sense of self and cultural norms. Children and young people's growing sense of their racial identity may also be revealed, as Ellis (1997) demonstrated in her observation of an infant and family of West African origin. This may be particularly helpful for making sense of the cultural and racial experiences of Jack, who is dual heritage but living with a white mother and siblings in a white-dominated society and having no contact with his father or black extended family. As a white worker, Tanya, like Ellis, will need to open herself up to Jack's different social and cultural experiences and consider whether and how he might be affected by racism and ethnocentrism. Self-awareness about her own habitus and an understanding of the impact of oppression on racial identity will be important here (Robinson, 2007).

As has already been identified, children do not always communicate directly through formal language. Thoughts, feelings and experiences are often emotionally and cognitively processed, encoded and conveyed through more indirect means. Body language and paralanguage may provide important clues as pieces of an overall jigsaw as workers listen to the music beneath the words (such as the child's tone of voice, eye contact and facial expression), and look for how these may support or belie their words (Malekoff, 1994). Children and young people's behaviour might also express much about how they are feeling. Unfortunately professionals and carers sometimes become preoccupied only with the difficult or concerning consequences of a young person's behaviour (such as violence or self-harming) rather than also wondering what the behaviour itself is trying to say for them. Children's play and interactions with parents and siblings are particularly rich sources of indirect communication and will be discussed later in this chapter.

How the child or young person interacts with professionals may signify a great deal. Some young people may convey their previous experiences of having been rejected, silenced or ignored by the ways they defend against engaging or communicating with workers. From a psychodynamic perspective, it might be worth considering whether the worker has become a transference figure (see Chapter Six). It can be helpful to talk with children about possible connections between past and present experiences where observation is alongside a direct work/keyworking relationship. A straightforward response to, or comment on, what a child says or does can be insufficient as it may mis-attune to the deeper thoughts and feelings beneath the basic message, or be too stark and shaming. Instead, a gentler and subtler process of noticing children's behaviour and helping them recognise, name and more directly express their thoughts, feelings and needs is preferable.

How workers might be affecting the observed situation must be taken into account. The experience of being observed, devoid of social interactions, cuts across normative social and cultural practices and can feel uncomfortable and disempowering. Fantasies may arise about what is being thought and felt (Tanner and Turney, 2000). Practitioners need to pay careful attention to boundaries and power relations, acknowledging the rights, dignity and sensitivities of children and their families (Hindle and Klauber, 2006). Many children, and their parents, feel anxious about being judged or misunderstood when they are being watched and this can make them behave differently. A parent who is nervous and anxious may be less able to pick up their child's cues and be misjudged for this. Children may become more challenging, or conversely more withdrawn, when faced with an anxious parent. The leap from observing to interpreting must consequently be a cautious one. Observing over longer periods and several occasions is likely to provide a more realistic appraisal.

Explicit and informed consent to the observation should always be sought not just from the parent but also from the child or young person as far as possible.

Methods of observation

Premature judgement and meaning making should be avoided in observation. Instead, practitioners are invited to take an attitude of 'respectful uncertainty' (Taylor and White, 2006) and to hold on to the intellectual and emotional anxiety that goes with 'not knowing' until things gradually become clearer. Observations, such as those which Tanya is planning with Isabella, offer an opportunity for workers to stand back from the 'me in role' and to concentrate on the 'observer me', a process of 'being' rather than 'doing' (Turney, 2008). Doing nothing but watching and taking in what is seen and heard heightens practitioners' capacity to pay close attention to subtle and complex dynamics and messages and to think carefully about what has occurred. This is qualitatively different from observations where the worker is concurrently interviewing or intervening, such as Tanya is doing with Jack. But observing while 'doing' also has its role. If practitioners can develop their 'reflection-in-action' skills (Schon, 1983), then they can use what they are perceiving in the moment to inform their communication with children and young people. Indeed, Austin and Halpin (1987) argue that it is only through also relationally interacting with a young person that who they are and how they are feeling and perceiving can truly be felt and understood.

Two broad approaches to child observation are commonly found within professional practice. The first derives from the physical sciences: natural world phenomena are observed and what is seen and heard is recorded as it happens in as objective a manner as possible. The second is a reflective approach that has its roots in psychoanalytic theory and concerns the subjective realm, thoughts, feelings and inferences that contribute to an overall interpretation (Fleming, 2004). Both approaches have strengths and can usefully inform an understanding of children and their experience. See Fawcett (2009) for a thorough overview and practical guidance on difference approaches to child observation.

Scientific approach

The natural sciences approach to child observation aspires to an objective, rational and accurate collection of data. The observer is encouraged to remain 'detached' and 'neutral' to maintain the validity of the data and just record what is seen and heard (Karp et al, 2004). There is an attempt to see the child directly as he or she is through observers 'bracketing off' (suspending, placing to one side) any feelings and assumptions which may influence how the child is perceived. A picture of a child-in-environment may result.

Naturalistic method

The simplest approach from this scientific paradigm is the 'naturalistic' method. Here the child is observed in a natural setting, such as home, nursery or school. Everything that happens, who says what to whom and so on, is written down as a 'running record'. This method can provide a wealth of data, requires no advance preparation or specialist training, feels natural and records the ecology of the environment (Fawcett, 2009). The worker is not pre-selecting what to record, so this can reduce the danger of pre-determining bias creeping in. However, a mass of unstructured data is produced, all 'lumped together', which is difficult for observers to thematise and make sense of. There are dilemmas regarding what and how much to record. When writing down everything that is seen and heard, workers may miss events that might have been significant.

An alternative is to decide in advance to observe and collect only certain kinds of data. When what the observer is seeking is a better understanding of a particular event or phenomenon it might be more helpful to focus on and record only that phenomenon; for example, how the child relates to his mother, interacts with his sister, uses fine motor skills or employs formal language. Data could be recorded at one-minute intervals. A large amount of precise, focused information can be gathered in a short time, providing an abundance of detail to assess a particular aspect of the child's current emotional, physical, social or cognitive development or functioning. Studying the fine grain of a behaviour in this way may reveal unexpected patterns.

Target child method

The 'target child' method of observation enables several aspects of a child's behaviour or functioning to be considered (Fawcett, 2009). A pre-prepared grid is used to note down data in each category, aiding later analysis. This includes one column where 'activities' are noted, that is, everything the child does. Another column records use of language, specifying who says what to whom. The next column enables activities in the first column to be categorised into particular kinds of task, such as problem solving, games with rules, waiting or watching. The final column picks out social behaviours.

This is quite a complex method and practitioners will find that they need practice to become proficient. It is difficult to concentrate on so many aspects at once and much may be missed while the observer is recording. Most practitioners are likely to be observing children in the family home, school, nursery or similar. However, if it were possible to video-record the observation, the video could be viewed a number of times, with the worker adding to the notes through several viewings. This would minimise the likelihood that important information is missed.

Time sampling

'Time sampling' is an alternative way of narrowing down data by observing and recording events that occur at specified intervals, such as every 15 minutes, or once every hour. Unlike the previous methods which enable a narrative picture of a child to be formed over relatively short periods of time, time sampling enables 'snapshots' to be taken of a child's functioning through the course of a day or within particular settings. Patterns or surprising occurrences may be revealed. Indeed this was the method used by James Robertson in his film *A two-year-old goes to hospital* (Robertson, 1953) which demonstrated the distressing and unrecognised nature of young children's experiences in institutional settings and led to changes in the way hospitalised children all over the western world were treated.

However, the data collected via time sampling might potentially be quite fragmentary and difficult to analyse. It does not necessarily provide insight into the quality and meaning of a child's experiences or why behaviours are occurring. Significant events might be missed between the snapshots which would render what is seen later more meaningful. The method is also less suitable for making sense of more imaginative play by children that cannot easily be reduced to 'behaviours' (Fawcett, 2009).

Role of subjectivity in observation

Despite the scientific aspiration of those methods, there remains the question of the extent to which subjective impressions, preconceptions and beliefs can be truly 'bracketed off' and not influence how the data is interpreted. Indeed, it has been contended that people's values, culture and previous experiences will always influence what they see, that humans interpret the world through their own subjective assumptions and constructs about what children's behaviour represents, symbolises or intends (Cox, 2005).

Think back to the child or young person you observed in the earlier exercise. How well behaved did you think they were? Your view on this will probably be influenced by the following:

- your personal and cultural values and norms about children's behaviour (whether children should be free to express themselves or 'seen but not heard');
- your views on discipline and boundaries ('I wouldn't tolerate this from my child', 'children today get away with too much');
- gendered expectations ('boys will be boys', 'she's putting herself forward too much').

The same behaviour by children of different genders or within particular cultures might lead to the same child being described by different people as 'well-behaved', 'quiet', 'shy', or 'withdrawn'; each term paints quite a different picture. While practitioners are, of course, entitled to hold their own views in their personal lives, these views and norms may not be socially, culturally and ethically appropriate when applied to children and young people encountered within the professional role. Workers' views should be underpinned and justified by research evidence and theoretical perspectives, not just personal preference (Macdonald, 2000).

When observing children and young people in professional practice it is arguably much more difficult to be objective. These individuals are not simply 'data' from a research study; they and their family contexts are known to practitioners. They could well evoke feelings of warmth, concern, protectiveness, irritation or fear in workers in the course of their assessments and interventions. It has been suggested that trying to adhere to the more 'scientific' approaches above, witnessing and noting down events and behaviours and attempting to 'cut off' subjective perceptions in a vain attempt to achieve 'objectivity', is likely to result in personal bias and cultural stereotyping simply being pushed below the surface:

> Emotion holds a cardinal place; it has to be observed and recorded and it will occur in the observer.... It is not a distraction or a contaminant. Correctly grasped, the emotional factor is an indispensable tool to be used in the service of greater understanding. (Miller, 1989, p 3)

An alternative method is one where professionals strive to create a reflective space in themselves where they not only look and listen, but also feel and think, using their emotions and responses as data, and checking out whether their assumptions and prejudices are unduly and inappropriately influencing them. Workers are encouraged to stay with uncertain/ambivalent feelings and thoughts, learn to tolerate uncertainty and avoid premature judgement.

The Tavistock method

The Tavistock method of infant observation is the most common reflective approach to observation that enables subjective perceptions to be considered. Rooted in psychodynamic theory, it was developed originally as a training method within child psychotherapy programmes (Bick, 1964) and traditionally involves observation of a baby with his or her parent or primary carer for an hour at the same time each week for one or two years. As a training method it aims to teach practitioners as much about themselves and their own subjectivity and internal worlds as it does about the experience of the child so that the skills of self-awareness and reflective practice that have been developed can be brought to future work (Briggs, 1999). Observers watch without interacting, intervening, conversing or recording. Instead they are involved in a continuous internal dialogue in which the relationship between the professional self and the personal self is kept alive and thought about. No notes are taken at the time but observers attempt to recall as much detail as possible after the session, writing down what has been noticed in an everyday fashion. Initial theorising is halted in an attempt to render the experience more immediate and personal.

The traditional Tavistock approach has been adapted for qualifying (Miles and Trowell, 2004) and post-qualifying (King, 2002) social work training where a much briefer framework is employed, often involving just six observational sessions. Observations of older children and young people as well as infants are encouraged. Reflective seminars in which practitioners discuss what has been observed and their cognitive and affective responses to this remain at the heart of the training approach. A particular aim is for the observer to produce a holistic appraisal of the child's well-being, development, relationships and inner world experiences. The practitioner will attempt to form an empathic hypothesis of what the child is experiencing, thinking and feeling, understand unconscious and indirect aspects of communication and behaviour and convey the felt atmosphere of the child's environment.

In bringing reflective approaches to child observation into social work, a link is made 'between knowledge of human growth and development, observational skills and effective social work communication with children' (Luckock et al, 2006a, p 39). A detailed picture of children's world and experience (particularly their emotional experience) is created, which may include how they interact with and respond to parents, carers, siblings and peers, depending on the setting. This may then be used to inform assessment and care planning, including the assessment of neglect (Tanner and Turney, 2000), child protection assessments (Fleming, 2004), multidisciplinary assessments for the family courts (Youell, 2002) and the supervision of contact (Hindle and Easton, 1999).

While this method requires no specialist materials and uses everyday language, it is demanding emotionally. It requires a real engagement by the self of the worker and a willingness to consider how his or her own assumptions, perceptions and responses may inform assessment and interpretation. If emotions, values and cultural preferences of the worker are not acknowledged and examined then, it is believed, subjectivity and proactive counter-transference (see Chapter Six) may reduce the validity of the information gathered and the interpretation made.

Observing parent–child interactions

Observation can shed light on the different ways in which children and young people have been parented, display norms of family and peer interaction and even facilitate prediction of whether a child may be parented safely and adequately in the future (Hill et al, 2008). It is a central component of many parenting programmes, such as those focused on increasing consistency and reducing harshness of discipline practices, improving early problematic parent–infant relationships and enhancing parental responsiveness to children's cues (for example, Webster-Stratton, 1981; Sameroff et al, 2004). Observations may be of 'normal' family life, such as meal times, or may involve watching a specific activity the family have been asked to undertake. Workers may notice the extent to which the child experiences child-centred interactions from their parent or carer (such as the parent attending, praising, smiling, mirroring or inviting the child) compared to child-directive behaviours (questioning, criticising, commanding, teaching, punishing), and how the child responds to either approach (Jenner, 2008). Contact between children in care and their birth parents or siblings may be observed to provide information as part of a protection plan or care proceedings (Hindle and Easton, 1999).

Setting up the observation

The venue could be the family home, the community (such as playing in the park or a shopping trip) or a specially designed venue such as a family centre, depending on the purpose of the observation. Seeing an infant and child together at home, as Tanya is doing with the Doyle family, will maximise the likelihood of family members demonstrating their usual patterns of interaction and family practices (Karp et al, 2004).

Practitioners will need to carefully explain the purpose and process of such observations to parents and to the children if they have the capacity to be aware of what is happening. It would be important for Tanya to clarify to Theresa that she will be operating in a different way on the days that she comes to observe her with Isabella (where she will be observing without interacting) than on the days she meets with Jack and his mother together and observes as part of the intervention. Having a worker just sitting and watching them for an hour can be quite unnerving for parents like Theresa and she may be helped by Tanya explaining that this is to help her gain a better understanding of how the mother and baby are in their daily interactions. Working collaboratively may help to ease the power imbalance a little in such situations. So, as well as providing clear information and gaining Theresa's informed consent to the observation, Tanya should negotiate in advance with Theresa the best times to visit and where to sit when she comes. She can also offer to spend some separate times with Theresa where she will talk with her about any issues that are arising.

Observing attachment

Detailed observations of parent–child interactions are one way of assessing younger children's affectional bonds and attachment style. It is beyond the scope of this book to provide a detailed description and analysis of attachment theory and how this may be assessed. This is amply provided by Howe (2005) and Prior and Glaser (2006), for example. Some general points will be made here, however, as to what workers might particularly seek to observe and make sense of.

Attachment theory explains children's preference for and proximity-seeking behaviour towards primary carers. By between three to six months babies are already showing more discriminating social responsiveness to their carers and a marked preference for one or two carers (most commonly, but not exclusively, the mother). So, Tanya might expect to see this behaviour by Isabella Doyle towards her mother. Between seven months and three years children are actively initiating proximity and contact with the attachment figure and have embarked on idiosyncratic developmental pathways, patterned according to their earlier parenting experiences and their response to these. The quality and consistency of caregiving an infant receives is thought to dictate a kind of 'internal working model', a psychological template for how children approach the world and make sense of future experiences. This internal working model is made up of enduring, pervasive mental representations of the self, other people and relationships. It includes expectations and beliefs about one's own behaviour and that of other people, the lovability, worthiness and acceptability of the self, the emotional availability and interest of others and the ability of carers to provide protection. Observing young children with their parents, then, is one way of helping children 'tell' professionals about how family life has been for them, who they are frightened of or feel safe with, and so on.

Through systematically observing parent–child dyads through the Strange Situation test, Ainsworth et al (1978) and Main and Solomon (1990) set out categories of attachment style centred round secure/insecure and organised/disorganised behaviour.

Secure attachment

Where children have had a sufficient amount of predictable, consistent, nurturing, attuned and safe experiences, they tend to be more *securely attached*. They will generally seek to remain within protective range of their primary attachment figure, with the range determined by age and temperament of the child. This carer provides a 'secure base' that gives them the confidence to explore their environment. Children will become distressed, protest and cling to this figure when unwillingly separated and seek proximity with this person whenever a threat appears or they are hurt. Securely attached children are more likely to be readily soothed when a parent returns and comforts them. Their initiating behaviour reflects the expectation of this; for example, a child putting his arms out to his mother knowing he will be picked up.

A securely attached child may demonstrate some uncertainty or fear when a new person, such as a professional, appears and will take their cues from their attachment figure. If the parent seems positive and relaxed, the child is more likely to approach and interact with the worker, although younger ones tend to scamper after the parent if he or she leaves the room.

These experiences of being consistently attuned to and cared for enable children to 'download' parents' and carers' views of them so that they grow to think of themselves as loved and effective, and others as loving and available. Feeling safe and confident enough means they are freer to explore and learn and to become sociable and pro-social in their behaviour. Secure attachment also promotes thinking, reflection and perspective-taking skills and enables children to better manage their emotions and behaviour.

Insecure attachment

Children who have not received parenting which is positive and predictable enough may become *insecurely attached* to a primary carer. Where the previous parenting was more consistently rejecting, intrusive, cool or hostile then their attachment style is more likely to be *avoidant*. These children have learned not to rely on their parents/primary carers for nurture and safety and have developed strategies to help them defend against the anxiety and distress that they are left with. Rather than protesting at a separation or threat and seeking proximity with a secure base, they may become quiet and withdrawn; they have learned that protest does not bring the required comfort and safety, but provokes indifference, irritation, helplessness or rejection by the parent, so they give up. Over time, children may become compulsively self-reliant, shutting down their feelings, over-intellectualising or focusing on activities, not allowing others to become close. The practitioner may notice that young children seem rather indifferent to their primary carer's presence, tolerate her absence and fail to protest if hurt or frightened. The play of older children may seem lifeless, lacking affect and spontaneity. Some may become controlling, even bullying towards others as they seek to control their environment in order to feel safe.

Where children's earlier parenting experiences were more unpredictable, insensitive and mis-attuned, they may develop an *ambivalent* or *resistant* insecure attachment. The lack of consistency means that these children have sometimes received comfort, care and protection and so, unlike avoidantly attached children, have not given up. Instead (unconsciously) their strategy is to amplify their affect and behaviour in the hope that it will elicit caregiving from the parent. They can never relax and trust but rather become preoccupied with their feelings and other people's responses to them. Professionals may observe a child who seeks attention and seems always dissatisfied, demanding and needy without being able to be comforted. Younger children become distraught at separation from the attachment figure and fail to be comforted and consoled at reunion, perhaps even pushing away from the parent in their anger and distress. Others become coercive or coy in their attempts to get their needs met. Distrust looms large for these children and the world is often split for them into good or bad, friends or enemies.

Disorganised attachment

Children who have developed an avoidant or ambivalent style have at least been able to attach to a parent, albeit insecurely, and organise their experiences and responses into a coherent internal working model for how to approach the world. By contrast, where children have had completely unpredictable experiences, often driven by abuse, neglect and discontinuity of care, their attachment style may become *disorganised*. These children lack a coherent strategy for dealing with separation anxiety and threat because they have been faced with a paradox: attachment behaviours (clinging, protesting etc) are designed to bring the primary carer closer, but this person is also the source of the threat to their safety or integrity. The danger may be posed by a parent who is directly harmful to them (for example, violent or sexually abusive) and is *frightening*, or it may be a parent who is helpless and *frightened* themselves and cannot protect or console them (for example, a mother who is as terrified as the child is of a violent partner) (Main and Solomon, 1990). Threatening situations normally activate attachment behaviours to access physical and psychological safety but these children are trapped between proximity-seeking and avoidance behaviours as neither works to keep them safe.

Such infants and toddlers may display chaotic or oddly organised behaviour as they simply do not know which way to turn. They lack coherence and direction and may appear more wary of the parent than of the visiting professional who is not known to them. As they grow older they may develop a range of behaviours associated with both ambivalent and avoidant attachment styles; they may seem sad or depressed; have developed compulsively care-giving, dependent or compliant behaviour; conversely they could be aggressive, controlling or manipulative, perhaps even attacking other children, adults or animals. Children with disorganised attachment styles are 'telling' professionals how unsafe and mistrustful they feel and that they will attack, control and unsettle others because these are the feeling states that are familiar to them (Prior and Glaser, 2006).

Using attachment theory in assessments

During observational assessments, social workers should aim to describe and explain children and young people's behaviour or strategies rather than categorise them. Definitive statements regarding a child's attachment style are best made by experienced clinicians, such as child psychiatrists, psychologists and psychotherapists, who may use diagnostic tests such as the Strange Situation (with babies and young children), story stem completion (ages 4–8), and the adult attachment interview (generally used from age 16 upwards). However, experienced social workers and other practitioners should be able to use their own observations of children's attachment behaviours as a lens to make sense of what they are conveying about their experience of parental care. Attachment alone can never be the full story, but should be considered alongside a more holistic appraisal of children and young people's cognitive, emotional and social development, including peer friendships, functioning at nursery and school, and so on.

Key questions for the worker to consider are:

- To what extent does the child use the parent or carer as a 'secure base'?
- How does the child or young person react to the worker's presence? Does he or she look to the parent for reassurance and seem more confident and friendly if this is positive?
- How does the child behave when frightened or threatened? Does he or she seek proximity with the parent, seek and receive comfort and reassurance?
- Is the child able to play freely, imaginatively and creatively?
- Is the child or young person able to express his or her thoughts and feelings in age-appropriate ways? Is a range of feeling states expressed, including joy, excitement, distress, contentment, penitence and anger?
- Does the child or young person demonstrate care-giving or controlling behaviour with toys, other children and animals?

Parent–child observations must be seen in the light of the wider family assessment that they are contributing to. It is crucial to take into account the parent's state of mind at any one time and whether this is different from usual because of a crisis and/or the involvement of professionals, as this may significantly affect the presentation of both child and parent. Theresa Doyle, for example, could well be depressed following the ending of her relationship with Janek and his disappearance from their lives, leaving her to raise a third child as a single mother. If Tanya feeds back to Theresa what she is observing then this offers Theresa an opportunity to reflect on and discuss her relationship with her children and how she feels about her parenting currently.

Observing children's play

Tanya has arranged to observe Jack Doyle during play sessions with him in order to gain a further dimension on his world and experiences. Such observations may provide vivid insights into children's inner worlds and family practices through the way that they design the rules of games, create stories, assign roles in fantasy play, and so on. This is because stories, play, drawings, even toddlers' scribbles, are meaningful activity, reflecting children's perceptions of the environment (Matthews, 2003). In order to consider the significance of children's play the role of symbolism in the development of the self is first explored.

Symbolic representation of experience

Before infants and toddlers develop language they do not have chronological memories of events to help shape their perceptions of the world, themselves and others in a logical or coherent form. Instead their thoughts, feelings and experiences are believed to be represented in *symbolic* form within their inner worlds (Winnicott, 1971). This internal realm is deeply subjective; the figures that inhabit it are not literally the same as the physical people, places or objects the infant has experienced. Instead they are mental and emotional representations, formed from these subjective perceptions – 'an amalgam of actual experience and perception' (Horner, 1991, p 8). The internal world will manifest itself in symbolic form through the infant's spontaneous play and can be communicated to others in this way. So simple games, such as Peekaboo, which develop between infants and their primary carers, can represent a child's awareness of and feelings about what is there and then not there, such as the parent leaving them and returning (Bruner and Sherwood, 1979, quoted in Dubowski, 1990). Children's earliest scribbles can be understood as 'a symbolic substratum upon which representation develops' (McGregor, 1990, p 51). Such play is, then, a significant part of a child's developing understanding of and comfort with themselves, others and the environment.

Well beyond infancy children continue to need opportunities for spontaneous play and creative image making either on their own or with peers or carers in order to be able to explore and process their experiences, thoughts and feelings. Just as with infants, simple images (such as a drawing of a house) and games (like 'hide-and-seek'), as well as being fun, often have a deep metaphorical meaning and purpose (Scarlett et al, 2005). Gradually, as intellect develops and language forms, the ability of most children to recognise, name and communicate their thoughts and feelings in more direct ways increases.

However, for some children, much of their internal life will remain unprocessed and in symbolic form for much longer than might be expected because of factors such as abuse, trauma and insecurity of attachment. Some young people reach adolescence still with neither the language to name their experiences nor the conceptual and affective frameworks through which to interpret and process them (Winnicott, 1996). Where earlier emotions, feelings and experiences have been pushed away or repressed, perhaps because they felt unbearable or were not contained and regulated by the parent or attachment figure, they remain unprocessed and can rarely be brought back simply in the same form (Bion, 1962; Schore, 1994; Howe, 2005). Instead the internal world offers them back later as 'seemingly irrelevant bits and bobs, like jigsaw pieces of a window, or in code as play, metaphor and image' (Bolton, 1999, p 62).

This is particularly so with pre-verbal trauma, which cannot usually be accessed consciously through language. Feelings tend not to be connected to event memories as they would be if the young person were older. Instead, what happened to them is 'remembered' by the body, with the child remaining unclear as to why they are frightened, angry, distressed, and so on. Such experiences can really only be processed and communicated through symbolic forms (McMahon, 2009).

This will be the case for many of the children and young people professionals come into contact with, who find it hard to interpret their bodily sensations, explain their motivations, describe their emotions or give opinions. In Chapter Eight it was noted how direct questions may feel 'loaded' or confusing to children. Rather than the response that is hoped for, professionals may find their questions just provoke a response of 'don't know', a shrug or a blank look. Some of these children and young people simply have no frame of reference for such a conversation as their experience is locked inside. This is why additional ways of communicating, which are less direct and verbal, must be found.

Making sense of children's play

Cox (2005) provides an example of how she observed a three-year-old girl's communication as she sat drawing on her own, in the writing corner of a nursery classroom:

> As she continued, she began to talk to herself, unaware that I was listening.... She identified the shape as a duck pond and the marks she was making as ducks. She then made a final dot within the shape, and declared it to be the plug where the water goes out.... There were no easily recognisable visual referents which would identify the marks as an aerial view of ducks on a pond.... Significantly, it was Leanne's commentary, apparently spoken only to herself, which provided the clues to how the various marks were distinguished and ascribed meaning. (Cox, 2005, p 118)

Cox suggests that, rather than the observer seeing Leanne's accompanying talk as overriding the meaning of her drawing and being the 'real' communication, instead it is the interplay of the different ways of meaning making and dialogue which matters. The drawing itself is a form of language and what is felt and experienced within Leanne is encoded and decoded between the verbal and expressive arts languages. Children have a multiplicity of ways, means, modes and materials through which they make meaning and express themselves, constructing signs for themselves and others which carry these complex meanings (Matthews, 2003). Practitioners will be entering a process of meaning making alongside the child, observing the content of play and artwork and considering what may be being conveyed.

While a process of meaning making in observation is encouraged, attempts to *interpret* children's play should be made very cautiously. There is currently no reliable framework that has been tested empirically that can explain precisely how children's play or creative artefacts reflect their life experience. Drawings, for example, are rarely literal statements, providing authoritative evidence of what has happened to a child. Even when children are asked to draw their home and family, the image is likely to reflect feelings and experiences from the internal subjective world as much as the outer 'reality'. Free painting or creative work is even more likely to reflect a fantasy realm and to be abstract rather than representative. It may be far more likely, for example, that children would communicate abusive experiences through '"making a mess" ... rather than through a drawing depicting who did what to whom, on a particular occasion' (Case and Dalley, 1990, p 4). As imaginative recall and reconstruction are generally involved, play and artwork should generally be treated as symbolic or semi-symbolic rather than factual unless children have directly and clearly indicated real-life parallels. However, if children constantly and consistently replay the same kinds of themes, then this may be more reliably included as part of a wider assessment alongside other information collected.

The narrative story stem technique, a formalised assessment tool, comes closest to providing an indication of children's experiences and perceptions of social relationships. It has found 'relationships between children's narratives with play figures and measures of their social behaviour or experience' (Page, 2001, p 172). Children are provided with a number of 'story stems' or beginnings of stories. Where they complete the stories with endings reflecting predictable order and positive outcome, this has been found to indicate sufficient experience of sensitive caregiving to enable them to develop security of attachment. Endings showing violent problem resolutions or tangential responses to problems reflect the reverse. It should be noted that it is only the formal and structured use of the narrative story stem technique (which requires specialist training) that provides more firm and reliable statements regarding children's projected experiences. Professionals may wish to commission such specialist assessments as part of care proceedings or planning.

Talking with children and young people about their play and artwork, rather than just observing it, is covered in Chapter Ten.

Cultural considerations in observation and meaning making

The cultural and social meanings of children's manner of communication, body language, play and relational style and the ways in which professionals' own sociocultural frameworks shape their interpretations, need to be carefully considered. Body language, such as eye contact, smiling and posture, might sometimes operate to different norms from what the worker might be used to, depending on cultural background. Children have been found to play quite differently depending on culture, gender, environment and socioeconomic status.

Gosso et al's (2007) observational study of children of a range of backgrounds in Brazil, for example, found that children engaged in differing amounts and kinds of play depending on cultural groupings. While all the children in the study engaged in make-believe play, those from a higher socioeconomic status and urban background engaged more in pretending play than Indian children, than those from a low socioeconomic status, and than those living in a small coastal town. The researchers suggest that this is because the latter cultures have simpler communication codes, are less technologically advanced and are more concerned with material survival issues, so they are focusing more on concrete and immediate solutions to daily life problems rather than the kind of symbolic and abstract thought which is demonstrated within and developed by play. It was also thought that the higher exposure of children in Indian and seaside cultures to contact with nature and having freer environments for unsupervised play might mean fantasy play is less of a requirement for them than those living in more restricted environments.

Gosso et al's findings regarding gender differences in play also reflected those found more generally within the literature; for example, girls are more likely to enact family and domestic themes whereas boys play out more fantastic themes and bring in transportation (cars, trucks, trains, planes and so on) (Smith, 2005); girls tend to focus more on interacting personally and socially with each other in their play than boys (Tarullo, 1994). Such research findings mean professionals should, when drawing conclusions about what they have observed, think carefully about the influence of the child's current and previous environments, their gender, their socioeconomic status, and so on, on their play in order to consider what kinds of norms to judge the situation against.

Cultural considerations are equally important when practitioners are observing parent–child relationships. Given that attachment theory has been tested with a range of children across different continents and cultures over the last 50 years, with similar needs for children to seek proximity to a primary carer or carers, and the same types of classification having broadly been found, it is believed that there is a sufficiently robust empirical base for cross-national generalisations to be made. However, the cross-cultural robustness of assessments of attachment and other measures of parent–child relationships have been called into question (Cleary, 1999). Comparative studies suggest that parenting norms may differ widely according to macro- and sub-culture; consequently professionals' assessments of parenting may be riven with cultural relativity. Western cultures, for example, tend to promote children developing autonomy and independence at an early stage, emphasising the 'self as agent', whereas non-Western cultures tend more to valorise children remaining in warmer and closer multiple interactions, with the self conceived as 'coagent' (Keller et al, 2004). In more individualistic cultures, parents are thought more likely to value their children's independence, privacy, achievement, competition, self-promotion, selfishness and open expression of negative emotions, whereas in collectivistic cultures, people seem to prefer 'we instead of I', affiliation more than achievement, closer relationships and harmony among people, and deter expression of negative emotions in children (Gosso et al, 2007). From their comparative study of parents and children in Japan and the US, this has led Rothbaum and colleagues (2000) to contest that some of attachment theory's core assumptions are culturally determined rather than universal and biological, that is, sensitivity, competence and the concept of a safe base are viewed and practised differently in these two cultures. Consequently care must be taken when assigning approval to one form of attachment over another.

Based on such arguments it seems clear that observers should always attend to the specific culturally based experiences of the children and families involved as well as to their own assumptions, values and prejudices. At the micro level, this might include learning more about a particular family's set of practices and cultural expectations (Minde et al, 2006). A child who has experienced regular caretaking from extended family members or a child minder, or has been in day care, is likely to respond differently to a separation or the presence of a stranger from a child who has been constantly in the presence of just one carer. At a macro level, workers should consider issues of difference between themselves and those they are observing and interrogate the assumptions and norms they bring to assessments of parenting so that they do not pathologise family structures they are unfamiliar with (Sudarkasa, 1988).

Conclusion

Observation can play a crucial role in informing assessment of children, young people and their families. When using the assessment framework (DH et al, 2000) and CAF (CWDC, 2008), for example, it can inform an appraisal of the three domains of children's development, parenting capacity and children's social environments. Of course, information gained via observations must be used alongside that obtained directly from children, young people and their carers. However, where children do not communicate directly via a formal language system observation (or not yet), or are avoiding or are unable to speak directly about their wishes, feelings, concerns and experiences, observation provides an invaluable opportunity for workers to gain insight into what has not been directly expressed.

Practitioners who aspire to be competent observers need to develop skills not only in noticing what occurs but also in making sense of what has been witnessed. The analytical interpretive process ('doing') that this involves requires careful attention to subjectivity and bias so should be informed by research, theoretical perspectives ('knowing'), ethical standards and rigorous self-reflection ('being'). As discussed in Chapter Six, supervision can provide a containing and challenging space to facilitate such reflection, to enable the worker to 'take in' the child or young person, hold them in their mind and process complex and difficult feelings which are evoked, while they attempt to give meaning to what has been heard.

Key questions

1. Describe the key differences between the target child, time sampling and Tavistock methods of child observation.
2. What differences in behaviour might you notice between a child who demonstrates an insecure-ambivalent attachment style and one with a more avoidant style?
3. How might cultural beliefs and norms affect how parenting practices are seen?

Further reading and resources

Fawcett, M. (2009) *Learning through child observation* (2nd edn), London: Jessica Kingsley Publishers.

Hindle, D. and Easton, J. (1999) 'The use of observation of supervised contact in child care cases', *Journal of Infant Observation and its Application*, vol 2, Special Issue: The application of infant observation to social work, pp 33-48.

Robinson, L. (2007) *Cross-cultural child development for social workers: An introduction*, Basingstoke: Palgrave Macmillan.

Turney, D. (2008) 'The power of the gaze: observation and its role in direct practice with children in care', in B. Luckock and M. Lefevre (eds) *Direct work: Social work with children and young people in care*, London: BAAF, pp 115-29.

Communicating with children and young people through play, activities and the expressive arts

10

Introduction

It has already been noted that direct forms of verbal and written language are not always the best way to learn more about what children and young people think, feel, want and have experienced, and that more of the 'hundred languages of childhood' might need to be used. This chapter considers how more child-centred approaches such as 'tools', games, activities, play and artwork[1] might be used to build rapport and explore thoughts and feelings as part of assessment and intervention. Practice approaches are illustrated through social worker Tanya's work with Jack Doyle (age 6) and Caz Doyle (age 14).

The role of activity-based work

> "The good thing about my social worker is she helps me when I'm upset and she gives me advice. I do lots of things with her, like playing games." (Jamie, aged 10, quoted in Headliners, 2009)

Chapter Nine highlighted how children and young people are not always able to identify, name and convey their inner thoughts and feelings. For younger children, this may be because they have not yet developed the vocabulary or cognitive capacity to do so, which comes with maturation if there is no learning disability. Other children and young people, even when they do have the ability to process and communicate their views and emotions to professionals, still do not do so. Neglectful or abusive parenting experiences may mean that some children are not used to adults really listening to, understanding and validating them, and they do not know how to begin to express themselves. They may be wary of adults generally, and feel it is safer to keep their thoughts to themselves. The power and status professionals have may cause them to worry about what may happen as a result of them talking about their lives.

With such young people, direct dialogue through talking, writing, signing or other communication systems may simply not be enough to engage them or help them discuss issues. Activities, playing games and having fun together can help a rapport to develop and create an atmosphere of trust and safety within which they can relax and feel safe (Thomas and O'Kane, 2000). Exploration of difficult matters and expression of emotions and perceptions may be facilitated when a more metaphorical language, such as artwork or stories, is also used. Approaches such as playing with toys, dolls or building bricks (McMahon, 2009), engaging in board or computer games (Ahmad et al, 2008), talking about or playing with pets or animals (Hoelscher and Garfat, 1993) or chatting about the child's hobbies or shared interests to help establish a connection can also act as what Clare Winnicott (1964) called a 'third object' or 'third thing', something for the worker and child or young person to focus on together which takes them away from the uncomfortable intensity of their interaction.

These more indirect forms of dialogue are not just helpful with younger or disabled children but can be very helpful with teenagers, some of whom do seem to go through a less communicative stage (Corcoran, 1997). A face-to-face situation where the worker is attempting to verbally interact with a silent young person who glares or averts eye contact can reduce the confidence of even the most experienced worker to rock bottom. A conversation about football, a wander round the shops together or being prepared to learn about a young person's favourite band can shift this dynamic and gives the message that the social worker is interested in him or her as a person.

Practice vignette: Beginning to engage with Caz Doyle

Through her visits to the house to see Jack and Theresa, Tanya has managed to make contact with Caz. On one occasion Theresa was absent, having gone to a doctor's appointment, and Caz was left babysitting. Tanya suggested they might have a coffee together while they waited for Theresa to return. While Caz is making the coffee, Tanya notices the MP3 player hanging from Caz's neck and asks her what she is listening to. Caz names several bands that Tanya has never heard of. Rather than being embarrassed or defensive about this, Tanya laughingly refers to her own lack of knowledge and asks Caz to play her some of the music so she can learn more about it. Caz is pleased that Tanya is showing an interest and acknowledging where she knows more about something. This encourages her to start to 'open up' to Tanya.

Comment on the vignette

Workers must involve themselves fully in a person–to–person relationship if activity-based approaches are to work; a distanced 'professionalism' will not be enough. This will call on their personal qualities such as their capacity to be playful, creative, fun, real and non-defensive (Prior et al, 1999), as Tanya has illustrated. Arguably, if a practitioner does not have these qualities, or is not prepared to draw on them in their professional role, then they should reconsider whether they should be working with children and young people at all. The professional use of personal qualities is, however, something that can be developed where the practitioner is motivated and committed to doing so. Chapter Six contains suggestions regarding this.

Introducing play and activities into direct practice with children

Professionals will need to feel confident and capable in understanding and using as many of the 'hundred languages of childhood' as possible if they are to communicate effectively with a particular child (Clark and Statham, 2005). A worker's choice of medium with a particular child or young person (for example, drawing, playing with dolls or figurines, using electronic media) should be based on their response to what is available in the environment and whether the social worker thinks that certain tools or approaches might help them express or work through a specific issue. However, workers are likely to be drawn to what they have been trained to use, what they have read about and the modes of communication and expression most familiar or comfortable to them. While this can offer many creative possibilities it can also be limiting. Where workers feel confident in using a range of approaches they are more likely to find a mode of communication that works between them and children. This means moving out of their comfort zone and into the child's.

Practitioners might work in a non-directive way, where the child leads the activity, or introduce focused activities, specific exercises or tools for a particular purpose.

> ### Practice vignette: Beginning to use play with Jack Doyle
>
> Tanya starts to meet weekly with Jack in the school counselling room as part of the core assessment. She begins with free play for the first few weeks to build some trust and to get to know more about him through letting him express

himself without her 'leading' the process. She will then move on to some more structured exercises and activities to find out some specific information.

Non-directive play and activities

A period of non-directive play and activities can be a helpful way of beginning an assessment, just as Tanya is doing with Jack Doyle. It can help children and young people engage and assist workers in learning more broadly about their strengths, way of communicating, habitus and family practices, rather than jumping too quickly to what the professionals think they want to learn about. To facilitate this workers should attempt to create a 'holding' and permissive space that encourages children and young people to engage in activities or play freely. They should let the child lead by playing alongside them rather than directing them, seeking guidance from the child about how they want them to take the game or story forward. To show interest and attention without leading the child in any particular direction, practitioners could also comment out loud in neutral tones on what is happening (Oaklander, 1978). For example, the worker might comment during play with dolls or little figures, "I see that the little dog has now been told off by its mummy". Such 'noticing' comments can encourage children to keep playing and perhaps to engage in their own commentary. This process helps children and young people begin to construct and express narratives which make connections between their inner and outer worlds, between experience as it is felt, as it is understood, and between what children would like it to be (Ahn and Filipenko, 2006). Such narratives also enable young people to convey how they see themselves in relation to others and their environment, which helps inform assessment.

Age, cultural or gender preferences may influence children and young people's preferences for certain kinds of play or activities. In my own work I found that many younger girls preferred doll play, dressing up and singing; teenage girls often loved going 'window shopping' where they could show me the clothes and music they liked as a way of me getting to know them; whereas I found I bonded better with some of the boys once I kicked a ball around the park with them. I learned that it was important, however, not to make presumptions about preferences in advance but to provide opportunities and options for a range of activities that children and young people could choose from.

When the purpose of the work is more therapeutic, it is often sufficient for workers just to provide a safe space for children in which their play is supported and facilitated without interference or interpretation (Ryan et al, 1995). Workers just follow, mirror and amplify the child's play and activities so that they feel met, appreciated and contained (Oaklander, 1978).

This follows the philosophy of non-directive play therapy which advises that humans' self-regulating and self-healing capacity means that children often tend to 'know' unconsciously what they need if the opportunities are available (McMahon, 2009).

Sometimes busy social workers do not feel they have time for such non-directive pursuits in their task-driven, short-staffed environments. But non-directive play and interactions with children are purposeful activities at the centre of the social work role, not added extras. They can help to engage children who are particularly wary, distant or angry in a safe and trusting relationship where difficult issues can be worked through. They inform assessment; providing information on how the child functions, relates and communicates. They can enable areas of feeling that children may not be able to put into words or would deny in conversation or questioning to be opened up for exploration and expression (Thomas and O'Kane, 2000).

Practice vignette: Play sessions with Jack Doyle

When she has seen him at home, Jack has mainly played with computer games. In her first session with him, Tanya notices that Jack seems rather at a loss when faced with props that require imaginative play. He moves around the paints and crayons in a desultory fashion. Eventually he locates a water pistol and pretends to shoot first Tanya then all of the dolls and cuddly toy animals he can find. He then takes a big stuffed tiger and beats the smaller dolls and animals with it.

Tanya makes comments to Jack about what she is noticing, for example, "I can see that the little bunny has been shot and now it's being hit over the head by the tiger". This encourages Jack, too, to comment on his play: "That bunny's had it, that bunny's going to get it!". He seems excited to be able to name what is happening and pleased that Tanya is interested in what he is saying. Tanya is then able to encourage Jack to share what feelings and experiences he is projecting on to the toys, for example, "So, is the tiger saying anything? ... What does the bunny want now?".

Comment on the vignette

Tanya is making an assessment rather than trying to work therapeutically with Jack, so her main purpose here is learning more about his world through his play, rather than pursuing therapeutic goals. Consequently she adopts a non-directive approach to observe what kind of spontaneous play he engages in. She keeps the situation safe while creating a permissive atmosphere; this encourages Jack to engage with her and with the sessions. The level of violence in Jack's play and the fact that he identifies with the powerful tiger, showing little pity or empathy for the smaller animals, gives rise to questions for Tanya as to whether this indicates anything about his inner or real world experiences. She does not seek to interpret this yet as the assessment is only just beginning; she is aware that it is only when a picture builds up over time that any inferences formed are more reliable. So, she seeks to keep him communicating by noticing, commenting and prompting. Her questions remain at a metaphorical level, rather than trying to push Jack to make any connections with his real world experiences at this stage.

Structured and focused activities

Structured exercises and focused activities will be more appropriate for other circumstances, such as when a broader picture is already formed and the worker is clearer about what specific information is needed from a child or young person. Many young people engage better with worker-led activity once a connection and some working trust has already been established, particularly when the content of the work is distressing or worrying to them.

Pre-designed resources can provide guidance and ideas for structured activities. Some are available specifically for assessment (such as Hutton and Partridge, 2006) while other imaginative and projective exercises, such as magic castles which are designed to provoke children's imagination and enable them to give a vivid picture of their thoughts and feelings, can be used for more therapeutic or intervention-based purposes as well (for example, Sunderland and Engelheart, 1993; Geldard and Geldard, 2008). However, workers will want to move beyond these into being able to draw on their own creativity to respond in the moment to children and young people. When there is something specific that needs to be conveyed to a child, such as explaining why they need to move to a different placement, workers could provide a visual representation of this using dolls or little animal figures, for example.

An important guide with worker-led activities is still to go at the child's pace wherever possible. Children who are very young, are insecure in their attachments, have learning difficulties and/or who are still very traumatised by their experiences are likely to struggle most with engaging in and concentrating on a structured activity and workers will need to re-assess and reconsider more non-directive work if this occurs.

Using artwork to communicate with children and young people

Non-directive painting and drawing

Free drawing is a form of meaning making and signing that young children engage in spontaneously from infancy onwards (where they have the motor capacity for this). Even their earliest scribbles are a way of helping children to identify, classify, order, conceptualise and express their experience and perceptions:

> When a child is including, or excluding, features of the world in a drawing and when they are encoding and decoding intentions in their drawings in a playful and on-going way, they are experimenting with the language of materials and marks and building concepts at the same time. (Cox, 2005, p 122)

Younger children tend not to have internalised yet notions of what 'proper' art should be. They do not usually constrain themselves by trying to characterise 'real' images of objects and people per se, but are satisfied with representing their understanding of 'the way objects operate in the world, the way they behave in space and time' (McGregor, 1990, p 39). Encouraging children to begin free painting, modelling or drawing in a safe and trusting environment harnesses this innate creativity and enables feelings and symbolic thoughts to be expressed (Case and Dalley, 1990). The complexities of their experience can be processed and children may convey what is important to them and/or significant in their internal world. This enables a picture shaped in their own terms to emerge, often a richer one than that acquired when they are constricted by the conceptions and assumptions underpinning social workers' suggestions about what to draw.

By providing a safe and unconditional space in which they can work at their own pace and in their own way, children and young people can be supported to make whatever colours and shapes they want, rather than just aiming for aesthetically pleasing images. Rather than questioning them directly about the significance or meaning of aspects of the image, workers can comment in a neutral manner on the visual qualities of the specific tree, animal, colour or shape that has been drawn; for example, "I can see you've poured lots of black paint over the house you drew" (quoted in Oaklander, 1978). Such comments enable the child and worker to stay connected and support the child in what they are doing so that they do not feel led or criticised. Very open questions also offer encouragement, such as "Maybe you'd like to tell me about your picture – I'm really interested in it". If, by contrast, workers jump too readily to questions and comments like, "Is that your house?", "Is that the boy's mother?", they are already constraining the possibilities of associations and meanings.

Worker-led activities using visual imagery

Practice vignette: More direct work with Jack Doyle

After a few sessions of non-directive play work with Jack, Tanya has formed an appraisal of how he is functioning developmentally and understands more about how he relates and communicates. Jack has built up a rapport with Tanya and is now better able to respond to her and concentrate in her presence. Tanya feels he might now be able to cope with the kinds of focused tasks that might help her comprehend more about his experiences, feelings and views.

Tanya suggests that Jack draw a picture of his home and family and asks him to tell her all about the different things and people he has placed in the picture. She then moves it on by asking, "If someone was going past and looked through the window, what might they see inside?... Who would be doing what?".

Comment on the vignette

Tanya keeps the pace gentle and looks at the picture rather than at Jack so that pauses feel natural. By concentrating on his drawing as well as the conversation, Jack seems quite relaxed and talks quite freely. Tanya begins to learn more about how he sees different family members, the relationships between them and what a typical day at home is like.

More structured and directive exercises using visual imagery such as these may be used both to elicit children's views and feelings regarding their circumstances and as a focus for intervention. Tasks introduced might be thought up by the worker, tailored to the child and his or her situation. Alternatively, ready-made exercises and tools, such as the genograms, ecomaps and 'life rivers' described below, are a simple but effective way of engaging collaboratively and dynamically with children and young people of all ages and abilities to enable them to convey their understanding and experience of family dynamics, social relationships and community networks (Walton and Smith, 1999). Younger children and those who have learning difficulties will find their visual and concrete nature particularly helpful. Where children have physical impairments that prevent them from picking up and using arts materials, they may use electronically based systems to support them, or issue instructions to the worker to create the image in the way that they visualise it.

Genograms

Genograms, also called family trees, are often placed in professionals' files to provide a quick visual picture of 'who's who' in a family. They are particularly useful for showing family structures over several generations and mapping extended families where siblings do not share both birth parents. The process of drawing up a genogram, however, can also be an effective way of exploring with families their histories and relationships. Constructing genograms with children can help identify the gaps in their knowledge about their family; this may be particularly important for children in care, young unaccompanied asylum seekers and as part of life story work. The genogram may also be used as a tool for the worker to explain to the child about their family history, rather than just to gather information. Additional information may then need to be sought from other family relationships, chronologies, and so on.

Genograms are most commonly shown as a diagram using common symbols, for example, a circle to denote a female and a square to indicate a male. Lines may then be used to indicate formal relationships between people. They could include photographs or drawings of people, too, or be constructed in 3D, using figurines of people, fairy tale characters, superheroes, animals, and so on, to represent different individuals. Further guidance and examples may be found in the free e-resource available on the SCIE website mentioned in the 'Further resources' section at the end of this chapter and in the Department of Health (2000) practice guidance on the assessment framework.

A word of caution should be struck, however, about the use of genograms and other similar tools such as ecomaps (below) with black children and their families. It has been suggested that such tools, often being designed by those from the dominant white Western culture, tend to construct and impose Eurocentric worldviews and value systems. They may not reflect the family systems and structure of Black African families, for example, which traditionally take differing views on the nature and importance of extended family relationships and the role of the wider community in child rearing. It has already been noted that black and dual heritage children in this country often experience their personhood, ethnicity and culture as being devalued and do not always feel they are given an opportunity to narrate their lived experiences of family life, school and public care (Graham and Bruce, 2006). Being asked to work with tools that do not make sense to them and further negate their experience may compromise their psychological well-being and identity development (Graham, 1999). A more ethnic-sensitive method (Schiele, 1997) might be to offer a more open-ended approach that enables an understanding and appreciation of a young person's racial, cultural and social diversity to emerge on its own terms. This also promotes a shift away from deficit models which view black young people's difference as a problem to providing a better appraisal of their strengths and competences (Graham, 2007).

Ecomaps

Ecomaps are another simple and visual way of helping children and young people explore and discuss their own views and subjective impressions of their family and community networks and supports (with the caveats above). Like genograms they can be constructed in a very basic way just using paper and pens. Young people should be asked to place themselves in a circle at the centre of the page; they can do this by writing their name, using a photograph or drawing themselves. They then place other circles on the page to represent significant figures in their lives, such as family members, foster carers, school friends, pets and professionals. It is up to the child or young person how many people he or she includes. Relationships between themselves and other people are then shown in a range of ways. This could include how the circles are spaced out: those closest to them emotionally could be drawn closest to them on the page. Different colours might be used, such as the child writing the name of those they feel closest to with their favourite colour. Different kinds of lines might be used to demonstrate connections between people, such as a thick line to show a strong or positive relationship, a dotted line to indicate a weak relationship or a wiggly line where a relationship is problematic. As with genograms, some children might prefer using dolls or toy animals or buttons of different size, shape and colour instead of pens and paper.

A variation on the ecomap is the sociogram suggested by Messiou (2009), which can reflect children and young people's perceptions of the relationships and preferences between family members or in other social groupings. A child could be asked to write down all their family members across a page and then to draw arrows between them, indicating particular relationships and preferences. For example, the child might draw an arrow pointing from their mother to their brother, from their father to their mother, from their brother to their mother and from the family dog to themselves when asked to show who seemed to like who best.

Life rivers

'Life rivers' or 'life paths' (Sunderland and Engelheart, 1993) are a way of helping children and young people map out how their life has gone so far and provide an overview. The worker can just draw a winding line on a page, writing the young person's date of birth at the beginning and the current date at the end. Then the worker would support the child or young person to gradually map along the pathway the significant things that have happened to them, showing what age these things happened and perhaps noting down feelings and thoughts that they remember from that time. Symbols, drawings, colours or even cut-out pictures can all be used instead of or as well as words to convey events, relationships and feelings.

With young people in care who have had a number of moves or refugee children who have moved across continents in the wake of war or other conflicts or disasters, these can be factually based, perhaps to help inform a new worker about their history. But, as with genograms and ecomaps, they can also be used as a reflective tool, helping the worker to understand the thoughts and feelings associated with life events. In this way, life rivers can support assessment, provide a focus for therapeutic interventions such as life story work and provide a 'third thing' activity to help difficult conversations to begin.

The window

The 'window' provides another creative opportunity for children to consider their perceptions, hopes and fears about their past, present and future (Sunderland and Engelheart, 1993). This is quite a vivid way of enabling a child not only to depict how things are, their aspirations and fears, but also enabling them to really see and explore these for themselves.

Practice vignette: The 'window' exercise

Drawing a simple window with four panes of glass, Tanya suggests to Caz that she could imagine looking at her life through this window. In one square she should draw or sketch the 'view' of her past. In another square, she should draw how things are for her in her life right now. In the third square, she should sketch how she would want her future to look and, in the fourth, what she fears it may be like.

Comment on the vignette

Such exercises enable a young person's imagination to be sparked in a way that verbal questions about concrete matters do not always achieve. In this way they are thus an intervention even when the aim is for information gathering in assessment. If children and young people seem very uncomfortable or under-confident in drawing they could use pictures cut out of magazines or downloaded from a computer to stick into each space, or even just write words in there.

Rating scales

Rating scales, such as those used in Chapter Eight with Caz, sketched quickly and using basic imagery, can provide spontaneous ways of gathering views and opinions (Mattaini, 1995). Different facial expressions may be provided as an alternative to words or numbers at either end of the scale. These could be drawn by the worker or illustrated using cut-outs from magazines, computer 'clip art' icons or getting the young person to help with the drawings. It is important to offer enough options for emotional responses (such as 'sad', 'angry', 'frightened', 'hopeful') so that the options for the child are not restricted.

Practice vignette: Using rating scales with a child and his mother

Tanya uses different kinds of rating scales with Jack Doyle and his mother than those she used with Caz. On a big sheet of paper she draws several lines and places cut-out images of different kinds of facial expressions along each line. One scale had a very happy face at one end and a very upset, tearful face at the other. Another scale had an angry face at one end and a content face at the other. The third had a frightened face at one end and a powerful looking face at the other. The fourth had 'bored' at one end and 'excited' at the other. Tanya asked Jack and Theresa to indicate where on each line they were in relation to different things, such as 'what things were like at breakfast time', and how they felt about Jack's school experiences. She also asked them to point to where they had thought each other was on the line.

Comment on the vignette

A different approach to the rating scales exercise is used to tailor it to the needs of a younger child this time. Approaches such as these help a professional find out not just what the child or parent's own thoughts and feelings are, but what their perceptions are about each other. It can also help them learn more about each other's feelings and experiences.

Communication through stories and creative writing

Plots and characters

Children, young people and their workers may find themselves communicating together through the medium of fictional characters or plots. Children (and adults too!) may engage and identify powerfully with particular characters or story lines from fairy tales, story books, novels, films or television programmes. These often have polarised archetypal characters (such as hero/villain, fairy godmother/witch) which allow children to consciously or unconsciously identify with certain qualities, allocate traits to others, understand their own and others' motivations, learn about different kinds of choices and play with new ways of looking at things (Barker, 1985). Exploring children and young people's thoughts and feelings about characters and story lines can help them learn about themselves and expand their opportunities for making sense of the world and the behaviour of others at many different levels (Sunderland and Armstrong, 2001). These can then be conveyed to the worker either directly or through the medium of the story. *The story of Tracy Beaker* (Wilson, 1992), for example, tells the tale of a young person in care in an engaging way and can help children and their social workers begin to talk about difficult subjects.

There is now a wide range of story books written about specific issues available that carers and workers can use with children and young people. Some (such as Sunderland et al, 2003) have additional sections or supplementary publications to alert carers and/or professionals to issues to be aware of and how to further open up areas for discussion following the story.

More direct conversations may be held with older young people about their favourite book, film or television programme and which characters they fear, admire or identify with. Learning about or meeting any 'virtual' identity they use in computer games or on the internet might also provide a way of exploring their perceptions of themselves.

Playing out stories

In play-based sessions, children could be encouraged to embody roles and enact plots, experimenting with aspects of their personality and history. The worker should enter the spirit of the child's play, inhabiting any story characters assigned to them. The child should be encouraged to lead so that they choose who the worker will 'be' and what they should behave like. Empathically 'tuning in' to children's needs helps workers know how to respond. With children who are less able to play, because neglect, trauma or emotional deprivation has not helped them develop this capacity, practitioners might take more of a lead, 'egging on' the child by being very playful themselves. Workers will have to put aside their own embarrassment and self-consciousness at such times!

Providing information through stories

Stories can be a way of giving information and explanations to children who are too young or distressed to make sense of what has been said. Hendry (1988) turned the account of why two very young children had to move placements into a story, presenting it as a book that could be read to them. She illustrated it with drawings and pictures to make it more appealing visually. Telling the story to them in the third person meant the children could engage with it gradually and make their own connections; consequently it was less threatening. Other play materials, such as small figures and dolls house furniture, were added in at a later stage to illustrate what would be happening when they moved placement. The mutable nature of these also enabled the children to be actively involved in the story and for changes to be incorporated as they occurred.

A reference is provided at the end of this chapter to a free e-learning resource on working with children and young people. Among many other resources, it contains an example of a simple story I wrote about four kittens who went to new homes as a way of helping a sibling group explore their experiences of coming into care. The children I worked with enjoyed the story at a basic level initially and empathised with the kittens' experiences; this may well have supported their emotional processing and healing at a subconscious level. The children were then able to begin to make more conscious connections between the kittens' lives and their own and to discuss some of the complex issues and dynamics involved. This led naturally on to more direct dialogue and explanations of why they could not return home, which facilitated their cognitive processing of events.

Developing such stories with children does not have to require any great talent on the part of professionals. The stories can be simple and practitioners can illustrate them with photographs or magazine images if they do not feel confident to illustrate them with their own drawings.

Communication and self-expression through creative writing

With older children and young people and those who feel comfortable using written language, encouraging them to turn their feelings and experiences into stories or poems might be a helpful adjunct or even alternative to them exploring their feelings and experiences in a direct manner. Stories may provide a 'container' for complex emotions, where they can be examined and reflected on at the safer distance of the metaphor. Changing or developing the story can be part of a child or young person beginning to process and move on from earlier trauma. Poems can be simple to produce where the aim is self-expression rather than producing an aesthetic artefact. The worker may need to do no more than give young people some help and guidance on how to begin, such as encouraging them to pick words and phrases which are expressive of what they think and feel and which matter.

The first stage of creating a poem or story may be cathartic. It is an opportunity for children's unconscious to be given sway, so their inner subjective world can emerge. Some young people want the worker to be involved at this stage, perhaps even to write down what they say so that it can be shaped into a poem. Others want to write while on their own, such as on the computer at home or in the foster placement, but want the worker to hear the poem once written, to witness the personal and intimate expression of the inner experience. Their initial outpourings are tangible, visible on the page and can be related to, worked on, organised, clarified and understood over time. They can return to them again and again to re-experience them in different frames of mind, different stages of life (Bolton, 1999). The stage of re-working this cathartic expression is important, not just to turn it into a coherent art object, but because it enables the writing to be reflected on and brought closer to what the child or young person thinks or feels.

For those who feel less confident in the creative element of story or poem writing, diaries offer a private way of thinking about and reflecting on personal experience. They may be shared with a worker or can be locked with a key or hidden away to keep private. For many young people today, an electronic medium might feel more appealing than pen and paper. It can be possible on most computers to protect documents and files with passwords to keep them private. 'Blogs' (online diaries) are very common nowadays so young people may need to be warned of the risks attached to putting any personal information into the public domain.

Communication through interactive and electronic media

"I preferred it when I didn't have to answer too many questions. I hated that. I liked it better when we did stuff on the computer together." (14-year-old boy describing his experience of coming to counselling, quoted in Sharry, 2004, p 57)

Professionals will want to make use of more interactive and technologically based play and activities, too, as these are now integral to children's daily lives and are highly valued in youth culture (Cowan, 2000). In Chapter Eleven electronic means of communication with children such as email and text messaging are discussed. Here, it is worth considering some of the ways technology may support communication.

There are now many interactive computer-based packages that have been designed for direct work with children and young people. They are in a similar format to the kinds of learning approaches now used in school and children are likely to feel familiar with their use. Young people are able to input their own thoughts, feelings and perceptions on screen and print them out in a format that looks good and creates a permanent record for them. Some packages also use fictional characters and situations so that issues can be explored at a safer metaphorical distance. Programmes often include humour, animations, sound effects and cartoon characters that make them appealing to use. One example is *Bridget's taking a long time* (Betts and Ball, 2004) which is a CD-ROM to use within a family where a child is coming to join them through adoption. The resource includes an on-screen story for children aged between 5 and 12, with animations, sound effects, music and interactivity in every screen, printable worksheets corresponding to the key issues and feelings, and a video of interviews with birth children speaking about their experience of being part of an adopting family.

Some packages are quite expensive and there may be resource constraints that preclude their regular use. However, practitioners and children may have access to other props that can support them. Many young people have their own mobile phones that have games, a camera, sound card or movie maker. Some social workers have phones provided by their organisation with these facilities, too. Practitioners could encourage a young person to make a diary, documentary or story through photographs, audio recording or video that they could then look at and work on together. Some phones have very basic cartoon or art packages on which images may be created; these can be used as a form or self-expression or just as a fun 'third thing' to aid rapport-building.

Where a dedicated room is being developed for direct work in an organisation, the inclusion of a computer should be a priority. Most nowadays have the facility to turn photographs into slide shows and video clips into films, both with added music, as well as art packages. Where there is a computer in the family home, residential unit or foster home, this, too, might be commandeered.

Children and young people sometimes feel intimidated or powerless in direct work, knowing that the adult is in control of the process, particularly in assessments where information is being gleaned from them. Electronically based media can turn the tables on this a little as most young people are a lot more comfortable and confident with them than adults. This was certainly the case for Edwin, the social worker in his forties, who we met in Chapter Six, who moved to work in the youth offending team and was finding himself feeling rather 'left behind' by the way such technologies were moving on. As Ahmad et al (2008, p 171) note,

> This reversal of power dynamics between child and adult can further aid the engagement and communication process. Simply using the mouse puts the child or young person in greater control, boosting their confidence and raising their value.

Workers can find that they learn a lot simply by allowing the young person to show them how everything works! They can also boost their own confidence in advance by familiarising themselves with equipment, including how to scan, download and print digital imagery. These computer-based tools do not generally require high levels of literacy skills so can be particularly inclusive where children have learning difficulties, have missed out on schooling or where English is not their primary language.

Communication through music

Performing, composing and listening to music may all be forms of communication and self-expression.[2] Music is often likened to a language enabling people to communicate about feelings, relationships and internal world experiences (Di Franco, 1993). Babies, for example, express their feelings and negotiate their way around relationships by altering the pitch, intensity, rhythm and timbre of their own vocalisations (paralanguage) to express their feelings to others (Heal and Wigram, 1993). Parents and carers often spontaneously and unconsciously further this communication by singing to the infant to soothe and delight it (Diaz de Chumaceiro, 1995). When children and young people are encouraged to engage musically in direct work, their self-expression and communication happens more at a symbolic level; just as with spoken language, their inner thoughts and feelings (meta-messages) are 'encoded' by the child (into musical sounds rather than words) and need to be received and successfully 'decoded' by the worker using their habitus and empathic emotional attunement. Playing together over time, the child and worker can generate a relationship where a musical idiom is developed which has meaning for them both.

Improvising with percussion

How the music will be used will depend on the musical capabilities of the practitioner, the interests of the child or young person, the resources available, the purpose of the worker's involvement and the setting of their interactions. Family centre workers, for example, may have access to a variety of instruments in which they can engage in free, rhythmic improvisation. This can enable the young person to express feelings in a safe and contained manner. As they create a desired sound with little or no musical skill, percussion instruments offer the opportunity for any child or worker to improvise freely without needing to be constrained by creating melody or harmony. A non-directive approach would tend to support, encourage and reflect their improvisations both verbally and musically. Alternatively, communication may occur through an interplay, with the child and the adult taking turns to initiate and respond in a succession of musical statements (Scovel, 1990). The musically and therapeutically skilled practitioner will be more able to improvise in a number of different styles using children's 'language', enabling them to feel that their expression has been heard and accepted. There is a long and successful history of such music therapy approaches with disabled children and young people (Sutton, 1995).

Singing

Non-musical practitioners without access to such resources could simply engage in the spontaneous singing of songs with children and young people, perhaps being prompted by the radio being on during a home visit or car journey. Nursery rhymes might be used with younger children. Singing is an ideal engagement tool, offering 'a safe musical starting point' from which 'the potentially unsafe world' of a new child/worker relationship can begin to be explored – 'rather like having a musical hand to hold' (Flower, 1993, p 42). A relationship of trust can develop through building up over time a 'collective memory of feelings and facts which binds you together … based on a common emotional experience' (Alvin, 1966, p 132).

Such songs become very familiar to the children and may provide a 'secure base' (Bowlby, 1988), or act as transitional objects (Winnicott, 1971); young people may return to them when difficult subjects are under discussion or when events threaten their security or well-being. The songs a child chooses to sing with the worker may also have a symbolic content deriving from associations with where the song was previously heard, or from the mood or the words or as a manifestation of a transference[3] relationship (Diaz de Chumaciero, 1995). Similarly, songs that the worker spontaneously sings when with, or thinking about, a child may be counter-transferential.

Listening to music together

Listening to music together may also be beneficial. The example at the beginning of the chapter showed Tanya engaging with Caz's music as a rapport-building tool. While on the one hand it might be good to keep up with the latest youth trends as a way of demonstrating an interest, in fact fashions do change rapidly and it is hard for adults to stay on top of them. Many young people, too, can be scornful of older people who they see as trying too hard to seem 'cool'. Following Tanya's example, letting the young person be the expert can share the power. It also allows for exploration of what is important or expressive in the music, which can give a good insight into the young person's world.

Guided music listening is where the practitioner introduces some music into the session with a child for a particular purpose. Structures and qualities inherent in the music, such as patterns of tension-inhibition-resolution, pitch, tempo and dynamics, may be chosen to connect with the child's emotions and provide a contained way for these to be re-experienced in a safe place and resolved. Such work has been linked to therapeutic healing and pain relief (Scovel, 1990).

Children and young people's responses to guided music listening will not be a simple matter of cause and effect but influenced by a number of extra-musical influences, such as their mood, the styles of music they are familiar with and prefer, their culture, social class, education and ethnic origin (Meyer, 1956; Gfeller, 1990; Bright, 1993). For example, certain styles selected by the worker might feel culturally or socially alienating to some children, preventing them hearing through this to the underlying musical mood. It is important not to rely on stereotyped notions of what might be acceptable to the child as this runs the risk of stunting experimentation and patronising or pigeonholing the child.

Previous experiences can also influence the child's response to the music, leading to a mismatch of expectations and possible miscommunications. It is possible that the music might even arouse a painful or frightened response in the child or young person, if there are associations to traumatic or abusive experiences, such as when the music was last heard. This can also happen for workers and pre-preparation should include exploring their own feelings in relation to different musical styles and sounds. Otherwise, their own counter-transferential reactions might intrude.

Some issues to bear in mind

A few cautionary notes need to be struck. First, while children and young people's play and artwork can help us understand something about their internal experience, there are questions about the extent to which play and artwork can be interpreted reliably. Bolton (1999, p 67) stresses, for example, that:

> … there is no one meaning in any image. The image is a window on a whole other world, not a two-dimensional picture.

The gaining of understanding from play and imagery should be a process of exploration and creation, 'of connotation rather than interpretation' (Bolton, 1999, p 66). Children's images, stories or games should be attended to with respect and care, so that they are allowed to tell their own story. Interpretation would be the reverse of this, a process of 'denotation', where the worker attempts to impose a specified meaning, which may or may not be accurate or the whole picture.

Second, practitioners should always consider whether children and young people additionally need direct dialogue about specific issues and should not allow activity to be a way of avoiding difficult conversations – for either the child or the worker.

Third, communication using experiential methods can be extremely powerful. It is imperative that workers are sensitive in their use, providing sufficient time to round off the session and being available for further support or reflection where painful issues have been triggered. Parents or carers may also need to be forewarned in case difficult feelings are evoked.

Also, unless they have undertaken additional training social workers should not try to use these approaches as primary methods in intensive or therapeutic work with children or young people who are significantly traumatised. That would be the role of play and art therapists who would work more dynamically with children's symbolic and metaphorical material. When in doubt, the safest approach is the non-directive one, which is to follow children's leads and support their play by providing a safe space and attuned responses, 'tracking' what the child is doing, rather than deliberately setting out to work through these issues. In this way play and art forms become bridges to communication between children's inner and outer worlds.

In order to provide the emotional sensitivity and containment for children that is required, practitioners are urged to practise these methods on themselves or on a colleague before they use them with children (Walton and Smith, 1999).

Conclusion

This chapter has discussed a range of more creative, play- and activity-based methods that might be introduced into professional contact with children and young people to utilise more of the 'hundred languages of childhood'. There are no absolute rules about what approach to use for different situations, age groups or cultures. What is most important is working out the best approach for the individual child or young person within the professional role and context. This will involve some careful prior reflection, learning about the child, experimentation and monitoring their response to different kinds of activity. As well as knowledge about methods ('knowing') and skills in using them ('doing'), practitioners will need a willingness to be imaginative and creative ('being') in their quest to get 'in touch' with children.

Notes

[1] Some material in this chapter draws on Lefevre (2008b) with the permission of its publisher, the British Association for Adoption and Fostering (BAAF).
[2] I have previously explored ways in which social workers both with and without musical skills might introduce music as a communicative tool with children, and refer readers to Lefevre, 2004 for a fuller discussion.
[3] See Chapter Six for a definition of and discussion on transference.

Key questions

1. How might a particular book, television programme or film that you know provide a useful focus for a discussion on bereavement with a child?
2. Name a song or piece of music that you think would be suitable to play to a child who was feeling hurt or let down.
3. What activity might be useful to try with a child who is feeling angry?

Further reading and resources

Geldard, K. and Geldard, D. (2008) *Counselling children: A practical introduction* (3rd edn), London: Sage Publications [the appendix contains lots of activity-based or creative worksheets to use with children].

Hutton, A. and Partridge, K. (2006) *'Say it your own way': Children's participation in assessment: A guide and resources*, Ilford: Barnado's Publications (www.barnardos.org.uk/sayityourownway).

Lefevre, M., Richards, S. and Trevithick, P. (2008) *Using play and the creative arts to communicate with children and young people* (www.scie.org.uk/publications/elearning/cs/cs08/index.asp) [this is an interactive e-learning resource, available to use free of charge on the SCIE website].

McMahon, L. (2009) *The handbook of play therapy and therapeutic play* (2nd edn), Hove: Routledge.

Sunderland, M. and Engelheart, P. (1993) *Draw on your emotions*, Bicester: Winslow Press [a photocopiable resource book containing lots of creative and interactive exercises and tools which can be used with children or adults].

Communication as the heart of social work practice

11

Introduction

This final chapter considers the way in which effective communication lies at the heart of all aspects of social work practice with children and young people. Different interventions and issues are explored through the practice vignette of the Doyle family, with the developing situation raising challenges and dilemmas. The chapter, and book, ends with a summary of the key principles for effective communication and engagement that have been presented along the way.

Providing children with information and explanations

> "If I was confused she would unconfuse me." (satisfied comment of a nine-year-old girl about her social worker, quoted in Prior et al, 1999, p 134)

Children and young people do 'not want to be kept in the dark or patronised' about matters which affect them (DH et al, 2000, p 38). They have both a right to and a need for information from professionals about a range of matters, such as services that are available (Dearden and Becker, 2000), their family and personal histories (Prior et al, 1999) and the progress of any legal proceedings that involve them (Bourton and McCausland, 2001). They also want the reasons for particular interventions or decisions to be carefully explained to them, such as why they have been placed in foster care or adopted (Harper, 1996; Holody and Maher, 1996) or why they must move to a new placement (Hendry, 1988). Such complex, worrying and distressing matters need to be clarified and explored with children clearly and sensitively using the language and methods that are most appropriate for them.

Professionals' capacity to do this effectively in a way that is appropriate to their age, ability and culture is highly valued by children and young people. For example, almost half of young people in one study identified their guardian ad litem's[1] ability to explain matters relating to their care proceedings to them in a child–centred way as their second most important attribute (Bourton and McCausland, 2001). Children with learning difficulties found that when more visual and concrete methods were used by professionals they could make better sense of events and chronologies and understand why they were being adopted (Moroz, 1996).Young people involved in child protection conferences found information regarding them was most meaningful and comprehensible when provided in the form of leaflets with pictures, cartoons and word games (Howes, 2005).

Children and young people often need ongoing information and explanations to deal with the questions that arise for them (see Box 14). Researchers hearing from young people who had been through investigations and interventions following the disclosure of their sexual abuse advised that, 'given the potential for confusion, it may be necessary to repeat the information and explanation until everyone especially the child, has a clear understanding' (Prior et al, 1999, p 141). Shelley, a young woman previously in care, emphasised how social workers might need to 'translate' the complex concepts and jargon often used by carers or other professionals so that the child is able to participate in the conversation (quoted in Lefevre, 2008a).

Helping children and young people to be better informed about their lives is particularly important for those who have been in care over a number of years. Some end up with a sense of 'discontinuity between past and present' and 'an inner feeling of holes' due to never have been told some of the basic facts about their lives such as why, when and how they came into care (Harper, 1996, p 21). One child's life was likened to 'a badly constructed jigsaw' (Connor et al, 1985, p 34). Confusion, guilt, blame and fantasies abound for children and young people without these anchors (Moroz, 1996).

Burnell and Vaughan (2008) advise that practitioners thoroughly read through agency files to ensure that they are fully in possession of the facts. They should help children put these together with what they already know or remember so they can then check out any mis-information or misperceptions. Of course, agency files may sometimes be wrong, too, or simply not have the level of detail that the young person has held on to so it is important not to assume that, if the child's account and the file differ, it must be the child who is necessarily wrong. The information sharing and understanding process is often two-way, a careful co-construction of a narrative. Facts and reflections from other family members should also be brought into this to help flesh out the picture and to substantiate unclear or conflicting stories.

Box 14: The kinds of information children and young people say they need from their social workers

- More information to keep me up to date with what is happening that affects me
- More information about leaving care
- More information on people to turn to for friendly advice and help
- Information on different topics such as training, jobs, entitlements and counselling
- Being kept in touch more with what is happening in my birth family, to help move back there one day
- Information on my family and background, such as 'why I'm in care and why I can't see my dad'

How information should be provided

- Information to be available whenever I ask for it
- No secrets
- No telling other people before me, like my mum
- Keeping confidences

Source: Morgan (2006, pp 23-4)

Providing information about reports

A child-centred approach might mean providing clear and simplified summaries of reports, assessments and plans to young people. However, this should not necessarily be presumed. Children subject to care proceedings in one study advised that they wanted to be able to read the whole of reports about them and were not satisfied with having parts or summaries read to them (Masson and Oakley, 1999). Interest in full reports was not confined to teenagers. Some of the younger children just needed additional time to read and absorb information. Children did not mention being upset by the reports or finding them too long: 'It was the right to know and not have information concealed which was important' (Masson and Oakley, 1999, p 106).

Discussing particularly difficult or painful issues

Comment on the vignette

In situations such as that in which Tanya has found herself, social workers may become very preoccupied by what might be termed 'external' or 'outer world' matters (Schofield, 1998). They may focus on the 'doing' side of their role, such as identifying a foster placement, liaising with other professionals, parents and carers and ensuring the paperwork is completed. While such considerations are, of course, important, there is a danger that the time and attention needed for these may squeeze out the 'being' aspects of their role, those which enable them to get 'in touch' with children's 'inner' worlds. Yet it is these that help workers discover what children are feeling and experiencing when such distressing and unsettling things happen and what their needs, views and preferences might be.

In a busy work context it might feel easier for Tanya to get on with identifying a foster placement and simply then inform Caz and Jack that their mother has been unwell and that they and their baby sister, Isabella, need to go and stay with foster carers for a while until Theresa has recovered. Operating in this way neglects, however, four fundamental and interrelated aspects of communication.

Calibrating how much information children and young people need
The first relates to providing the right degree of complexity and explicitness in information and explanations provided to children. While all children have a right to information that concerns them, the integrative position set out in Chapter Two demands that practitioners should also consider the impact on children of learning very distressing or frightening information. How much detail they are given will also depend on the child's maturity and capacity to comprehend complex matters. Being told that his mother is 'unwell' may be enough information for a six-year-old, like Jack, to hear both cognitively and emotionally.

However, it is important also not to make assumptions about vocabulary, emotional resilience and conceptual understanding. Alderson (2000, p 244) generously provides an example of what happened when she became over-concerned with not using over-complex language when interviewing children about their response to surgery. She had asked a 10-year-old girl '"So you're having your legs made longer?" and the girl replied, "I suffer from achondroplasia and I am having my femurs lengthened"'. Mediating the level of explanation to protect a vulnerable child from distress may also relate more to the professional's over-protectiveness than the child's need. Young children have often seen matters deteriorate in the family home (such as in situations of domestic violence) and may need more honest and specific explanations to address their worries and confusion.

Jack Doyle, for example, has seen his mother become steadily more depressed; he has witnessed her not getting dressed, staring into space and alternating between ignoring the children and shouting at them. He has heard her yell at Caz, "I've had enough, you're pushing me to the edge. What do you want? Do you want me to just do myself in?". He has been frightened and bewildered by this and needs clarification and reassurance about whether or not his mother is going to be okay. Caz, at 14, will need a much more up-front and detailed conversation, particularly as she was the one who found her mother unconscious from an overdose and called for an ambulance.

Providing information in a way children and young people can make sense of
Second, children and young people will be able to understand more complex information and deal with more unsettling material when it is conveyed in a supportive and child-centred manner. Relying solely on direct verbal dialogue is not always the best way to help a child understand what has occurred and what might need to happen next, particularly with very young children or where there are learning difficulties or sensory impairments. It might help for Tanya to draw a picture for Jack showing the house where the family have originally lived, the hospital where Theresa is currently and the foster home. She might alternatively use small dolls or figures to represent each of the family members and show how they move around from one place to another according to the situation.

Ensuring children and young people are able to hear what is said
Third, children and young people's state of mind and 'inner world' need to be discerned to ensure that what professionals attempt to convey is received and decoded by them. While Caz might be expected to be able to comprehend the words of the explanation provided by Tanya, how she is feeling at that moment may mean that the 'meta-message' cannot be 'decoded' by her. Caz might feel responsible for her mother and worry that the suicide attempt was her fault. Her mind may well be in disarray and she will need patient and careful help disentangling her feelings.

This is also likely to be true of Jack, so Tanya might need to help him make sense of how and why his mother was often very sad, upset and angry if she is to help him comprehend what has happened. Isabella, a baby, cannot receive a straightforward verbal set of explanations but she will be emotionally and psychologically 'taking in' the mood of all those around her. The information that is transmitted to her inner world, through others' body language and paralanguage, might be that 'my mum is gone, no one is here for me, the world is unsafe'. Tanya must make sure that calmer, more containing messages are also provided for Isabella through both a sensitive physical 'holding' (Winnicott, 1965) by the foster carers and a psychological 'containment' by the whole system (Bion, 1962).

Consulting, not just telling
Fourth, a focus by a professional on explanations might ignore the *consultation* process that should also be included at such times. Tanya might feel that consulting with the children at this stage is pointless as the situation is a fait accompli: Theresa is unavailable to care for them; they have to live somewhere else; no extended family members are regularly in contact; a dual heritage foster placement is available which seems appropriate to the sibling group's mixed cultural and racial identity needs. Tanya might worry that if she asks the children what they want in this situation, they could ask for something

they cannot have; for example, they may come up with the idea that they should remain in the family home with Caz looking after the younger ones and a neighbour popping in to keep an eye on them.

This would be a misunderstanding by Tanya of what consultation means, however. It is not about presenting children with a simulacrum of open choice ('Where would you want to live right now?') when there are, in fact, very limited options. Instead consultation is about realistic and informed choices. It entails clarifying to children what the parameters might be, helping them understand and explore what their thoughts and feelings are about this and identifying what they *can* influence about the situation. This is more transparent and recognises the competence children often have to deal with difficult realities.

Reflective exercise

Reflect on the following questions to consider how you might deal with a situation where you have to discuss very difficult issues with a child or young person. The questions are based on guidance provided by Trevithick et al (2008b) to help practitioners prepare for breaking bad news to service users and carers. If you are not already working in a context where this is immediately applicable, imagine a situation where you might need to do so in order to carry out this exercise:

1. First of all, identify a situation where you need to explore and discuss difficult or worrying issues with a child or young person. Identify the issues, the characteristics of the child or young person and, where possible, base this on a real person or situation and your usual work role.
2. Now imagine that you are about to receive the same kind of information, advice or explanations as the child or young person in your scenario:
    a. How might you feel about this?
    b. What might you need from the person communicating this to you to help you understand this and manage the feelings evoked?
3. Now think about what you know about the child or young person:
    a. How might they feel about what you are discussing with them?
    b. How might they react to the content of the discussion?
    c. What might they want from you in the communication?
4. Think about how best to discuss these issues in terms of:
    a. the setting and where best to communicate with the child or young person;
    b. who else might need to be present to provide comfort, support or assistance within the bounds of their role;

   c. your choice of words, tone and timing and other non-verbal forms
      of communication that could be helpful and provide comfort and
      reassurance;
   d. how to avoid being interrupted.
5. What additional or follow-up work may be needed in order to ensure
   that the child or young person is able to cope and to manage the feelings
   and reactions that they are experiencing?
6. What support might you need? How are you likely to react or be left
   feeling? Who could provide you with that support?
7. Think about how to tie up any loose ends, including any practical
   arrangements that need to be dealt with.

Issues of confidentiality

> "I don't trust my social worker because she tells other people my
> business. For example, if I have a fight she might tell my school or
> the police. My perfect worker would keep my problems to herself
> and help me out more." (Mica, age 12, quoted in Headliners, 2009)

Discussing sensitive and concerning issues with children and young people
raises the thorny issue of confidentiality. Many young people feel strongly
that they need a confidential space to think through difficult issues and are
deeply unhappy when what they have disclosed has been shared with others
without their permission or perhaps even their knowledge (Munro, 2001).
Some become reluctant to share their thoughts and feelings with social
workers because they know it will be written down in files and might be
shared with strangers (Carroll, 2002). Once the information is out of their
mouths they can no longer control where it goes or what the consequences
may be. It has been suggested that this lack of confidentiality has 'a real and
detrimental effect on the quality and depth of the relationship' that children
and their social workers form and may mean that young people, in particular,
might 'at times withhold topics of concern' (Ryan et al, 1995, p 139).

  This can present practitioners with an ethical dilemma regarding the
best way to proceed. A common law duty of confidentiality exists between
social workers and people who use services and their carers. This means
that, generally, information given by an individual that they wish to be kept
confidential should not be passed on to a third party without permission.
This common law duty also applies to practice with children and young
people, but with certain caveats. While a 16- or 17-year-old is normally
treated like an adult, with the entitlement for them to give or refuse their
consent to information about them being passed on, for children under
16 this is dependent on their capacity to understand and make their own

decisions. If professionals believe them to have this capacity, then children can withhold their consent to information being shared.

Children aged between 12 and 16 are generally assumed to have sufficient understanding to give, or refuse, their consent. This draws on the principle of 'Gillick' or 'Fraser' competence, case law which sets out that it is not children's chronological age which determines competence but whether they have sufficient understanding and intelligence to comprehend what is being proposed and to make a choice in their own best interests. If children under the age of 16 are thought to demonstrate sufficient maturity and understanding, then they may be treated for all intents and purposes as if they were 16 and thus able to make reasoned decisions. A fuller assessment is generally required with children younger than 12 to ensure that they understand the issues being discussed (DfES, 2006b).

Some of those who align themselves more with a children's rights perspective[2] emphasise the sanctity of this common law duty to protect children and young people's confidences and suggest that it is often inappropriately transgressed under the guise of protection. They urge professionals to respect children and young people's inherent capability to know and express their wishes and feelings regarding confidentiality and to allow them to operate as the experts in their own lives. Daniels and Jenkins (2000, p 553), writing about therapeutic work from this paradigm, suggest that young people who disclose abusive experiences are not always asking for protection but are trying to establish solutions to their difficulties through exploring the situation with a professional, and are capable of a 'mature decision' regarding this. They advise practitioners to clarify whether their anxieties about the repercussions of not sharing information are a powerful 'rescuer fantasy' or 'omnipotent counter-transference' which should be contained and discussed in supervision rather than being acted on.

By contrast, those who are concerned with children's vulnerability more than their capability talk of seeing children struggling to make sense of what has happened to them and comprehend the significance and impact of their disclosures. They advise that such children need the professional to 'be the adult' and look after them (Gewirth, 2001). Few professionals work in isolation; most are part of multidisciplinary networks or 'Teams Around the Child' within integrated children's services. It is often only when information is shared that a fuller picture can emerge and this prompts government guidance regarding information sharing, such as that contained in *Working together to safeguard children* (HM Government, 2006).

An ethical dilemma regarding confidentiality

Practice vignette: A young person's wish for confidentiality

All three children are now in foster care. Tanya is visiting them regularly and spending time with Jack and Caz separately to explore their thoughts and feelings about Theresa's suicide attempt, their move to foster care and what their hopes and fears are for the future. Caz is initially quite cagey and Tanya needs to take time to carefully build a relationship and a safe space for her to talk. Eventually Caz blurts out that she hopes Theresa stays in the psychiatric unit as life is much better in care: "At least we all get fed here". Almost as quickly as she has said it, Caz tries to bite it back: "I didn't mean it, please don't tell anyone I said it, don't tell my mum". Tanya is very disconcerted as she realises she has not carefully explained the confidentiality ground rules with Caz as she should have done. She is worried about destroying the slender trust that has been established between them.

Comment on the vignette

Professionals such as Tanya need to make a carefully considered judgement as a young person's refusal of consent does not necessarily preclude the sharing of confidential information (see Box 15). It is permissible to breach confidentiality if it will mean the practitioner preventing a crime or acting in the public interest. One example of this could be where a young person has confessed criminal behaviour and intentions to their social worker. Another is where what the child or young person has said indicates that they are suffering or at risk of suffering significant harm. For Tanya, the picture is less clear-cut. What Caz has said has real implications for the welfare of all the children, but this leads to suspicions of significant harm rather than any clear evidence.

The Doyle family live in England, where Section 47(10) of the 1989 Children Act does not oblige practitioners to disclose all concerns about a child to the interprofessional safeguarding system 'where doing so would be unreasonable in all the circumstances of the case'. This might include situations where a child or young person has expressed strong feelings against this. Tanya will need to weigh up with her supervisor what might happen if what Caz has said is shared with others (and her mother) against what might happen if it is not. They would need to consider very carefully how Caz's wishes being overridden might possibly rupture the burgeoning therapeutic relationship and cause Caz to feel more powerless.

Sometimes this is an issue of timing. When concerns are immediate and serious, then action needs to be taken quickly. In other situations, such as this one, the children are safe and cared for at present, so it might be more constructive to allow some negotiated space for Caz to think and talk some more before the information is discussed within the system, or with Theresa (Cooper et al, 2003). Tanya does, however, need to give Caz very clear guidance now about the confidentiality parameters of what she says (as she should have done at the beginning of their involvement) and not make any promises about keeping information secret. Research suggests that when boundaries and limits to confidentiality are clearly explained to children and young people in a manner that is appropriate to the situation and their level of understanding then they are empowered to make better decisions for themselves (Ryan et al, 1995; van Rooyen and Engelbrecht, 2001). Even quite young children may understand reasons why workers might need to pass on information about them (Carroll, 2002).

It is helpful to follow up verbal discussions about this with written information (Bell, 2002), such as the sample written agreement that is provided in Chapter Seven.

Box 15: Key questions to guide whether a child or young person's request for information to be kept confidential should be overridden

1. Is there a legitimate purpose for you or your agency to share this information with parents, carers or other professionals or should it be viewed as confidential?
2. Has the child asked you to keep it confidential?
3. Is there a statutory duty or court order to share the information?
4. If the child refuses consent for you to share certain information, or there are good reasons why you should not seek the child's consent, is there a sufficient 'public interest' to share the information, such as safeguarding concerns?
5. If the decision is to share, are you sharing the right amount of information in the right way with the right people?
6. Have you properly recorded your decision?

Guidance

1. Wherever possible, explain at the outset to children, openly, honestly and clearly, what and how information will be shared.
2. Seek their consent to sharing confidential information.

3.   Only share information if, in your judgement, there is sufficient need to override their lack of consent. Always consider both children's rights to confidentiality and their safety and welfare.
4.   Seek advice where you are in doubt.
5.   Ensure the information is accurate and up to date, necessary, shared only with those people who need to see it and shared securely.
6.   Always record the reasons for your decision, whether it is to share information or not.

Source: Based on DfES (2006a)

Involving children and young people in meetings

"When I was eight years old I started going to Team Around the Child meetings with my mum. There were lots of adults there. At first I was shy but now they ask me things and I can say what I would like to happen and they listen to me." (Tilly, age 9, quoted in Youth Pathways to Employment, 2008)

Children and young people are keen to be involved in meetings about them. They want to know what is going on, to have the opportunity to 'have their say' and to be supported through this process (Cleaver et al, 2004, p 590); and, indeed, they have a right to this. Including children in meetings such as reviews and child protection conferences where a number of professionals are attending and difficult subjects are under discussion should not be undertaken lightly, however. They need to be fully prepared for their attendance (Howes, 2005). This includes receiving explanations in advance of what the purpose of the meeting is, who will be there and what their own role is. They may also need support in the conference from an advocate or similar person who is independent of the other professionals attending the conference. Children and young people will often want reassurance, too, about how sensitive topics will be discussed. They may not want certain information about them discussed openly in front of them and they may be worried about how parents or carers will react if certain things are said.

Calibrating children and young people's level of involvement in a meeting

Practice vignette: Involving the Doyle children in a review

The children's first looked-after child review is approaching. Tanya needs to consider whether and how to involve each of them in the meeting. Even if they do not appear in person, she must ensure that their views are fully represented and taken into account in decision making and planning.

Comment on the vignette

Young people of Caz's age and cognitive ability may well feel able to participate in the whole of a meeting, once they have been well briefed. It is essential that professionals at meetings, however, remember that a young person may feel intimidated by them because of the authority, status and 'cultural capital'[3] their role and education bring. Many children and young people interviewed about their participation in child protection conferences said they had felt intimidated by the size and formality of meetings (Bell, 2002). Careful attention to seating, language (particularly no jargon), breaks and body language can help a young person feel comfortable and welcomed. The chair of the meeting should take responsibility for ensuring young people are following proceedings and that their views on discussions are carefully elicited and noted. Without this, they are likely to feel marginalised and dismissed (Biehal et al, 1995; Williamson and Butler, 1995; Dearden and Becker, 2000).

It may not be appropriate for a child or young person to attend the whole meeting, however. One reason for this would be where a meeting is held to discuss a whole sibling group. A young person might then only be invited in to the part of the meeting that refers specifically to him or herself. Another reason is where a child's age or capacities make attendance throughout unhelpful for them. Promoting children's participation is not about lip service. Jack, for example, is only six years old and has some difficulties with concentration. He is likely to find sitting through a long meeting quite intolerable and the discussion often impossible to follow. Coming in to a carefully managed part of the meeting, perhaps with fewer people present, might feel much safer or manageable to him.

Advocating for children

Whether they have been able to attend in person or not, children and young people's views must be fully represented to a meeting. Even if they have prepared what to say, their views may not come across clearly. Their keyworker should ensure information is clarified and repeated if necessary. Including an advocate in the meeting may be particularly beneficial. Advocates support other people in expressing their views, preferences and decisions, but do not make choices or decisions for them (see Box 16 for a summary of the skills involved in advocacy). If Jack Doyle, for example, told an advocate he wanted to go straight back home to live with his mother, the advocate's role would be to ensure that the meeting understood this was Jack's preference. It would then be for the other professionals to hear this view and to take it into account within their decision making and planning. Where independent advocates have been involved to support children in addition to the work carried out by their key social workers, children's participation in decision making and planning forums appears to have been strengthened (Howes, 2005).

Box 16: The main communication skills involved in advocacy

- Careful listening
- Accurate note taking
- Explaining the process
- Taking instructions from clients
- Gathering relevant information
- Feeding back lucidly
- Negotiating for improvements

Source: Brandon (2000, p 7)

Working with difficult, aggressive or threatening behaviour

Practice vignette: Managing difficult behaviour by Jack

Jack's behaviour, which had been challenging in both the family home and school environment, is no better in foster care. In fact, it deteriorates as the uncertainty about his mother's well-being and his future care continues. Tanya is working closely with the foster carers to support them in management of this using behavioural strategies (Jenner, 2008). She has also made an appointment to consult with the local child and adolescent mental health service to discuss what else she might try and whether play therapy or family therapy might be appropriate. She recognises, however, that it is essential she keeps engaged with Jack to explore his feelings and help him make sense of his situation, so she continues to meet weekly with him in the school counselling room. Tanya has become anxious, however, about how to contain Jack and keep them both safe as he has starting kicking out at her.

Comment on the vignette

Some children and young people (particularly girls) deal with emotional distress, trauma and disruption in their lives through *internalising* their feelings. These difficult emotions and thoughts are turned in on the self and may manifest themselves through self-harming behaviour, depression, eating disorders or low self-esteem, for example. Others (especially boys) *externalise* their inner experience, projecting it outwards on to others as anger, aggression, disruptiveness, violence or criminal activity. Professionals may not only be working with parents and carers to help them manage their child's difficult behaviour, but, like Tanya, may well find themselves on the receiving end of it, struggling with children and young people who swear or spit at them, prod or poke them, threaten them, throw things at them or damage property. The following principles should be followed in such situations.

Helping children and young people express their feelings in less challenging ways

When children and young people are exhibiting difficult behaviours such as those enacted by Jack, practitioners must strive to remain empathically in touch with where this behaviour has originated from and recognise it as an additional form of communication, another of the 'hundred languages of childhood'. Words can act as a container of emotions, so verbalising what is felt can be an excellent way of releasing affect. Where children cannot fully articulate the pain, terror, hurt and insecurity they feel, these emotions fill them up until they are overflowing – so they then have to be either repressed (internalising) or spilt out over others (externalising). Psychodynamic theories would also suggest that such feelings may be 'split off' and 'projected' into workers, so that they end up feeling the same shame, pain, fear, and so on, that the child is experiencing.

Helping children and young people find a more constructive way of naming and expressing their inner feelings might improve matters, perhaps using some of the methods described in Chapter Ten, such as writing poetry, banging drums or painting.

Individual therapy might additionally be needed for children such as Jack, but it is *always* the role of the keyworker in situations such as this to keep helping children explore and express their feelings. The link that social workers have between children, their siblings and their parents, between foster homes, birth homes and school, uniquely positions them to help children make the necessary links between their 'inner and outer worlds' (Schofield, 1998). Feeling heard and understood in these ways can often help difficult behaviour to dissipate.

The role of workers in provoking difficult feelings in children and young people

Workers should also recognise and acknowledge any part they may have played in provoking angry feelings in children and young people, however unwittingly. Jack may be kicking out at Tanya because she is the person who told him what had happened to his mother and took him to foster care. He may well associate her with these events, even blame her for them. Tanya could try to name this to Jack and explore his feelings towards her.

Tanya has done her best to be sensitive, caring and empathic in the way that she has worked with Jack. However, a practitioner who is not always thoughtful, reflective, gentle or compassionate, who misses appointments, turns up late and forgets what she has been told, may be partly liable for inflaming a situation – although they cannot be held responsible for causing aggression or violence in another. Workers must always consider whether their own behaviour may be at fault and always apologise if they think it may be. Genuine regretfulness can go a long way to repairing ruptured relationships and allowing someone's anger to make way for deeper feelings such as loss or sadness. It is no loss of professional authority to apologise; indeed it models excellent qualities of maturity, self-awareness and humility that are very helpful for children and young people to experience.

Containing children and young people's behaviour

Dangerous, aggressive or violent behaviour by children needs to be contained at both a psychological and physical level. Children like Jack often feel frightened or out of control themselves and have a psychological need for a boundary to be placed around them until they can begin to introject an inner sense of safety and security. This need to deal with the fear and distress underlying anger and aggression is as true of teenagers (and adults) as it is of younger children and can be easy to forget when the worker, too, becomes frightened or irritated by a young person's behaviour. Boundaries can be best provided through clear ground rules for behaviour (written into a contract) and the worker's own manner, which should be calm, kind and empathic but also firm and authoritative. Personal authority and professionalism is essential to maintain, so that the worker is able to project a sense that they can manage the situation and keep it safe for everyone.

In all situations it is important to make sound organisational arrangements to maintain safety (see Box 17) and to know the agency procedures regarding restraint in case a child or young person's behaviour becomes unmanageable or dangerous to themselves or others. It is vital to work closely with parents, carers and all other professionals involved with the child so that information is shared regularly about how they are and whether anything has happened which might make them particularly volatile on a given day. If, for example, Tanya is to be telling Jack that his mother remains unwell and he will be remaining in the foster home for at least a few more weeks, it might be sensible to do so in the presence of the foster carer. The two adults should carefully prepare how to talk with Jack about the situation and to deal with his feelings both during the meeting and afterwards, as the carers are likely to have a very difficult evening with him.

Box 17: Organisational arrangements to keep situations safe if a child or young person has a history of frightening, aggressive or violent behaviour

When seeing children and young people in an establishment or office setting, work out a contingency plan beforehand:

- Know the location of alarm/panic buttons.
- Ensure colleagues are available in the vicinity and aware of the situation.
- Position yourself within easy reach of the door but ensure that the exit path for the young person is not blocked.
- Ensure there are no obviously dangerous implements available (such as sharp scissors).
- Work in a room where windows only open a small amount so the child cannot climb out and put themselves in danger.

When meeting with children and young people in their family or foster homes, in other settings or out in the community:

- Make a careful risk assessment with your manager/supervisor.
- Carry a mobile phone.
- Ensure that your agency are aware of your whereabouts and movements.

- Work with another colleague when considered appropriate for your safety and the safety of others, including the young person.

In all cases regularly share information with parents and carers and be particularly alert when something has happened to distress, anger or unsettle the child or young person.

Source: Based on Trevithick et al (2008b)

Communication through touch

Whether and when it might be appropriate or permissible to touch children and young people is not always clear to professionals. The custom and practice of many organisations is that social workers do not normally touch children or only for particular purposes and in certain ways. However, this is not necessarily written into agency guidelines or into professional codes of conduct, such as the GSCC (2002) code of practice. This suggests that there is uncertainty about if and when certain kinds of touch might be appropriate. In fact, in what has been called our 'risk society' (Webb, 2006), there seems to be a great deal of fear attached to touch, both in relation to the risk posed to children but also the risk posed to practitioners if a child or young person were to misinterpret any touch.

Touch for practical purposes

Tanya's work with the Doyle family helps uncover some aspects of when touch might or might not be appropriate. When Tanya was taking baby Isabella to the foster home, she needed to pick her up and carry her at times. She also needed to touch Jack in passing when making sure he was safely strapped into her car. She did not need to touch Caz to do that as Caz was able to carry this task out for herself. If Theresa had been present, it would have been more appropriate for her to carry Isabella and strap Jack in. Now the children know the foster carers, they would be the first choice to manage any physical assistance the children needed in future.

Through this example it can be seen that the appropriateness of touch is, then, *based on the help the child or young person needs.* This derives from their age and capacities, the professional role and the availability of their primary carers. When working in a play-based way with children, for example, physical touch might be a practical and natural part of the work (Johnson, 2000). Children's hands may become covered in paint and glue and they may well need help cleaning them and drying them off. A practitioner who did not do so might actually be rather neglectful.

This highlights the point made in Chapter Eight about why some children with complex healthcare needs or other physical disabilities can be more vulnerable to abuse: more adults are entitled to touch them as part of daily care practices and so unsafe touch can more easily take place.

Touch to communicate comfort

Physical touch can promote connection, be reassuring and share warmth, particularly where a child or young person is frightened or distressed (Davidhizar, 1991). However, physical touch by professionals is not always welcomed by children and young people, nor is it always appropriate for their needs. Those who have been sexually abused might feel very unsafe with touch, as they might perceive a reassuring pat on the arm as similar to the 'grooming' process their abuser initiated. A worker who gives a child an affectionate hug or cuddle when distressed could also set up a child's expectations of a closer relationship than the social worker can provide and may leave the child very unclear about boundaries. The meaning of touch can also vary between cultures, and could result in a very different message being transmitted between worker and child than was intended. For these reasons, affectionate touch is normally not sanctioned between field social workers and children and young people.

However, in a residential setting, where workers are acting in a caring capacity towards children and young people, physical affection and touch as part of caregiving will be much more the norm. Indeed, where this was forbidden it could leave children very touch-deprived, which would be damaging to their emotional well-being. Residential units will have their own guidance for practitioners to follow, which might include ensuring that cuddles generally happen in the presence of others, that workers do not touch certain parts of the child's body (for example, legs or buttocks) and that there is no physical chastisement.

A particular area of struggle for practitioners is children who initiate affection towards them; for example, a child who jumps on their lap while they are on the sofa, or holds out their arms for a cuddle, saying "I love you". In my own experience, this has usually tended to happen with children I have not known for very long and who have been very neglected and/ or sexualised. They have responded to my friendliness in a way that has illuminated their emotional hunger or lack of clarity about boundaries. Practitioners should aim to find a way of managing such situations which ends the physical contact as quickly as possible but also does not shame or reject the child. I have found it helpful to say warmly but firmly as I lift the child off my lap, "Let's sit you back on the sofa, though, as that will be much more comfortable for us both".

Keeping in regular contact with children

Practice vignette: Maintaining ongoing contact with children in care

Theresa has left the psychiatric unit and is now home, receiving outpatient care, including medication, counselling and support from a community psychiatric nurse. She is starting to re-engage in assessment work, although not yet feeling strong enough to contemplate if, when and how the children might return to her care. However, she is having regular supervised contact with the children. As lead professional, Tanya is working closely with Theresa, liaising with all the other agencies, supporting the foster placement and organising contact sessions. One of the most important aspects of her role, however, is continuing to see the children regularly, keeping them informed, giving them a space to reflect on what is happening, hearing what they have to say and helping them with their feelings.

Comment on the vignette

As the vignette highlights, it is a central aspect of the social work role for there to be regular contact with children and young people in care. Social workers can keep in contact with children not just by visits but also through telephone calls, letters, email and text messages.

Telephone calls

"If something is wrong you should be able to ring them…. Every social worker could have an emergency care phone so you could ring the number." (quoted in Morgan, 2006, p 13)

Young people often welcome telephone calls, finding them an important way for their social worker to check that they are okay or pass on information to them quickly. Being able to ring the worker themselves is also important and helps accessibility and availability. Just leaving messages on impersonal answerphones or with people they do not know is not good enough. Instead, young people suggest, all social workers should be given a mobile phone to help them remain in contact with the children and young people on their caseload and to be available when they are needed (Morgan, 2006).

Letters

Written communications by the worker to children and young people are not only helpful in providing clear information, but can also have therapeutic benefits. Marner (1995) and Wood (1985) describe letters they have written to children after meeting with them in which they summarise the strengths, insights, actions and intentions that the child had demonstrated or discussed in the session. Rather than this being just a way of communicating a record of progress (in itself of use), it can demonstrate to children that they have been witnessed and understood. A particular advantage of such written communication can be that 'in letters words do not fade away but may be read and re-read' (Marner, 1995, p 171).

Email

Some professionals, depending on their role and setting, are also now in contact with young people by email, harnessing the medium commonly used by them. A particular advantage of email is accessibility and availability – young people in care, for example, know exactly where they can leave a message for their social worker. But workers do need to be alert to possible miscommunications due to the absence of the non-verbal cues that usually provide contextual information in conversation and can influence interpretation of meaning (Hunt, 2002). This is likely to be particularly the case for younger children who are even more dependent on non-verbal gestural cues than teenagers (Doherty-Sneddon and Kent, 1996).

   If organisational guidance permits email contact, then it is important to warn young people that workers may not be able to respond as quickly as young people might like or expect. Sending emails into a non-responsive void can provoke anxiety in anyone, let alone distressed and insecure young people. They may need reassurance that a delayed response may simply mean the worker is dealing with urgent business. Setting up the 'out of office' message on the email system is helpful, too, as this automatically conveys that information to the young person.

Text messages

Text messages, although the most widespread manner by which young people in the UK keep in touch with each other, are not yet commonly used between children and their social workers. In part this may be because not all practitioners are allocated a work mobile phone. It also relates, however, to the concerns raised above by email. Messages can seem curt or brusque. In their private lives individuals often put a 'kiss' (x) at the end to signify humour or friendliness and 'warm up' the message. It would not be appropriate, of course, for social workers to do this, although smiley faces can be used, for example :-). Another issue is of managing the boundary of what to do if text messages are received late at night or at weekends and how quickly they should be replied to. Given these complexities, it is probably most appropriate to keep text messaging for situations where there is a need to remind young people about appointments, such as in youth offending services or sexual health clinics. However, it will be important for practitioners to negotiate with young people about this as they may feel marginalised or sidelined if their usual communicative practices are rejected.

Social networking

'Blogging',[4] 'tweeting' via Twitter[5] and social networking on sites such as Bebo, MySpace or Facebook[6] are a way of life for many young people now. It would not normally be appropriate for social workers to keep in touch with children and young people via these as the boundaries would be much harder to manage and there would be a danger of confidential information coming into the public domain. Conversations about why this is can be very important as it enables young people and their social workers to begin to explore together the complex nature of the professional boundary between them. Practitioners who use such sites themselves should be wary of young people seeking them out and accessing their personal information. Most sites have 'privacy settings' to enable careful management of this.

Ending interactions with children

It is always important to consider how best to bring an interaction or episode of communication to an end. Every ending is unique, with its nature and significance connected to whether it relates to a one-off meeting or the ending of a keyworking relationship spanning months or years. Even within very short-term interactions, such as an initial assessment, duty visit or a child protection investigation, the social worker's role may have been very momentous to a child or young person. Children still need practitioners to say goodbye properly to them, by making eye contact with them and demonstrating by their body language that the interaction has been meaningful for them both.

Koprowska (2008) distinguishes between endings that are planned and unplanned and those where the work is complete or incomplete, including some situations where the intervention with a child will be transferred to another worker. Where the work is successfully completed, there can be a sense of satisfaction, even pride, for both child and worker. Conversely, the work may have ended in a way that has left one or both of them with uncomfortable feelings. Either way it is most helpful if worker and child or young person can together find a way of honouring what has occurred between them during their time together, clarifying what has been covered and what information needs to be shared with others. This can help the child 'to "close down" and return to his or her usual ways of coping' (Bannister, 2001, p 137).

Endings of individual sessions can be models or precursors of the final ending between worker and young person that is to come. Where the worker has always been open and explicit about the length of sessions and the overall intervention, has prepared children and young people for holiday breaks and has given time at the end of each session to 'clearing up time', this has already communicated to them that endings are something to be managed. The reverse is also true.

Where the contact has been longer term, children and young people may have formed a significant affiliation to a worker. This needs particularly sensitive handling for those who have experienced significant losses and disruptions or have an insecure attachment pattern. Elbow (1987) suggests worker and child complete something like a 'memory book' together as a way to enhance their communication about the ending. The book could include a review of reasons for the worker and young person initially coming together, the issues that were dealt with, what was accomplished, the reason for termination and the meaning of termination for both the child and worker. Elbow emphasises that (as with life story work) the process is as important as the content. The worker should use the book as a means of facilitating the termination work, not to replace it.

Where workers, themselves, have difficulties with facing endings, this is likely to be enacted in their work with children and young people. One aspect of the 'knowing oneself' aspect of the core capabilities model will thus be self-awareness regarding how the worker has previously faced up to significant endings in his or her life. If the worker's usual pattern is to avoid or downplay endings it may be more difficult for them to appreciate the importance to children and young people of having plenty of warning for endings and of having them talked about.

Reflective exercise

Think about ending the work with a child or young person you had known professionally for some time.

- What were your feelings and thoughts about this work coming to an end? Can you notice any ways in which your own common relational patterns emerged? (For example, how hard you found it to let go, or talk about the ending, or your tendency to acknowledge the reality that you might not ever see this child or young person again.)
- How well prepared for the ending was the young person? Did he/she know it was coming?
- Was the child or young person clear about the reasons for the ending and the outcomes of the work? (For example, did you verbally explain decisions and recommendations, following this up in written form where necessary?)
- Did you talk directly with them about their feelings about endings? If so, how? If not, what prevented you?

Now do the same exercise in relation to a child or young person where the contact was very brief.

- Are any of the processes/issues similar? Should you be giving more attention to how you end brief interventions?

Conclusion

This book has covered a range of ways in which social workers and other professionals might communicate with children and young people. It has highlighted and discussed the kinds of knowledge, personal qualities, emotional capacities, ethics, values, skills and techniques that workers will need to draw on to underpin their practice. These were grouped together under the 'core capabilities' model of 'knowing, being and doing', set out in Chapter Five. In particular the book has emphasised the right children and young people have to be informed, involved, consulted and supported by competent practitioners who fully engage themselves in caring professional relationships with them.

There have been a number of exercises through the book to help practitioners develop their communicative capabilities. In the 'Key questions' section at the end of this final chapter, readers are asked to reflect on what they have learned through the book as a whole and how they might try to develop their communication with children and young people in the future.

The final words should be given over to the voices of the children and young people cited through this book who, through the time and effort they have given to research studies and consultations, are able to inspire us all to more effective relationship-based practice with them. I have chosen a quote from one of the young people who responded to the Children's Commissioner for England (Morgan, 2006) about what they thought an ideal social worker should be like. It summarises some of the main messages that have underpinned the 11 chapters of this book regarding what a social worker should both 'do' and 'be':

> "… support, advice, friend, someone I can trust, someone I know really cares about me, not just a number or a client who they really don't care about … not just someone who just read the textbook." (in Morgan, 2006, p 28)

Notes

[1] The functions of the guardian ad litem in care proceedings have now been taken over by children's guardians in Cafcass (Children and Family Court Advisory Support Service) in England and Cafcass Cymru in Wales.

[2] The importance of attending to both needs and rights, both vulnerability and capability, seeing children as 'both beings and becomings' (Uprichard, 2008) was discussed in Chapter Two.

[3] Cultural capital was defined in Chapter Six.

[4] Blogging is the common term for a 'web log' or online journal written for public consumption. See www.blogger.com for more information.

[5] Twitter is an online forum for social connection, enabling people to respond to the question 'What are you doing?' and follow others' responses to this. Postings must be under 140 characters in length and can be sent via mobile texting, instant message or the web. See www.twitter.com/about

[6] Facebook, Bebo and MySpace are social networking sites providing opportunities for comments on one's own and others' activities, sharing photographs, video and music, undertaking quizzes and making new friends. See www.facebook.com, www.bebo.com, www.myspace.com

Key questions

1. What do you think were the most important messages in this book about effective communication with children and young people?
2. What have you learned about yourself as a communicator?
3. What other knowledge, personal qualities or skills might you need to further develop and how will you go about this?

Further reading and resources

Luckock, B. and Lefevre, M. (eds) (2008) *Direct work: Social work with children and young people in care*, London: BAAF.

Thomas, N. (2005) *Social work with young people in care: Looking after children in theory and practice*, Basingstoke: Palgrave Macmillan.

Trevithick, P. (2005) *Social work skills: A practice handbook* (2nd edn), Maidenhead: Open University Press and McGraw-Hill Education.

Trevithick, P., Richards, S. and Lefevre, M. (2008) *Communicating in challenging situations*, London: Social Care Institute for Excellence (www.scie.org.uk/publications/elearning/cs/cs07/index.asp) [this is an interactive e-learning resource, available to use free of charge on the SCIE website].

References

Augmentative Communication in Practice: Scotland (ed) (2003) *Augmentative communication in practice: An introduction*, Edinburgh: Scottish Executive Education Department (http://callcentre.education.ed.ac.uk/SCN/Intro_SCA/IntroIN_SCB/introin_scb.html).

Ahmad, A., Betts, B. and Cowan, L. (2008) 'Using interactive media in direct practice', in B. Luckock and M. Lefevre (eds) *Direct work: Social work with children and young people in care*, London: BAAF, pp 169-80.

Ahmed, S. (1986) 'Cultural racism in work with Asian women and girls', in S. Ahmed, J. Cheetham and J. Small (eds) *Social work with black children and their families*, London: B.T. Batsford Ltd.

Ahmed, S. (1994) 'Anti-racist social work: a black perspective', in C. Hanvey and T. Philpot (eds) *Practising social work*, London: Routledge.

Ahn, J. and Filipenko, M. (2007) 'Narrative, imaginary play, art, and self: intersecting worlds', *Early Childhood Education Journal*, vol 34, no 4, pp 279-89.

Ainsworth, M.D.S., Blehar, M.C., Waters, E. and Wall, S. (1978) *Patterns of attachment*, Hillsdale, NJ: Erlbaum.

Alderson, P. (2000) 'Children as researchers', in P. Christensen and A. James (eds) *Research with children*, London: Falmer Press, pp 241-57.

Aldgate, J., Jones, D., Rose, W. and Jeffery, C. (2006) *The developing world of the child*, London: Jessica Kingsley Publishers.

Aldridge, J. and Becker, S. (1993) *Children who care: Inside the world of young carers*, Loughborough: Young Carers Research Group, University of Loughborough.

Alvin, J. (1966) *Music therapy*, London: Hutchinson.

Anderson, P.A. (1990) 'Explaining intercultural differences in nonverbal communication', in L.A. Smovar and R.E. Porter (eds) *Intercultural communication: A reader*, Belmont, CA: Wadsworth.

Applewhite, L.W. and Joseph, M.V. (1994) 'Confidentiality: issues in working with self-harming adolescents', *Child and Adolescent Social Work Journal*, vol 11, no 4, pp 279-94.

Archard, D. and Skivenes, M. (2009) 'Hearing the child', *Child & Family Social Work*, vol 14, no 4, pp 391-9.

Atkins-Burnett, S. and Allen-Meares, P. (2000) 'Infants and toddlers with disabilities: relationship-based approaches', *Social Work*, vol 45, no 4, pp 371-9.

Austin, D. and Halpin, W. (1987) 'Seeing "I to I": a phenomenological analysis of the caring relationship', *Journal of Child Care*, vol 3, no 3, pp 37-42.

Axline, V. (1969) *Play therapy*, New York, NY: Ballantyne Books.

Bannister, A. (2001) 'Entering the child's world: communicating with children to assess their needs', in J. Horwath (ed) *The child's world: Assessing children in need*, London: Jessica Kingsley Publishers, pp 129-39.

Barker, P. (1985) *Using metaphors in psychotherapy*, New York, NY: Brunner/Mazel.

Barthes, R. (1972) *Mythologies* (translated by Annette Lavers), New York, NY: Hill and Wang.

Bell, M. (2002) 'Promoting children's rights through the use of relationship', *Child & Family Social Work*, vol 7, pp 1-11.

Betts, B. and Ball, N. (2004) *Bridget's taking a long time*, CD-ROM, Information Plus.

Bick, E. (1964) 'Notes on infant observation in psychoanalytic training', *International Journal of Psychoanalysis*, vol 45, pp 484-6.

Biehal, N., Clayden, J., Stein, M. and Wade, J. (1995) *Moving on: Young people and leaving care schemes*, London: HMSO.

Bion, W. (1962) *Learning from experience*, London: Heinemann.

Blom-Cooper, L. (1985) *A child in trust*, Wembley: London Borough of Brent.

Bolton, G. (1999) *The therapeutic potential of creative writing: Writing myself*, London: Jessica Kingsley Publishers.

Bourdieu, P. (1991) *Language and symbolic power*, Cambridge: Polity Press.

Bourton, A. and McCausland, J. (2001) 'A service for children and a service for the courts: the contribution of guardians ad litem in public law proceedings', *Adoption and Fostering*, vol 25, no 3, pp 59-66.

Bowlby, J. (1969) *Attachment and loss, Volume 1: Attachment*, London: The Hogarth Press and The Institute of Psychoanalysis.

Bowlby, J. (1988) *A secure base: Clinical applications of attachment theory*, London: Routledge.

Brandon, D. (2000) 'Advocacy', in M. Davies (ed) *The Blackwell companion to social work* (2nd edn), Oxford: Blackwell.

Braye, S. and Preston-Shoot, M. (2005) 'Emerging from out of the shadows? Service user and carer involvement in systematic reviews', *Evidence & Policy*, vol 1, no 2, pp 173-93.

Briggs, S. (1999) 'Links between infant observation and reflective social work practice', *Journal of Social Work Practice*, vol 13, no 2, pp 147-56.

Bright, R. (1993) 'Cultural aspects of music in therapy', in M. Heal and T. Wigram (eds) *Music therapy in health and education*, London: Jessica Kingsley, pp 193-207.

Broadhurst, K., Wastell, D., White, S., Hall, C., Peckover, S., Thompson, K., Pithouse, A. and Davey, D. (2010) 'Performing "initial assessment": identifying the latent conditions for error at the front door of local authority children's services', *British Journal of Social Work*, vol 40, pp 352-70.

Burnell, A. and Vaughan, J. (2008) 'Remembering never to forget and forgetting never to remember: rethinking life story work', in B. Luckock and M. Lefevre (eds) *Direct work: Social work with children and young people in care*, London: BAAF, pp 223-33.

Burnham, A. and Balls, E. (2009) Government response to the Social Work Task Force, letter to Moira Gibb, Chair, Social Work Task Force, 1 December.

Butler-Sloss, E. (1988) *Report of the Inquiry into child abuse in Cleveland 1987*, Cm 412, London: HMSO.

Caple, F.S., Salcido, R.M. and di Cecco, J. (1995) 'Engaging effectively with culturally diverse families and children', *Social Work in Education*, vol 17, no 3, pp 159-70.

Carroll, J. (2002) 'Play therapy: the children's views', *Child & Family Social Work*, vol 7, no 3, pp 177-87.

Case, C. and Dalley, T. (1990) 'Introduction', in C. Case and T. Dalley (eds) *Working with children in art therapy*, London: Routledge, pp 1-6.

Ceci, S.J. and Bruck, M. (1993) 'The suggestibility of the child witness: a historical review and synthesis', *Psychological Bulletin*, vol 113, pp 403-39.

Ceci, S.J. and Friedman, R. (2000) 'The suggestibility of children: scientific research and legal implications', *Cornell Law Review*, vol 86, pp 33-108.

Chand, A. (2000) 'Do you speak English? Language barriers in child protection with minority ethnic families', *British Journal of Social Work*, vol 35, no 6, pp 67-77.

Children in Scotland (2002) *What matters to me: Citizenship in practice* (www.childreninscotland.org.uk/docs/participation/Whatmatterstome.pdf).

Children in Scotland (2009) *Key principles for effective participation* (www.childreninscotland.org.uk/html/par_mak.htm).

Clark, A. and Statham, J. (2005) 'Listening to young children: experts in their own lives', *Adoption & Fostering*, vol 29, no 1, pp 45-56.

Clarkson, C. (1990) 'A multiplicity of psychotherapeutic relationships', *British Journal of Psychotherapy*, vol 7, pp 148-63.

Cleary, R. (1999) 'Bowlby's theory of attachment and loss: a feminist reconsideration', *Feminism Psychology*, vol 9, pp 32-46.

Cleaver, H. and Walker, S. with Meadows, P. (2004) *Assessing children's needs and circumstances: The impact of the assessment framework*, London: Jessica Kingsley Publishers.

Colton, M., Sanders, R. and Williams, M. (2001) *An introduction to working with children: A guide for social workers*, Basingstoke: Palgrave Macmillan.

Connor, T., Sclare, I., Dunbar, D. and Elliffe, J. (1985) 'Making a life story book', *Adoption & Fostering*, vol 9, no 2, pp 32-5.

Cooper, A., Hetherington, R. and Katz, I. (2003) *The risk factor: Making the child protection system work for children*, London: Demos.

Cooper, R. (1994) *The voice of the child: Piaget and the Children Act interpreted*, Social Work Monographs no 126, Norwich: University of East Anglia.

Corcoran, J. (1997) 'A solution-oriented approach to working with juvenile offenders', *Child and Adolescent Social Work Journal*, vol 14, no 4, pp 277-88.

Cowan, L. (2000) 'Interactive media for child care and counseling', in H. Resnick (ed) *New opportunities, new resources: Electronic technology for social work education and practice* (2nd edn), Orkney: Information Plus.

Cox, S. (2005) 'Intention and meaning in young children's drawing', *Journal of Art and Design Education*, vol 24, no 2, pp 115-24.

CSCI (Commission for Social Care Inspection) (2005) *Making every child matter: Messages from inspections of children's social services*, Newcastle upon Tyne: CSCI.

CWDC (Children's Workforce Development Council) (2008) *Common assessment framework*, Leeds: CWDC (www.ecm.gov.uk/caf).

Dalzell, D. and Chamberlain, C. (2006) *Communicating with children: A two-way process*, London: NCB (www.ncb.org.uk/resources/free_resources/communicating_with_children.aspx).

Daniels, D. and Jenkins, P. (2000) *Therapy with children: Children's rights, confidentiality and the law*, London: Sage Publications.

Davidhizar, R. (1991) 'The "how to's" of touch', *Advancing Clinical Care*, November/December, pp 14-15.

Davis, J.M. (1998) 'Understanding the meanings of children: a reflexive process', *Children & Society*, vol 12, no 5, pp 325-35.

DCSF (Department for Children, Schools and Families) (2007) *Care matters: Time for change*, Cm 7137, White Paper, London: The Stationery Office.

DCSF (2008) *Care matters: Time to deliver for children in care – An implementation plan*, London: The Stationery Office.

DCSF (2009) *About the Integrated Children's System* (www.dcsf.gov.uk/everychildmatters/safeguardingandsocialcare/integratedchildrenssystem/ics/).

Dearden, C. and Becker, S. (2000) 'Listening to children: meeting the needs of young carers', in H. Kemshall and R. Littlechild (eds) *User involvement and participation in social care*, London: Jessica Kingsley Publishers, pp 129-42.

Derrida, J. (1978) *Writing and difference*, London: Routledge and Kegan Paul.

de Winter, M. and Noom, M. (2003) 'Someone who treats you as an ordinary human being... Homeless youth examine the quality of professional care', *British Journal of Social Work*, vol 33, no 3, pp 325-37.

DfEE (Department for Education and Employment) and the Home Office (2000) *Framework for the assessment of children in need and their families*, London: The Stationery Office.

DfES (Department for Education and Skills) (2003) *Every Child Matters*, Green Paper, Nottingham: DfES Publications.

DfES (2005) *Common core of skills and knowledge for the children's workforce*, Nottingham: DfES Publications (www.dcsf.gov.uk/everychildmatters/strategy/deliveringservices1/commoncore/commoncoreofskillsandknowledge/).

DfES (2006a) *What to do if you're worried a child is being abused*, London: HM Government.

DfES (2006b) *Information sharing: Further guidance on legal issues*, London: HM Government.

DH (Department of Health) (1991) *Patterns and outcomes of child placement*, London: HMSO.

DH (2000) *Assessing children in need and their families: Practice guidance*, London: The Stationery Office.

DH (2002) *Listening, hearing and responding: Core principles for the involvement of children and young people*, London: The Stationery Office.

DH (2004) *National Service Framework for children, young people and maternity services*, London: The Stationery Office.

DHSS (Department of Health and Social Security) (1974) *Report of the Committee of Inquiry into the Care and Supervision Provided in Relation to Maria Colwell*, London: HMSO.

Diaz de Chumaceiro, C.L. (1995) 'Lullabies are transferential transitional songs: further considerations on resistance in music therapy', *The Arts in Psychotherapy*, vol 22, no 4, pp 353-7.

Di Franco, G. (1993) 'Music therapy: a methodological approach in the mental health field', in M. Heal and T. Wigram (eds) *Music therapy in health and education*, London: Jessica Kingsley Publishers, pp 82-90.

Doherty-Sneddon, G. and Kent, G. (1996) 'Visual signals and the communication abilities of children', *Journal of Child Psychology and Psychiatry*, vol 37, no 8, pp 949-59.

Dubowski, J. (1990) 'Art versus language (separate development during childhood)', in C. Case and T. Dalley (eds) *Working with children in art therapy*, London: Routledge, pp 7-22.

Dunhill, A. (2009) 'What is communication? The process of transferring information', in A. Dunhill, B. Elliott and A. Shaw (eds) *Effective communication and engagement with children and young people, their families and carers*, Exeter: Learning Matters, pp 17-30.

Edwards, C.P., Gandini, L. and Forman, G.E. (eds) (1993) *The hundred languages of children: The Reggio Emilia approach to early childhood education*, Greenwich, CT: Ablex.

Ekman, P. (2003) *Emotions revealed: Understanding faces and feelings*, London: Wiedenfeld and Nicholson.

Elbow, M. (1987) 'The memory book: facilitating terminations with children', *Social Casework*, vol 68, pp 180-3.

Ellis, L. (1997) 'The meaning of difference: race, culture and context in infant observation', in S. Reid (ed) *Developments in infant observation: The Tavistock model*, London: Routledge.

Faller, K.C. (2003) 'Research and practice in child interviewing: implications for children exposed to domestic violence', *Journal of Interpersonal Violence*, vol 18, no 4, pp 377-89.

Farnfield, S. and Kaszap, M. (1998) 'What makes a helpful grown up? Children's views of professionals in the mental health services', *Health Informatics Journal*, vol 4, no 1, pp 3-14.

Fawcett, M. (1996) *Learning through child observation*, London: Jessica Kingsley Publishers.

Fawcett, M. (2009) *Learning through child observation* (2nd edn), London: Jessica Kingsley Publishers.

Ferguson, H. (2005) 'Working with violence: the emotions and the psycho-social dynamics of child protection: reflections on the Victoria Climbié case', *Social Work Education*, vol 24, no 7, pp 781-95.

Fiske, J. (1990) *Introduction to communication studies* (2nd edn), London: Routledge.

Fleming, S. (2004) 'The contribution of psychoanalytical observation in child protection assessments', *Journal of Social Work Practice*, vol 18, no 2, pp 223-38.

Flower, C. (1993) 'Control and creativity: music therapy with adolescents in secure care', in M. Heal and T. Wigram (eds) *Music therapy in health and education*, London: Jessica Kingsley Publishers, pp 40-5.

Foley, P. and Leverett, S. (eds) (2008) *Connecting with children: Developing working relationships*, Bristol: The Policy Press.

Folgheraiter, F. (2004) *Relational social work: Toward networking and societal practices*, London: Jessica Kingsley Publishers.

Francis, J. (2002) 'Implementing the "Looking after Children in Scotland" materials: panacea or stepping-stone?', *Social Work Education*, vol 21, no 4, pp 449-60.

Freake, H., Barley, V. and Kent, G. (2007) 'Adolescents' views of helping professionals: a review of the literature', *Journal of Adolescence*, vol 30, pp 639-53.

Freed-Kernis, A. (2008) 'We're all human beings, aren't we? Working with lesbian, gay, bisexual and transgender young people in care', in B. Luckock and M. Lefevre (eds) *Direct work: Social work with children and young people in care*, London: BAAF, pp 258-72.

Garrett, P.M. (2009) *Transforming children's services? Social work, neoliberalism and the 'modern' world*, Buckingham: Open University Press/McGraw Hill.

Gaskell, C. (2009) '"If the social worker had called at least it would show they cared". Young care leavers' perspectives on the importance of care', *Children & Society*, Advance Access, February 2009, DOI:10.1111/j.1099-0860.2009.00214.x.

Geldard, K. and Geldard, D. (2008) *Counselling children: A practical introduction* (3rd edn), London: Sage Publications.

Gerhardt, S. (2004) *Why love matters: How affection shapes a baby's brain*, Hove: Brunner-Routledge.

Gewirth, A. (2001) 'Confidentiality in child welfare practice', *Social Service Review*, vol 75, no 3, pp 479-89.

Gfeller, K.E. (1990) 'Cultural context as it relates to music therapy', in R.F. Unkefer (ed) *Music therapy and the treatment of adults with mental disorders*, New York, NY: Schirmer Books, pp 63-9.

Gibb, M. (2009a) *First report of the Social Work Taskforce*, 1 May, Nottingham: DCSF Publications.

Gibb, M. (2009b) *Facing up to the task: The interim report of the Social Work Task Force, July 2009*, Nottingham: DCSF Publications.

Gibb, M. (2009c) *Building a safe, confident future: The final report of the Social Work Task Force*, Nottingham: DCSF Publications.

Goldstein, B.P. (2002) 'Black children with a white parent', *Social Work Education*, vol 21, no 5, pp 551-63.

Gosso, Y., de Lima Salum e Morais, M. and Otta, E. (2007) 'Pretend play of Brazilian children: a window into different cultural worlds', *Journal of Cross-Cultural Psychology*, vol 38, pp 539-58.

Graham, M. (1999) 'The African-centered worldview: toward a paradigm for social work', *Journal of Black Studies*, vol 30, no 1, pp 103-22.

Graham, M. (2007) *Black issues in social work and social care*, Bristol: The Policy Press.

Graham, M. and Bruce, E. (2006) '"Seen and not heard" – sociological approaches to childhood: black children, agency and implications for child welfare', *Journal of Sociology and Social Welfare*, vol 34, no 4, pp 31-48.

Griffin, E. (2006) *A first look at communication theory* (6th edn), New York, NY: McGraw-Hill.

GSCC (General Social Care Council) (2002) *Code of practice for social care workers*, London: GSCC.

Habermas, J. (1984) *The theory of communicative action, Volume One: Reason and the rationalization of society*, Boston, MA: Beacon Press.

Haddon, M. (2003) *The curious incident of the dog in the night-time*, London: Jonathon Cape.

Hague, G., Mullender, A., Kelly, L., Imam, U. and Malos, E. (2002) 'How do children understand and cope with domestic violence?', *Practice*, vol 14, no 1, pp 17-26.

Halliday, M.A.K. (1996) 'Language as social semiotic', in P. Cobley (ed) *The communication reader*, London: Routledge, pp 359-83.

Hargie, O. and Dickson, D. (2004) *Skilled interpersonal communication* (4th edn), London: Routledge.

Harper, J. (1996) 'Recapturing the past: alternative methods of life story work in adoption and fostering', *Adoption & Fostering*, vol 20, no 3, pp 21-8.

Hart, A., Saunders, A. and Thomas, H. (2005) 'Attuned practice: a service user study of specialist child and adolescent mental health, UK', *Epidemiologia e psichiatria sociale*, vol 14, no 1, pp 22-31.

Harvey, P. (1996) 'Assessment and treatment of children with moderate learning difficulties with particular reference to effective communication', *Adoption & Fostering*, vol 20, no 3, pp 29-34.

Hawkins, P. and Shohet, R. (2000) *Supervision in the helping professions* (2nd edn), Buckingham: Open University Press.

Headliners (2009) *Children's professionals: What I really think of my ...* (www.headliners.org/storylibrary/stories/2005/childrensprofessionals whatireallythinkofmy.htm?id=6787184094961558887).

Heal, M. and Wigram, T. (eds) (1993) *Music therapy in health and education*, London: Jessica Kingsley Publishers.

Hendry, E. (1988) 'A case study of play-based work with very young children', *Journal of Social Work Practice*, vol 3, pp 1-9.

Hill, C., Maskowitz, K., Danis, B. and Wakschlag, L. (2008) 'Validation of a clinically sensitive, observational coding system for parenting behaviors: the parenting clinical observation schedule', *Parenting*, vol 8, no 2, pp 153-85.

Hill, M. (1999) 'What's the problem? Who can help? The perspectives of children and young people on their well-being and on helping professionals', *Journal of Social Work Practice*, vol 13, no 2, pp 135-45.

Hindle, D. and Easton, J. (1999) 'The use of observation of supervised contact in child care cases', *Journal of Infant Observation and its Application*, vol 2, Special Issue: The application of infant observation to social work, pp 33-48.

Hindle, D. and Klauber, T. (2006) 'Ethical issues in infant observation: preliminary thoughts on establishing an observation', *Infant Observation*, vol 9, no 3, pp 269-79.

Hindley, P. and Brown, R. (1994) 'Psychiatric aspects of specific sensory impairments', in M. Rutter, E. Taylor and L. Hersov (eds) *Child and adolescent psychiatry: Modern approaches*, Oxford: Blackwell Science, pp 720-36.

HM Government (2006) *Working together to safeguard children: A guide to inter-agency working to safeguard and promote the welfare of children*, London: The Stationery Office.

Hoelscher, K. and Garfat, T. (1993) 'Talking to the animal', *Journal of Child and Youth Care*, vol 8, no 3, pp 87-92.

Holland, S. and Scourfield, J. (2004) 'Liberty and respect in child protection', *British Journal of Social Work*, vol 34, no 1, pp 21-36.

Holody, R. and Maher, S. (1996) 'Using lifebooks with children in family foster care: a here-and-now process model', *Child Welfare*, vol 75, no 4, pp 321-34.

Home Office (1945) *Report on the circumstances which led to the boarding out of Denis and Terence O'Neill at Bank Farm* (Monckton Report), London: Home Office.

Home Office (1992) *Memorandum of good practice*, London: Home Office in conjunction with the Department of Health.

Home Office (2002) *Achieving best evidence in criminal proceedings: Guidance for vulnerable or intimidated witnesses, including children*, London: Home Office Communication Directorate.

Home Office (2007) *Achieving best evidence in criminal proceedings: Guidance on interviewing victims and witnesses, and using special measures*, London: Home Office.

Horner, A.J. (1991) *Psychoanalytic object relations therapy*, Northvale, NJ: Jason Aaronson.

Horwath, J. (ed) (2009) *The child's world: The comprehensive guide to assessing children in need* (2nd edn), London: Jessica Kingsley Publishers.

House of Commons (2000) *Learning the lessons. The Government's response to 'Lost in care: The report of the Tribunal of Inquiry into the abuse of children in care in the former county council areas of Gwynedd and Clwyd since 1974'*, Cm 4776, London: The Stationery Office.

Howe, D. (1996) 'Surface and depth in social work practice', in N. Parton (ed) *Social theory, social change and social work*, London: Routledge, pp 77-97.

Howe, D. (2005) *Child abuse and neglect: Attachment, development and intervention*, Basingstoke: Palgrave Macmillan.

Howe, D. (2008) *The emotionally intelligent social worker*, Basingstoke: Palgrave Macmillan.

Hunt, R. and Jensen, J. (2006) *The school report: The experiences of young gay people in Britain's schools*, London: Stonewall.

Hunt, S. (2002) 'In favour of online counselling?', *Australian Social Work*, vol 55, no 4, pp 260-7.

Hutton, A. and Partridge, K. (2006) *'Say it your own way': Children's participation in assessment: A guide and resources*, Ilford: Barnado's Publications (www.barnardos.org.uk/sayityourownway).

James, A. and Prout, A. (eds) (1997) *Constructing and reconstructing childhood: Contemporary issues in the sociological study of childhood*, London: Falmer Press.

Jenner, S. (2008) *The parent/child game: The proven key to a happier family*, London: Bloomsbury.

Johnson, R. T. (2000) *Hands off! The disappearance of touch in the care of children*, New York, NY: Peter Lang.

Jones, D. (2003) *Communicating with vulnerable children: A guide for practitioners*, London: Gaskell.

Karp, J., Serbin, L., Stack, D. and Schwartzman, A. (2004) 'An observational measure of children's behavioural style: evidence supporting a multi-method approach to studying temperament', *Infant and Child Development*, vol 13, pp 135-58.

Keats, D.M. (1997) *Culture and the child*, New York, NY: John Wiley & Sons.

Kennedy, M. (1992) 'Not the only way to communicate: a challenge to voice in child protection work', *Child Abuse Review*, vol 1, pp 185-7.

King, R. (2002) 'Experience of undertaking infant observation as part of the post-qualifying award in child care', *Journal Of Social Work Practice*, vol 16, no 2, pp 213-21.

Kitayama, S., Markus, H.R., Matsumoto, H. and Norasakkunkit, V. (1997) 'Individual and collective processes in the construction of the self: self-enhancement in the United States and self-criticism in Japan', *Journal of Personality and Social Psychology*, vol 72, no 6, pp 1245-67.

Kohli, R. (2006) 'The sound of silence. Listening to what unaccompanied children say and do not say', *British Journal of Social Work*, vol 36, no 5, pp 707-21.

Koprowska, J. (2008) *Communication and interpersonal skills in social work* (2nd edn), Exeter: Learning Matters.

Krueger, M. (1997) 'Using self, story, and intuition to understand child and youth care work', *Child and Youth Care Forum*, vol 26, no 3, pp 153-61.

Laird, S. (2008) *Anti-oppressive social work: A guide for developing cultural competence*, London: Sage Publications.

Laming, Lord (2003) *The Victoria Climbié Inquiry: Report of an inquiry by Lord Laming*, Cm 5730, London: The Stationery Office.

Laming, Lord (2009) *The protection of children in England: A progress report*, London: The Stationery Office.

Leeson, C. (2007) 'My life in care: experiences of non-participation in decision-making processes', *Child & Family Social Work*, vol 12, pp 268-77.

Lefevre, M. (2004) 'Playing with sound: the therapeutic use of music in direct work with children', *Child & Family Social Work*, vol 9, pp 333-45.

Lefevre, M. (2008a) 'Knowing, being and doing: core qualities and skills for working with children and young people who are in care', in B. Luckock and M. Lefevre (eds) *Direct work: Social work with children and young people in care*, London: BAAF, pp 21-40.

Lefevre, M. (2008b) 'Communicating and engaging with children and young people in care through play and the creative arts', in B. Luckock and M. Lefevre (eds) *Direct work: Social work with children and young people in care*, London: BAAF, pp 130-50.

Lefevre, M., Richards, S. and Trevithick, P. (2008b) *Gathering information*, London: Social Care Institute for Excellence (www.scie.org.uk/publications/elearning/cs/cs04/index.asp)

Lefevre, M., Richards, S. and Trevithick, P. (2008c) *Using play and the creative arts to communicate with children and young people* (www.scie.org.uk/publications/elearning/cs/cs08/index.asp).

Lefevre, M., Tanner, K. and Luckock, B. (2008a) 'Developing social work students' communication skills with children and young people: a model for the qualifying level curriculum', *Child & Family Social Work*, vol 13, pp 166-76.

Le Grand, J. (2007) *Consistent care matters: Exploring the potential of social work practices*, Nottingham: The Stationery Office.

Lepper, J. (2010) 'London is slow to embrace the *Care matters* reforms', *Children and Young People Now*, 16-22 February, p 9.

Leveridge, M. (2002) 'Mac-social work: the routinisation of professional activity', *Maatskaplike Werk/Social Work*, vol 38, no 4, pp 354-62.

London, K., Bruck, M., Wright, D.B. and Ceci, S.J. (2008) 'Review of the contemporary literature on how children report sexual abuse to others: findings, methodological issues, and implications for forensic interviewers', *Memory*, vol 16, no 1, pp 29-47.

Lovell, T. (2000) 'Thinking feminism with and against Bourdieu', *Feminist Theory*, vol 1, no 1, pp 11-32.

Luckock, B. and Lefevre, M. (eds) (2008) *Direct work: Social work with children and young people in care*, London: BAAF.

Luckock, B., Lefevre, M. and Orr, D. (2006b) 'What counts as effective communication with children in social work practice?', *Teaching, learning and assessing communication skills with children and young people in social work education*, Knowledge Review, London: Social Care Institute for Excellence, pp 11-31.

Luckock, B., Lefevre, M. and Orr, D. with Tanner, K., Jones, M. and Marchant, R. (2006a) *Teaching learning and assessing communication skills with children in social work education*, Knowledge Review, London: Social Care Institute for Excellence.

Macdonald, G. (2000) *Effective interventions for child abuse and neglect: An evidence-based approach to evaluating and planning interventions*, Chichester: Wiley.

Mackewn, J. (1997) *Developing Gestalt counselling*, London: Sage Publications.

McGregor, I. (1990) 'Unusual drawing development in children: what does it reveal about children's art?', in C. Case and T. Dalley (eds) *Working with children in art therapy*, London: Routledge, pp 39-53.

McLeod, A. (2007) 'Whose agenda? Issues of power and relationship when listening to looked-after young people', *Child & Family Social Work*, vol 12, no 3, pp 278-86.

McLeod, A. (2008) *Listening to children: A practitioner's guide*, London: Jessica Kingsley Publishers.

McMahon, L. (2009) *The handbook of play therapy and therapeutic play* (2nd edn), Hove: Routledge.

Main, M. and Soloman, J. (1990) 'Procedures for identifying infants as disorganized/disoriented during the Ainsworth Strange Situation', in M. Greenberg, D. Cichetti and E. Cummings (eds) *Attachment in the pre-school years*, Chicago, IL: University of Chicago Press, pp 121-60.

Malekoff, A. (1994) 'A guideline for group work with adolescents', *Social Work with Groups*, vol 17, no 1-2, pp 5-19.

Marchant, R. (2008) 'Working with disabled children who live away from home some or all of the time', in B. Luckock and M. Lefevre (eds) *Direct work: Social work with children and young people in care*, London: BAAF, pp 151-68.

Marner, T. (1995) 'Therapeutic letters to, from and between children in family therapy', *Journal of Social Work Practice*, vol 9, no 2, pp 169-76.

Marsen, S. (2006) *Communication studies*, Basingstoke: Palgrave Macmillan.

Massinga, R. and Pecora, P.J. (2004) 'Providing better opportunities for older children in the child welfare system', *The Future of Children*, vol 14, no 1, pp 150-73.

Masson, J. and Oakley, M.W. (1999) *Out of hearing: Representing children in care proceedings*, London: NSPCC/John Wiley.

Mattaini, M.A. (1995) 'Visualizing practice with children and families', *Early Child Development and Care*, vol 106, pp 59-74.

Matthews, J. (2003) *Drawing and painting: Children and visual representation* (2nd edn), London: Paul Chapman.

Mattinson, J. (1975) *The reflective process in social work supervision*, London: Tavistock.

Maybin, J. (2001) 'Language, struggle and voice: the Bakhtin/Volosinov writings', in M. Wetherell, S. Taylor and S.J. Yates (eds) *Discourse theory and practice: A reader*, London: Sage Publications, pp 64-71.

Menzies-Lyth, I. (1988) *Containing anxiety in institutions: Selected essays, Volume 1*, London: Free Association Books.

Messiou, K. (2009) 'Listen to me, please…', in A. Dinhill, B. Elliott and A. Shaw (eds) *Effective communication and engagement with children and young people, their families and carers*, Exeter: Learning Matters, pp 31-42.

Meyer, L.B. (1956) *Emotion and meaning in music*, Chicago, IL: Chicago University Press.

Miles, G. and Trowell, J. (2004) 'The contribution of observation training to professional development in social work', *Journal of Social Work Practice*, vol 18, no 1, March, pp 49-60.

Millar, S. and Scott, J. (2003) 'What is augmentative and alternative communication?', in ACP:S (ed) *Augmentative communication in practice: An introduction*, Edinburgh: Scottish Executive Education Department (http://callcentre.education.ed.ac.uk/downloads/acpsbook/introbook.pdf#1).

Miller, L. (1989) 'Introduction', in L. Miller, M. Rustin, M. Rustin and J. Shuttleworth (eds) *Closely observed infants*, London: Duckworth, pp 1-4.

Minde, K., Minde, R. and Vogel, W. (2006) 'Culturally sensitive assessment of attachment in children aged 18-40 months in a South African township', *Infant Mental Health Journal*, vol 27, no 6, pp 544-58.

Morgan, R. (2006) *About social workers. A Children's Views report*, Newcastle upon Tyne: Commission for Social Care Inspection (https://www.rights4me.org/content/beheardreports/3/about_social_workers_report.pdf).

Moroz, K.J. (1996) 'Kids speak out on adoption: a multiage book-writing group for adopted children with special needs', *Child Welfare*, vol 75, no 3, pp 235-51.

Munro, E. (1999) 'Common errors of reasoning in child protection work', *Child Abuse and Neglect*, vol 23, no 8, pp 745-58.

Munro, E. (2001) 'Empowering looked-after children', *Child & Family Social Work*, vol 6, no 2, pp 129-37.

Murray, M. and Osborne, C. (2009) *Safeguarding disabled children: Practice guidance*, Nottingham: The Children's Society/DCSF Publications.

NCB (National Children's Bureau) (2004) *What young people thought would be the world's worst CAF assessor* (www.dfes.gov.uk/consultations/downloadableDocs/NCB%20CAF%20report.doc).

NSPCC (National Society for the Prevention of Cruelty to Children) (1996) *Childhood matters: Report of the National Commission of Enquiry into the prevention of child abuse*, London: The Stationery Office.

Oaklander, V. (1978) *Windows to our children: A Gestalt therapy approach to children and adolescents*, Moab, UT: Real People Press.

Ofsted (2009) *Learning lessons, taking action: Ofsted's evaluations of serious case reviews 1 April 2007 to 31 March 2008*, Manchester: Ofsted.

Oosterhoorn, R. and Kendrick, A. (2001) 'No sign of harm: issues for disabled children communicating about abuse', *Child Abuse Review*, vol 10, no 4, pp 243-53.

Outhwaite, W. (1994) *Habermas: A critical introduction*, Cambridge: Polity Press.

Page, T. (2001) 'The social meaning of children's narratives: a review of the attachment-based narrative story stem technique', *Child and Adolescent Social Work Journal*, vol 18, no 3, pp 171-87.

Paylor, I. and Simmill-Binning, C. (2008) 'Evaluating youth justice in the UK', *American Journal of Evaluation*, vol 25, pp 335-49.

Pinker, S. (1999) *Words and rules: The ingredients of language*, London: Wiedenfeld & Nicholson.

Prior, V. and Glaser, D. (2006) *Understanding attachment and attachment disorders: Theory, evidence and practice*, London: Jessica Kingsley Publishers.

Prior, V., Lynch, M.A. and Glaser, D. (1999) 'Responding to child sexual abuse: an evaluation of social work by children and their carers', *Child & Family Social Work*, vol 4, no 2, pp 131-43.

Qvortrup, J. (1987) 'Introduction: the sociology of childhood', *International Journal of Sociology*, vol 17, no 3, pp 3-37.

Reder, P., Duncan, S. and Gray, M. (1993) *Beyond blame: Child abuse tragedies revisited*, London: Routledge.

Richards, S., Lefevre, M. and Trevithick, P. (2008) *Communication across social and cultural differences*, London: Social Care Institute for Excellence (www.scie.org.uk/publications/elearning/cs/cs10/index.asp).

RNID (2004) *Communication tips: If you're deaf or hard of hearing*, London: RNID (www.rnid.org.uk/information_resources/factsheets/communication/factsheets_leaflets/communication_tips.htm).

Robertson, J. (1953) *A two-year-old goes to hospital*, London: Tavistock Child Development Research Unit (film).

Robinson, L. (2007) *Cross-cultural child development for social workers: An introduction*, Basingstoke: Palgrave Macmillan.

Rogers, C. (1951) *Client-centred therapy*, Boston, MA: Houghton-Mifflin.

Romaine, M. with Turley, T. and Tuckey, N. (2007) *Preparing children for permanence: A guide to undertaking direct work for social workers, foster carers and adoptive parents*, London: BAAF.

Rothbaum, F., Weisz, J., Pott, M., Miyake, K. and Morelli, G. (2000) 'Attachment and culture: security in the United States and Japan', *American Psychologist*, vol 55, pp 1093-104.

Rowe, J., Cain, H., Hundleby, M. and Keane, A. (1984) *Long-term foster care*, London: BAAF/Batsford.

Ruch, G. (1998) 'Direct work with children – the practitioner's perspective', *Practice*, vol 10, no 1, pp 37-44.

Ruch, G. (2005) 'Relationship-based practice and reflective practice: holistic approaches to contemporary child care social work', *Child & Family Social Work*, vol 10, pp 111-23.

Ruch, G. (2007) 'Reflective practice in contemporary childcare social work: the role of containment', *British Journal of Social Work*, vol 37, pp 659-80.

Ruegger, M. (2001) 'Seen and heard but how well informed? Children's perceptions of the guardian ad litem service', *Children and Society*, vol 15, no 3, pp 133-45.

Rustin, M. (2005) 'Conceptual analysis of the critical moments in Victoria Climbié's life', *Child & Family Social Work*, vol 10, pp 11-19.

Ryan, V., Wilson, K. and Fisher, T. (1995) 'Developing partnerships in therapeutic work with children', *Journal of Social Work Practice*, vol 9, no 2, pp 131-40.

Sameroff, A., McDonough, S. and Rosenblum, K. (eds) (2004) *Treating parent–infant relationship problems: Strategies for intervention*, New York, NY: Guilford.

Scarlett, W., Naudeau, S., Salonius-Pasternak, D. and Ponte, I. (2005) *Children's play*, Thousand Oaks, CA: Sage Publications.

Schiele, J. (1997) 'The contour and meaning of Afrocentric social work', *Journal of Black Studies*, vol 27, pp 800-19.

Schofield, G. (1998) 'Inner and outer worlds: a psychosocial framework for child and family social work', *Child & Family Social Work*, vol 3, no 1, pp 57-67.

Schofield, G. and Brown, K. (1999) 'Being there: a family centre worker's role as a secure base for adolescent girls in crisis', *Child & Family Social Work*, vol 4, no 1, pp 21-31.

Schon, D. (1983) *The reflective practitioner*, New York, NY: Basic Books.

Schore, A. (1994) *Affect regulation and the origin of the self*, Hillsdale, NJ: Lawrence Erlbaum Associates.

Schwandt, T. (1997) *Qualitative inquiry: A dictionary of terms*, Thousand Oaks, CA: Sage Publications.

Scovel, M.A. (1990) 'Music therapy within the context of psychotherapeutic models', in R.F. Unkefer (ed) *Music therapy and the treatment of adults with mental disorders*, New York, NY: Schirmer Books, pp 96-108.

Seden, J, (2005) *Counselling skills in social work practice*, Maidenhead: Open University Press and McGraw-Hill Education.

Shannon, C. and Weaver, W. (1949) *The mathematical theory of communication*, Champaign, IL: University of Illinois Press.

Sharland, E. (2006) 'Young people, risk taking and risk making: some thoughts for social work', *British Journal of Social Work*, vol 36, pp 247-65.

Sharry, J. (2004) *Counselling children, adolescents and families*, London: Sage Publications.

Shaw, I. (2009) 'Ways of knowing', in M. Gray and S. Webb (eds) *Social work theories and methods*, London: Sage Publications, pp 184-94.

Shemmings, D. (2000) 'Professionals' attitudes to children's participation in decision-making: dichotomous accounts and doctrinal contests', *Child & Family Social Work*, vol 5, no 3, pp 235-43.

Sheridan, M. (2008) *From birth to five years: Children's developmental progress* (3rd edn, revised and updated by A. Sharma and H. Cockerill), New York, NY: Routledge.

Shotter, J. (1993) *Cultural politics of everyday life: Social constructionism, rhetoric and knowing of the third kind*, Buckingham: Open University Press.

Smith, P.K. (2005) 'Social and pretend play in children', in A.D. Pellegrini and P.K. Smith (eds) *The nature of play*, New York, NY: Guilford, pp 173-212.

SSI (Social Services Inspectorate) with Jones, A., Clark, P.A. and Pont, C. (1997) *Messages from inspection: Child protection inspection 1992–1996*, London: Department of Health.

Stalker, K. and Connors, C. (2003) 'Communicating with disabled children', *Adoption & Fostering*, vol 27, no 1, pp 26-35.

Stein, M. (2009) *Quality matters in children's services: Messages from research*, London: Jessica Kingsley Publishers.

Stevens, J.W. (1998) 'A question of values in social work practice: working with the strengths of black adolescent females', *Families in Society*, vol 79, no 3, pp 288-96.

Sudarkasa, N. (1988) 'Interpreting the African heritage in Afro-American family organisation', in H.P. McAdoo (ed) *Black families*, London: Sage Publications, pp 27-43.

Sunderland, M. and Armstrong, N. (2001) *Using story telling as a therapeutic tool with children*, Brackley: Speechmark Publishing Ltd.

Sunderland, M. and Engelheart, P. (1993) *Draw on your emotions*, Bicester: Winslow Press.

Sunderland, M., Hancock, N. and Armstrong, N. (2003) *Helping children with loss: A guidebook*, Brackley: Speechmark Publishing Ltd.

Sutton, J. (1995) 'The sound world of speech and language impaired children', in A. Gilroy and L. Lee (eds) *Art and music: Therapy and research*, London: Routledge, pp 152-63.

Tanner, K. and Turney, D. (2000) 'The role of observation in the assessment of child neglect', *Child Abuse Review*, vol 9, pp 337-48.

Tarullo, L.B. (1994) 'Windows on social worlds: gender differences in children's play narratives', in A. Slade and D.P. Wolf (eds) *Children at play: Clinical and developmental approaches to meaning and representation*, New York, NY: Oxford University Press, pp 169-87.

Taylor, C. (2004) 'Underpinning knowledge for child care practice: reconsidering child development theory', *Child & Family Social Work*, vol 9, no 3, pp 225-35.

Taylor, C. and White, S. (2006) 'Knowledge and reasoning in social work: educating for humane judgement', *British Journal of Social Work*, vol 36, no 6, pp 937-54.

Thomas, C., Beckford, V., Lowe, N. and Murch, N. (1999) *Adopted children speaking*, London: BAAF.

Thomas, N. (2005) *Social work with young people in care: Looking after children in theory and practice*, Basingstoke: Palgrave Macmillan.

Thomas, N. and O'Kane, C. (2000) 'Discovering what children think: connections between research and practice', *British Journal of Social Work*, vol 30, no 6, pp 819-35.

Thompson, N. (2002) *People skills* (2nd edn), Basingstoke: Palgrave Macmillan.

Thompson, N. (2003) *Communication and language: A handbook of theory and practice*, Basingstoke: Palgrave Macmillan.

Thompson, N. (2006) *Anti-discriminatory practice*, 4th edn, Basingstoke: Palgrave Macmillan.

Trevithick, P. (2003) 'Effective relationship-based practice: a theoretical exploration', *Journal of Social Work Practice*, vol 17, no 2, pp 163-76.

Trevithick, P. (2005) *Social work skills: A practice handbook* (2nd edn), Maidenhead: Open University Press and McGraw-Hill Education.

Trevithick, P., Lefevre, M. and Richards, S. (2008a) *Overview of communication skills in social work*, London: Social Care Institute for Excellence (www.scie.org.uk/publications/elearning/cs/cs10/index.asp).

Trevithick, P., Richards, S. and Lefevre, M. (2008b) *Communicating in challenging situations*, London: Social Care Institute for Excellence (www.scie.org.uk/publications/elearning/cs/cs07/index.asp).

Triangle (2001) *Two-way street: Communicating with disabled children and young people – Communication handbook*, Leicester: NSPCC.

Triangle (2009) *Three-way street: Putting children at the centre of three-way communication*, Hove: Triangle.

Triseliotis, J., Borland, M., Hill, M. and Lambert, L. (1998) 'Social work supervision of young people', *Child & Family Social Work*, vol 3, no 1, pp 27-35.

Trotter, J. (2000) 'Lesbian and gay issues in social work with young people: resilience and success through confronting, conforming and escaping, Critical commentary', *British Journal of Social Work*, vol 30, no 1, pp 115-23.

Turner, C. (2003) *Are you listening? What disabled children and young people in Wales think about the services they use*, Cardiff: Welsh Assembly.

Turney, D. (2008) 'The power of the gaze: observation and its role in direct practice with children in care', in B. Luckock and M. Lefevre (eds) *Direct work: Social work with children and young people in care*, London: BAAF, pp 115-29.

Tyson, E.H. (2003) 'Rap music in social work practice with African–American and Latino youth: a conceptual model with practical applications', *Journal of Human Behavior in the Social Environment*, vol 8, no 4, pp 1-21.

Uprichard, E. (2007) 'Children as "being and becomings": children, childhood and temporality', *Children & Society*, vol 22, no 4, pp 303-13.

van Rooyen, C. and Engelbrecht, A.N. (2001) 'Confidentiality: investigating the impact of breaches of confidentiality on teenage children in care', *Maatskaplike Werk/Social Work*, vol 37, no 1, pp 84-97.

Vrij, A. (2002) 'Deception in children: literature review and implications for children's testimony', in H. Westcott, G. Davies and R. Bull (eds) *Children's testimony: A handbook of psychological research and forensic practice*, Chichester: Wiley, pp 175-94.

Wade, A. and Westcott, H. (1997) 'No easy answers: children's perspectives on investigative interviews', in H. Westcott, G. Davies and R. Bull (ed) *Children's testimony: A handbook of psychological research and forensic practice*, Chichester: Wiley, pp 175-94.

Wake, E. (2009) 'Children's voices: working with children and young people with additional needs', in A. Dunhill, B. Elliott and A. Shaw (eds) *Effective communication and engagement with children and young people, their families and carers,* Exeter: Learning Matters, pp 43–60.

Walton, E. and Smith, C. (1999) 'The genogram: a tool for assessment and intervention in child welfare', *Journal of Family Social Work*, vol 3, no 3, pp 3–20.

Ward, A. (2008) 'Opportunity-led work with children', in B. Luckock and M. Lefevre (eds) *Direct work: Social work with children and young people in care*, London: BAAF, pp 181–94.

Watson, D. and West, J. (2006) *Social work process and practice: Approaches, knowledge and skills*, Basingstoke: Palgrave Macmillan.

Wattam, C. and Woodward, C. (1996) 'And do I abuse my children… No!', *Childhood Matters Background Papers*, vol 2.

Webb, S. (2006) *Social work in a risk society*, Basingstoke: Palgrave.

Webster-Stratton, C. (1981) *BASIC manual*, The Incredible Years Parents, Teachers and Children Training Series, Seattle: Incredible Years.

Welsh Assembly Government (2005) *National Service Framework for children, young people and maternity services* (www.wales.nhs.uk/sites3/home.cfm?OrgID=441).

Westcott, H. and Davies, G. (1996) 'Sexually abused children and young people's perspectives on investigative interview', *British Journal of Social Work*, vol 26, no 4, pp 451–74.

Westcott, H. and Jones, D. (1999) 'Annotation: The abuse of disabled children, *Journal of Child Psychology and Psychiatry*, vol 40, pp 497–506.

Westminster Local Safeguarding Children Board (2006) *Serious case review: Executive summary* (www.westminster.gov.uk/councilgovernmentanddemocracy/councils/pressoffice/).

White, S. (2009) 'Discourse analysis and reflexivity', in M. Gray and S. Webb (eds) *Social work theories and methods*, London: Sage Publications, pp 161–71.

Whitfield, C. (2009) 'Communication: the historical and current social policy context', in A. Dunhill, B. Elliott and A. Shaw (eds) *Effective communication and engagement with children and young people, their families and carers*, Exeter: Learning Matters, pp 1–16.

Wickham, R. and West, J. (2002) *Therapeutic work with sexually abused children*, Thousand Oaks, CA: Sage Publications.

Williams, C. and Soydan, H. (2005) 'When and how does ethnicity matter? A cross-national study of social work responses to ethnicity in child protection cases', *British Journal of Social Work*, vol 35, no 6, pp 901–20.

Williamson, H. and Butler, I. (1995) 'No one ever listens to us: interviewing children and young people', in C. Cloke and M. Davies (eds) *Participation and empowerment in child protection*, London: Pitman.

Wilson, J. (1992) *The story of Tracy Beaker*, London: Random House.

Winnicott, C. (1986) *Face to face with children*, Working with Children Practice Series 13, London: BAAF.

Winnicott, C. (1964) 'Communicating with children', *Child Care Quarterly Review*, vol 18, no 3, pp 85-93.

Winnicott, C. (1996) 'Communicating with children', *Smith College Studies in Social Work*, vol 66, no 2, pp 117-28.

Winnicott, D.W. (1965) *The maturational processes and the facilitating environment*, London: Hogarth Press.

Winnicott, D.W. (1971) *Playing and reality*, London: Tavistock Publications.

Winter, K. (2009) 'Relationships matter: the problems and prospects for social workers' relationships with young children in care', *Child & Family Social Work*, vol 14, pp 450-60.

Wood, A. (1985) 'King tiger and the roaring tummies: a novel way of helping young children and their families change', *Dulwich Centre Review*, pp 41-9.

Youell, B. (2002) 'The relevance of infant and young child observation in multidisciplinary assessments for the family courts', in A. Briggs (ed) *Surviving space: Papers on infant observation; Essays on the centenary of Esther Bick*, London: Karnac, pp 117-34.

Youth Pathways to Employment (2008) *The common core for children and young people: What to expect!*, Leeds: CWDC (www.cwdcouncil.org.uk/common-core).

Index

The letters *b*, *f* and *t* following page numbers indicate information in boxes, figures and tables respectively.

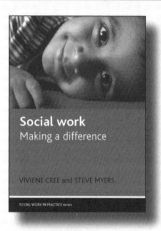